OYSTERS MACARONI & BEER

THURBER, TEXAS AND THE COMPANY STORE

GENE RHEA TUCKER

FOREWORD BY RICHARD FRANCAVIGLIA

Texas Tech University Press

This book is typeset in Palatino Linotype. The paper used in this book meets the minimum requirements of ANSI/NISO Z39.48-1992 (R1997). ∞

Designed by Kasey McBeath
Jacket design by Audrey Norman and Kasey McBeath
Jacket photographs courtesy Special Collections, University of Texas at Arlington Library

Library of Congress Cataloging-in-Publication Data
Tucker, Gene Rhea, 1979–
Oysters, macaroni, and beer : Thurber, Texas, and the company store / Gene Rhea Tucker ; foreword by Richard Francaviglia.
p. cm. — (Plains histories)
Includes bibliographical references and index.
ISBN 978-0-89672-768-7 (hardcover : alk. paper) — ISBN 978-0-89672-773-1 (e-book) 1. Thurber (Tex.)—Economic conditions. 2. Thurber (Tex.)—Social conditions. 3. Texas Pacific Mercantile and Manufacturing Company—History. 4. Company stores—Texas—Thurber—History. 5. Business enterprises—Texas—Thurber—History. 6. Texas and Pacific Coal Company—Employees—Services for—Texas—Thurber—History. 7. Company towns—Texas—Case studies. I. Title.
HC108.T48T83 2012
381′.1—dc23 2012021209

Printed in the United States of America
12 13 14 15 16 17 18 19 20 / 9 8 7 6 5 4 3 2 1

Texas Tech University Press
Box 41037 | Lubbock, Texas 79409-1037 USA
800.832.4042 | ttup@ttu.edu | www.ttupress.org

CONTENTS

ILLUSTRATIONS

MAPS

TABLES

PLAINSWORD

Of all the works created by mining corporations, few have been as reviled as the company store—establishments wherein the company provided retail goods, and sometimes even services, to workers. As immortalized by the line "I owe my soul to the company store" in the popular 1955 song "Sixteen Tons," the company played a powerful role in the lives of miners who lived in the company's privately owned towns. Merle Travis, who wrote "Sixteen Tons" in 1946, based the lyrics on his father's experiences in Kentucky coal towns in the 1930s, but company-controlled mercantile institutions had come under intense scrutiny and criticism at least half a century earlier. At that time, in the 1880s, labor and management locked horns in a titanic struggle that would ultimately determine who would call the shots.

To many observers, then and now, company stores seemed the antithesis of the free market. These stores were widely considered to be monopolistic by a society that was becoming increasingly populist and freely using strikes, and then the courts, to challenge the hegemony of companies. In the popular culture, the company store came to symbolize the inherent injustice of an impersonal corporation wielding control over a relatively helpless individual—the worker. Then, too, the issue of paternalism was palpable. What even well-meaning companies thought was best for workers (who would ideally not only benefit from largesse, but also be personally elevated by it) often backfired. Beginning in the nineteenth century, then, companies found themselves facing mounting labor organization, and growing public antipathy. Never mind the fact that labor unions often espoused another form of paternalism: they at least ostensibly represented the wishes of workers rather than management. Despite the growing power of labor, company towns persisted well into the late twentieth century in some areas, as did their infamous company stores. By this time, however, company stores were becoming much harder to find because, when companies did the math, they found mercantile operations to be losing propositions. Still, the legacy of the company store is rich and the lessons we can learn from it are profound.

That legacy is mired in considerable emotion. Even supposedly objective academic researchers who study the role of companies tend to sympathize with workers (labor), and to chastise corporations (management) as oppressive. In the bruising struggle for control over production—and concern about profits—that characterizes much of the industrialized world, corporations have tended to come out on the losing end of public relations battles. In both the popular mindset and the world of scholarship, then, the corporation is viewed as the natural villain. When companies operated company stores, they were almost universally viewed as taking unfair advantage of the individual worker and his or her family. The fact that many company stores offered "scrip" as a form of credit, the acceptance of which literally put workers in debt to the company, only added to the image of oppression.

Disdain for large-scale, heavy-handed mining companies remains popular, but it has its limits. In the tug of war between labor and management, workers are often depicted as if they have relatively little power, when in fact they may have gained considerable clout, either as individual workers with particular skills, or collectively through organizing. As historian Gene Rhea Tucker shows in this book, the common wisdom that workers were treated as helpless pawns overlooks the fact that workers in some places had significant clout—sufficient enough to make corporations hesitant to push too hard. Thurber, Texas, was one of those places in which proficient individual workers and organized labor had considerable power to make the company think twice. And yet, paradoxically, Thurber was first and foremost a company town—a type of community wherein virtually everything, including the land and infrastructure, was owned and controlled by a single corporation.

Company towns like Thurber were more prevalent than many people realize, and their economic activities were diverse. They could be found in all parts of the nation, and produced a wide variety of products—for example, lumber, fish, steel, and minerals. Thurber was tied to mineral resources, and coal put it on the map. This company town in Texas was but one of many nationwide underlain by bituminous coal; other areas where company coal towns could be found included much of Appalachia, southern Colorado, Wyoming, and the Cascade Range of Washington. In Texas, bituminous coal is found in a belt running from the north central to central part of the state, and a number of towns existed solely to mine this resource. In Thurber, however, coal mining was supplemented by another industrial activity, brick production based on shale deposits.

If readers find the idea of a coal mining town in a state known for its nearly limitless supplies of oil to be peculiar, that was just one of several paradoxes surrounding Thurber. A second paradox is that rural Texas is not normally associated with the domination of communities by corporations, although company lumber towns existed in east Texas, and some large ranches in west Texas were under corporate control. Still, the fact that the Texas and Pacific Coal Company owned Thurber lock, stock, and barrel made it a rare breed among the state's mining communities. Third, Texas is not normally associated with unionization, and yet—surprisingly—Thurber is said to have been one of the most heavily unionized towns in the entire nation—this in a state known for its right-to-work ethic, if not outright animosity toward unions. Fourth, although the popular image of Texas is that it is largely Anglo-American in terms of population, the state is actually highly diverse ethnically. So, too, was Thurber, where people of more than twenty nationalities coexisted. Fifth, Thurber is now a "ghost town," but this too is a paradox. Although such places are normally found in isolated locales, Thurber was located close to the main line of a major east-west railroad line (the Texas and Pacific Railway). Given the tendency for the nation's interstate highway system to essentially parallel major railroads (for intercity travel is the goal of both), it is not surprising that the route chosen for busy Interstate 20 figures in the later history of the town. What is surprising, though, is that Thurber's townsite is almost perfectly bisected by this freeway, something few ghost towns can claim.

Yet another paradox is that, for a ghost town, Thurber has been so well studied. As Tucker notes, about half a dozen informative books have been written about Thurber's history. Still, Tucker had a burning interest in this town of paradoxes, one of them being how the company provided a wide range of goods and services to workers here. The vehicle they used was the Texas Pacific Mercantile and Manufacturing Company, a subsidiary in the classic sense of the word. Surprisingly, this aspect of Thurber had never been studied in detail despite the fact that company records exist in several archives, most notably the Southwest Collection at Texas Tech University. I suspect most researchers had been lured by the social drama of about ten thousand people living under the rule of one company. Tucker, however, wisely realized that the mercantile operations of the company itself deserved closer scrutiny. Thurber, it should be noted, was not alone in this regard: Throughout the nation, most scholarship has focused on the fate of workers, while issues pertaining to business history are often barely mentioned. When he embarked on this study, Tucker plumbed the scanty secondary literature on company stores and found a gaping hole in our knowledge about how and why companies provided goods and services. This book, therefore, is one of the very few that analyzes a company's mercantile operations in detail, shedding new light on the subject and shattering assumptions in the process.

In researching this topic, Tucker did what all good historians should do: He questioned what had been written (and believed) about the subject by going to primary sources—recollections of miners, company records, legal documents, newspaper reports, and so on. If the book you are about to read is one of a handful to address the subject, it does something else; namely, it provides a rather objective look at what is still an emotional subject. Astute readers will note that Tucker sides neither with the company nor the workers—a stance that makes this book rather unique. As his research progressed, Tucker encountered material that made him question what was known, and especially what was believed, about the company and its subsidiary retailing operations. He thus scrutinized Thurber and its company anew, and the result is revisionist history in the best sense of the term. If some of Tucker's findings are startling or unsettling, it should be remembered that he backs them up with evidence. He answers some penetrating questions. For example, did—as was widely believed—the Thurber company store really charge higher prices for goods? Were—as was widely claimed—the workers really forced to patronize it? Were—as was often the case in Texas—non-Anglo workers treated differently by the company when it came to employment opportunities and access to services in the company store? To answer these questions, Tucker had to look deeply, going beyond the anecdotal and digging into specific data bases (such as advertisements for goods, and company ledgers to compare prices per item throughout the local area). His answers to some of these questions may surprise readers. Tucker's research revealed that our knowledge of this company's practices (and by extension, possibly the practices of other companies not yet compared) was based more on speculation and mythology than fact.

If, ultimately, Tucker discovered that perceptions of Thurber's mercantile operation and other services offered by the company were characterized by considerable cognitive dissonance, then that finding is especially noteworthy. His study is therefore not only eye-opening for Thurber, but, by extension, suggests something much deeper and broader about company stores and company towns generally. If, as Tucker discovered, the company store is emblematic of deep schisms in American culture—a culture that cherishes individual freedom while seeking collective solutions—then hopefully it will inspire researchers to study other company towns for what they reveal not only about labor-management relations, but broader American society in general. Moreover, Tucker's study has significant implications for business history generally, for it reaffirms the inherent economic advantages (and social liabilities) of vertically integrated, large-scale retailing, and its effect on local populations. Today, much the same kind of arguments are used against—and similar animosity felt against—large enterprises like Walmart as were used against the company store a century ago. Thus it is that important lessons can be learned from a nearly vanished Texas mining ghost town—lessons that may indeed be applicable far beyond kindred historic mining towns, and just might help us better understand the controversial role of corporate commerce in present-day America.

Richard Francaviglia, Salem, Oregon
Professor Emeritus, University of Texas at Arlington,
and author of *Hard Places: Reading the Landscape of America's Historic Mining Districts*

ACKNOWLEDGMENTS

My first debt is to the members of my master's thesis committee at Tarleton State University in Stephenville, Texas: T. Lindsay Baker, Chris Guthrie, and Patricia Zelman, for directing my research and shaping the text. Under their guidance, especially that of Dr. Baker (a noted historian of technology and ghost towns), I was able to place the interesting story of Thurber's company store into the larger context of industrial company towns and the labor history of Texas. Sincere thanks to Michael Pierce and Donald Zelman, who helped secure funds from Tarleton for research. Employees from several archival collections were instrumental in pointing the way to evidence and images: LeAnna Biles Schooley, Bethany Kolter Dodson, and T. Lindsay Baker at the W. K. Gordon Center for Industrial History of Texas; Glenda Stone at Tarleton State University; Tai Kreidler, Randy Vance, and Monte Monroe at the Southwest Collection/Special Collections Library at Texas Tech University; Jim Bradshaw at the Nita Stewart Haley Memorial Library; and Cathy Spitzenberger at the University of Texas at Arlington. Thanks also to the countless, nameless, and seldom appreciated graduate student workers of these institutions, who did the lion's share of the grunt work. Robin Deeslie, Robert Fairbanks, and Beth Wright of the University of Texas at Arlington helped defray some of my publication costs. I am immensely grateful to Richard Francaviglia, professor emeritus of the University of Texas at Arlington and jack-of-all-trades, for reading the manuscript, helping me to smooth rough passages, and writing a laudatory foreword. Finally, thanks to my parents for their never-ending love and support.

OYSTERS MACARONI & BEER

THURBER, TEXAS AND THE COMPANY STORE

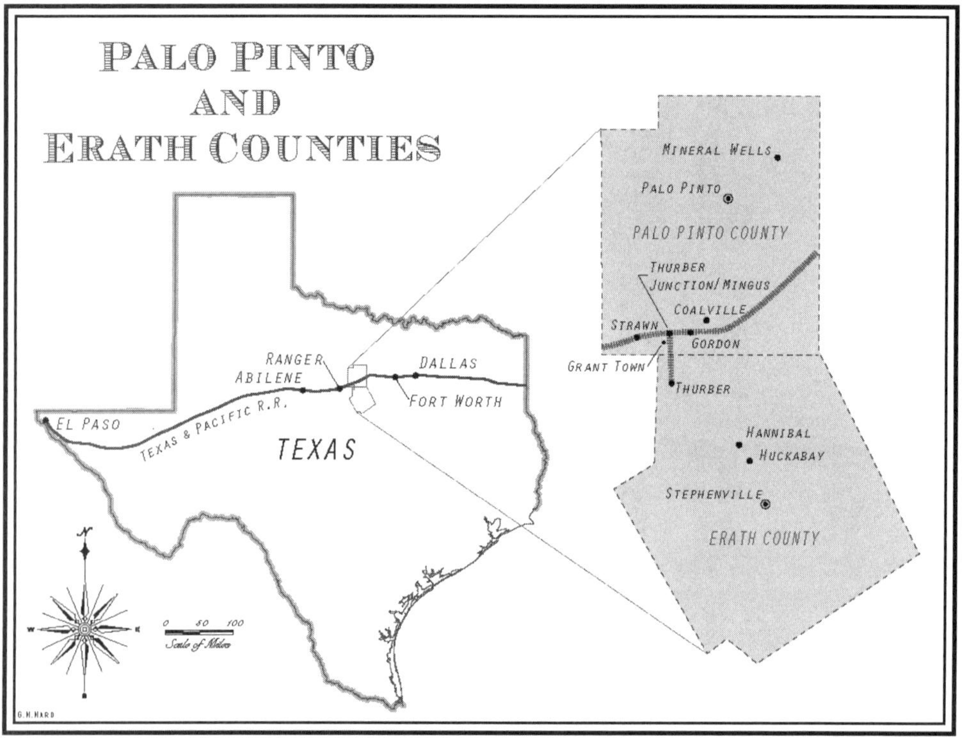

Texas and the Thurber area. Map by George Ward.

CHAPTER 1
THE COMPANY TOWN OF THURBER

About halfway between Fort Worth and Abilene on Interstate 20 lies perhaps the best-known ghost town in Texas: Thurber. For nearly half a century, from the 1880s until the 1930s, Thurber was one of the premier industrial cities in Texas. As a "company town," all the land, buildings, and stores were owned by the Texas and Pacific Coal Company. There were no elected city officials, no city taxes, and no school taxes. It was a kingdom unto itself, wholly owned and operated by the company. During its life, Thurber etched a place in the history of Texas. It was an almost completely unionized camp after 1903, playing an important role in the labor history of the Greater Southwest. The company and the residents made it the largest, most cosmopolitan town between Fort Worth and El Paso. Home to nearly ten thousand people from more than twenty nations at its height, it was the largest single producer of bituminous coal in the state and manufactured millions of vitrified paving bricks that survive in many streets throughout Texas and other states across the southern half of the United States. By 1920 the company, renamed the Texas Pacific Coal and Oil Company, had built at Thurber several dozen workhouses, stores, warehouses, and other buildings, as well as hundreds of homes. The functioning of Thurber so impressed Texas governor Joseph D. Sayers in 1902 that he declared it one of the greatest things he had ever seen in the state.[1] The company town's operations so pleased Edgar L. Marston, the company's second president, that he bragged about it in a personal letter to oil magnate John D. Rockefeller, comparing it favorably to the trouble-ridden coal mining camp at Ludlow, Colorado.[2]

A modern-day traveler would see much less, and, without investigation, would hardly believe such a town had existed at the site. On the north side of the highway is a red brick smokestack towering 150 feet. Described by one observer as "Thurber's Tombstone,"[3] the tower has at its base an old painted placard and historical marker that briefly describes the history of the town, leaving unmentioned the brickworks and extensive mercantile operations. Nearby is a restaurant in an old, large, similarly colored, crumbling brick building. Little else on this side of the highway gives evidence to the past of the site but a few aged, deteriorating buildings and a pair of old-fashioned ranch-style homes. On the south side of the road are a few more clues. A modern restaurant loaded with old memorabilia sits atop a rise oddly named "New York Hill." Surely that moniker, spelled out in large painted letters on the hillside, has a story behind it. At the bottom of the hill is the Thurber Historical Park, with a miner's home, the old bandstand, and St. Barbara's, Thurber's original and quaint Catholic church, beautifully restored. A modern brick museum, designed to look old, stands next to the park. Called the W. K. Gordon Center for Industrial History of Texas, honoring the town's longtime general manager, the building houses first-rate museum exhibits and a growing archival collection. With a little work, the modern-day traveler would discover eight historical markers in the immediate vicinity and a wealth of information about the history of Thurber.

Still, there is little visual evidence of coal mining in the immediate vicinity, except for the mentions in the historical markers or exhibits. Only in winter, when the cold thins the brush and grass in the pastures of the surrounding ranchlands, can some eroded humps of discarded rock—mine tailings—be seen in the distance. The Thurber Brick Company produced most of the bricks found at the empty townsite. Indeed, the vitrified paving bricks produced by the subsidiary of the coal company, still in place in numerous streets in places like Fort Worth, Austin, and Galveston, serve as some of the most lasting reminders of Thurber's industrial reach. The surviving landmarks of Thurber, however, all have connections to another subsidiary concern of the Texas and Pacific Coal Company: the Texas Pacific Mercantile and Manufacturing Company (TPM&M). Executives created TPM&M in 1894, about five years after the founding of Thurber, to oversee and manage the numerous commercial and service enterprises that were essential to the life and history of a company town. The smokestack provided draft for the boilers that powered the industrial-sized icehouse, which produced blocks of high-quality ice for the townspeople, the company's stores, and the refrigerated railcars of Jay Gould's Texas and Pacific Railway. The old building now housing a restaurant was once the company dry goods store, which sold everything from bolts of cloth to the choicest coffins. TPM&M carpenters built the homes of the managers that visitors can still spy from the base of the smokestack, as well as the miner's shack and bandstand on the south side of the highway, just as they erected and maintained countless others in Thurber's heyday. Even the modern museum resembles the long-gone town drugstore where TPM&M soda jerks, countermen, and pharmacists once plied their trade.

Although the Texas Pacific Mercantile and Manufacturing Company outlasted both the extraction of coal and the manufacturing of brick at Thurber, general histories of the town have yet to focus on the mercantile in any significant detail. Labor histories mention TPM&M in passing as a grievance of the miners. Other authors devote a few scant pages to it in a tangential manner. These writings do not examine the structure of the company, the makeup of its employees, or the importance of TPM&M to the history of the company town. The Texas Pacific Mercantile and Manufacturing Company touched the lives of all of Thurber's residents: coal miners, brickmakers, teamsters, smiths, accountants, bookkeepers, clerks, and the oft-unmentioned housewives and children. In addition to providing goods and services to the townspeople of Thurber, who encountered TPM&M every day, or attempted to ignore it, the mercantile company sought business from residents of the surrounding countryside and served those passing through the town as well. When work in the mines was slack or when labor troubles loomed, the TPM&M continued to operate and continued to generate revenue. For company towns, the subsidiary that ran the town's businesses and services was an integral component of the site's history, but no previous studies of Thurber have described in detail the role of TPM&M. To call the mercantile a pernicious monopoly or a mere contrivance to exploit laborers paints an incomplete portrait of the company store. To fully understand Thurber, the history, character, and perception of the Texas Pacific Mercantile and Manufacturing Company must be related.

Mining in the area predated the establishment of Thurber. The coal deposits in Erath and Palo Pinto Counties are of bituminous coal, a black or dark-brown coal lower in quality than jet black hard anthracite and better than brown soft lignite. The coal in the vicinity was probably known to local Indian tribes and was first described by geologists after explorations in 1855 and 1856. In 1881, eight miles northeast of what would become Thurber, the pick and shovel of miners working for the

James, Cowan, and Noltan Company began a drift-mining operation, cutting directly into the side of a hill. By 1884 Jay Gould's Texas and Pacific Railway Company owned and operated the rugged camp called Coalville, hoping to extract coal cheaply along its line, which ran east and west though the area. Despite intermittent labor disruptions prompted by the Knights of Labor, who formed a local union chapter for miners at the nearby town of Gordon in 1882, workers extracted perhaps three hundred tons a day from three tunnels, even boring one tunnel completely through a hill. Once the miners removed this coal from the earth, they dragged it by oxcart to a siding of the Texas and Pacific line for use as fuel in its locomotives. Poorly run and plagued by labor difficulties, the mines at Coalville were abandoned by the railroad company in 1886. The workers, still members of the Knights of Labor, drifted into the camp of the newly formed Johnson Coal Mining Company on the site of what would become Thurber.[4]

Fleeing massive debt in their home state of Michigan, brothers William W. and Harvey Johnson ended up in Texas in 1878 looking for new business opportunities along the frontier. In 1880 William Johnson discovered that farmers in northern Erath County were finding "black rocks" near the surface of the earth; he knew these rocks were coal. On October 7, 1886, the Johnson brothers purchased the Pedro Herrera survey, more than twenty-three hundred acres, in the northwest corner of Erath County, Texas, for twenty-five hundred dollars, purchasing more land over the next several months. The brothers hoped to reap substantial profits from selling coal to the Texas and Pacific Railway, which ran east and west about two miles north of their first shaft, sunk in December 1886. After months of negotiations, on May 7, 1887, the Johnson brothers agreed to sell a minimum of five hundred tons of clean coal a day to the railway, and the railway in turn agreed to lay a spur track from its main line to the mines and pay the Johnson brothers a fifty-cent profit on each ton mined, as long as the total price of coal was not more than $2.75 per ton. In the summer of 1887, the Johnson brothers incorporated their enterprise as the Johnson Coal Mining Company and immediately borrowed one hundred thousand dollars at 6 percent interest, issuing one hundred bonds to pay for the loan. In 1887 the Texas and Pacific Railway completed the spur to the mine, where some fifty carloads of mined coal sat ready for shipment.[5]

Labor difficulties and a lack of capital beleaguered the Johnson Coal Mining Company from the outset of its short business life. The workers at the new Johnson operation came from the defunct mines at Coalville and built a new Knights of Labor hall on union-owned land neighboring the Johnson mines, which they informally referred to as Johnsonville. The miners objected to working for a rate of $1.50 per ton, lower than the $1.75 per ton they had earned at Coalville, and went on strike for two months. The Johnson brothers capitulated and raised the rate to $1.95 per ton. Adding to the financial difficulties of the Johnson brothers, they opened and operated a commissary and agreed to build the workers houses. This mercantile operation was a necessary component to any coal camp, as the workers needed access to food and supplies, being located so far from any established community or store. The Johnson brothers, however, lacked the funds to build the promised homes, prompting the miners to erect their own shacks and shanties. The paucity of capital also meant that the brothers could only meagerly stock the small, all-purpose store. Also, while the first shaft was in operation and producing just four hundred tons of coal daily, the company spent what little money it had sinking a second shaft that brought no benefit. The Johnson Coal Mining Company continually fought off bankruptcy while it attempted to meet its monthly payroll demands.[6]

Johnson commissary. The Johnson brothers built a rudimentary commissary for their coal workers at the site that would later become Thurber. They were too cash strapped to build any other stores. Courtesy of Southwest Collection/Special Collections Library, Texas Tech University, Lubbock, Texas, Thurber, Texas, Photograph Collection, SWCPC 209.

Through 1887 and 1888, the bonds of the Johnson Coal Mining Company sold poorly, and their monthly fiscal burden prompted the Johnson brothers to seek outside sources of capital. In the summer of 1887, Harry M. Taylor, attorney for William and Harvey Johnson, approached Colonel Robert Dickie Hunter of Saint Louis to secure a loan of fifty thousand dollars. Hunter was born in Ayrshire, Scotland, on April 5, 1833, and immigrated to the United States with his parents at the age of nine. He grew up around Bunker Hill, Illinois, marrying in 1858, and the next year tried his hand in mining and prospecting in the Colorado and Arizona Territories. Settling in Missouri during the Civil War, without fighting (his colonelcy seems to be honorific, although it is unknown who gave it to him), he entered the young and burgeoning cattle industry, moving cattle from Texas to the railroads in Missouri. By 1871 Hunter had earned a fortune as a livestock trader, making contacts in places like Fort Worth and Dodge City, and encountering characters as diverse as cattleman John Chisum and railway tycoon Jay Gould. By the mid-1880s, the successful businessman was searching for new investment opportunities as the strength of his cattle enterprise waned. The Johnson mines intrigued the second-string robber baron. Hunter toured the site in August 1887, telling his friend Gould that the property would be valuable if he could obtain sufficient capital to exploit it properly. He did not give the Johnson brothers a loan, but began moving behind the scenes to purchase the property for himself. In the meantime, the loss of Harvey Johnson, "a successful manager of men," who died of typhoid fever on January 30, 1888, weakened the already struggling Johnson Coal Mining Company. William Johnson now had to run the undercapitalized mines without the support of his more labor-friendly brother.[7]

In the spring of 1888, William Johnson borrowed $25,000 from a Weatherford, Texas, bank, on unfavorable terms, in an attempt to remain solvent. In May he sold an option, the right to share in the profits of the company, to Colonel Hunter for another $25,000 in an attempt to raise much-needed funds. The Johnson Coal Mining Company faced more than financial problems in early 1888. On March 24, 1888, the receiver for the Texas and Pacific Railway Company, John C. Brown, sent an angry letter to the Johnson Coal Mining Company, declaring that the quality and quantity of coal mined by the Johnson operation had never reached levels specified by the contract of 1887. Brown also criticized the high cost of the coal and threatened to remove the spur track that led to the mines if a new agreement could not be negotiated. The Johnson mines had never had enough capital to purchase the machinery needed to properly separate unwanted slate from the coal or reach its promised production of five hundred tons a day. Hunter may have asked his acquaintance Jay Gould to put this added pressure on the Johnson operation.[8]

In June Hunter purchased two more options on the Johnson Coal Mining Company, which was enough money for Johnson to meet his pressing payroll obligations. This transaction gave Hunter the time to arrange his finances for his eventual takeover of the mines. For months, Colonel Hunter and his son-in-law Edgar L. Marston, a New York City banker, had been assembling a cadre of investors interested in the Texas coal mines. In mid-September 1888, William Johnson informed his workers that he could not afford to pay the August payroll. The miners obliged him by giving him an extra week to do so. When that deadline passed on September 22, 1888, the Johnson miners quit the mines and went on strike. Several sold their statements of earnings for pennies on the dollar or left the area; others angrily waited for their pay. Just over a month later, on October 27, 1888, Hunter gained control of the Johnson mines from William Johnson, and on November 12, 1888, transferred the property to the newly organized Texas and Pacific Coal Company.[9]

The Texas and Pacific Coal Company held its initial meetings in September of 1888, and the state of Texas granted it a corporate charter on October 4, 1888. Whereas the Johnson brothers had kept their capital stock among themselves, Hunter, president and general manager of the new company, spread the twenty thousand 100-dollar shares of stock among several investors. This generated a pool of capital, amounting to about two million dollars, and allowed Hunter's new venture to avoid many of the pitfalls encountered by the Johnson Coal Mining Company. The board named their new venture to flatter its principal customer and Hunter's friend, the Texas and Pacific Railway of Jay Gould. The coal camp at Johnsonville also received a new name: Thurber. This was to honor a principal investor in the new Texas and Pacific Coal Company, wealthy grocer Horace Kingsley Thurber of New York City, an associate of Edgar L. Marston. Many of the investors and directors of the new corporation were from the Northeast, and several were successful New York businessmen.[10]

When the Texas and Pacific Coal Company took possession of the mines in November 1888, Colonel Hunter immediately set out to break the striking miners and their Knights of Labor organization. Hunter first announced a reduction in the rate paid to miners per ton of coal excavated, lowering it from Johnson's $1.95 to $1.40, ostensibly to discourage the striking men from returning to the mines. He also announced that the company would "screen" the coal before payments were calculated. In the process of screening, weighmen passed coal over a gratelike screen. The smaller pieces that passed through the screen would not be weighed, which meant the company would pay a smaller wage to the miner than before. The company would either utilize or sell the nut- or pea-sized coal that passed through the screen, boosting their profits. There were some threats of violence; so Hunter ensured that a detachment of Texas Rangers under Captain Sam A. McMurray was stationed at Thurber for most of 1889. Still, none of the striking miners joined the new operation and the coal company found itself without workers. To remedy this, at a cost to the company of $10,833.64, Hunter began recruiting men from the nation's various coal mining districts. Many of the miners Hunter transported to Thurber refused to work once they learned that a strike was on, but in February 1889 about 170 black miners began working the coal at Thurber. Some people labeled these black men professional strikebreakers, and indeed some used aliases: Robert Henry Smith, Thurber's "Negro Boss," was better known as Bob Rogers, and one laborer, Albert Alcorn, registered with the company as Albert Whitehead. Later that year, the National Progressive Union's *National Labor Tribune* declared that according to union rules, there was not a legitimate strike in Thurber because the striking miners had never worked for Hunter's company. With this development, Hunter was able to recruit more men, many of them foreign immigrants willing to work for his wages. Colonel Hunter declared that the Knights of Labor had called the strike "off" by the middle of 1889.[11]

With these labor difficulties ongoing, Hunter engaged himself in building a new company town from scratch. A company town is a settlement where one corporation wholly owns the real estate, homes, and commercial buildings. The employees of such a town are mainly dependent on the company for employment, housing, and supplies. Though company towns are not a purely American invention or phenomenon, they reached their zenith in terms of prevalence and development in the United States during the late nineteenth and early twentieth centuries. In this heyday of company towns between the Civil War and the Great Depression, perhaps as many as twenty-five hundred such places dotted the land. Numerous factors contributed to this phenomenon, among them: a lack of state-run industry, a vibrant laissez-faire capitalism, and the widespread but oftentimes remote locations of natural resources. Because these raw materials were often located far

The "Bob Rogers" family. Thurber's coal-mining population was racially and ethnically diverse. Colonel Hunter hired black miners to break an early strike, and many worked for the company for decades. "Bob Rogers" was the alias of Robert Henry Smith, who was probably a professional strikebreaker. Courtesy of Nita Stewart Haley Memorial Library, Midland, Texas, Miles B. Hart Collection.

from established population centers or there was no adequate access to well-worn transportation routes, the company town was essential to extract the resources and turn a profit. Factories or other industries located near towns could draw their workers from the local population; extractive industries—coal, ores, and lumber—were usually not so conveniently located. Like the coal towns of southern Appalachia or the lumber camps of the great Northwest, Thurber, Texas, was created for drawing workers to a remote resource on the frontier.[12]

Access to natural resources was not the only reason for building and operating all company towns, as some such communities also sprang up around factories, like Pullman, Illinois, built just outside Chicago by the Pullman Palace Car Company. The primary incentive for a company to build its own town was the maximization of profit: a happy worker was a more productive worker. Operators of company towns could take steps to ensure the contentment of employees and attempt to counter the spread of unionism, which most companies viewed to be detrimental to their bottom line. The Stonega Coke and Coal Company of Virginia, for instance, built its own towns believing that a good town would attract the best workers, tie them to the community, and help deter unionization. A Stonega Coke and Coal Company report in 1916 concluded: "Contentment is necessary for the stability of labor and prevention of unions and lockouts."[13] Industrialist George Pullman claimed his company town of Pullman, Illinois, would counter the "baneful influences" of Chicago, a hotbed of labor radicalism, and hasten a new era of labor relations by creating a problem-free workforce. The Colorado Fuel and Iron Company, a steel concern with coal mining towns in southern Colorado, built its towns recognizing that they could keep the workers happy and the unions out if they could shape the lives of their workers.[14] Hunter built Thurber for the Texas and Pacific Coal Company with such ideas in mind: to lure and maintain a labor force, preferably a non-union labor force. He immediately had laborers building stores, boarding houses, schools, and two hundred homes.[15]

The majority of company-owned coal towns founded in the late nineteenth century began as rough-and-tumble frontier-type communities with few amenities beyond the necessities of life. These towns were impermanent, built without specific plans for growth, and provided the bare minimum needed for the workers. The first shelter for miners was often temporary, usually tents or barracks-style dormitories. The first mercantile buildings were often all-purpose company stores and saloons. The company stores provided miners and their families with food and tools and supplies for mining like picks, shovels, and blasting powder. The saloons provided the necessary lubricant for the worker: alcohol. More permanent housing came next, followed by buildings such as schools, specialty stores, and amusement halls. Most companies constructed these latter improvements only years after a town's founding, when profits ensured the operations' viability. Many American coal company towns, like those of southern Appalachia and southern Colorado, went through such an early "frontier" phase, building amenities later. The Stonega Coke and Coal Company began building such facilities in its town of Stonega, Virginia, two years after its founding because of local competition for workers from other collieries. The company constructed schools and hospitals to attract workers and their families and, of course, keep them content. In southern Colorado, the Colorado Fuel and Iron Company added a "Sociological Department" twenty years into its existence to build and run schools, hospitals, and recreation facilities. A happy worker was a stable worker: he would stay in town, shun the unions, be more productive, and buy from the company store.[16] Hunter and his investors were more farsighted in Thurber.

Colonel Hunter busied his firm in late 1888 and early 1889 constructing his new company town and beginning its mercantile operations. The financially strapped Johnson Coal Mining Company had offered only the least of amenities to its miners, constructing only a rickety commissary and saloon. The Johnson commissary was a nondescript building offering only rudimentary food and mining supplies. With little spare capital, the store was chronically understocked. The saloon was a small building leased to a private individual named John L. Ward, once coproprietor of Fort Worth's famous White Elephant Saloon. The homes the Johnson brothers promised to build for their workers never completely materialized, and the miners had built small shacks for themselves.[17] Hunter first ordered the removal of the primitive shanties set up by the striking Johnson miners, offering their "owners" a pittance in return, telling his investors: "No one is now allowed to erect a house for any purpose."[18] He then hired a number of local workers to erect a barbed-wire fence around nine hundred acres, lay out and clear streets, build water tanks, and construct numerous permanent buildings. Many of these structures would become the core of the Mercantile Department for the Texas and Pacific Coal Company, which would eventually evolve into the Texas Pacific Mercantile and Manufacturing Company. According to Hunter's 1889 annual report to his stockholders, the Texas and Pacific Coal Company spent $56,494.29 on a "large general store with warehouse attached, drug store, hardware store, boarding houses, offices, stables, shops, school houses, churches, and over two hundred two, three, four and five room houses."[19] Hunter and his company were desperately in need of miners, and wanted to lure workers and families to a location that was not only on the faraway frontier but also already known for its labor strife. Designing and erecting a company town with features usually found only in more evolved camps would make Thurber an enticing place to work.[20]

Operations at the Mercantile Department of Texas and Pacific Coal Company centered on the commercial buildings first built by Hunter and his work crews: the general commissary, drugstore, and hardware store. With direct access via spur track to the growing web of railroads that crisscrossed the United States, these outlets provided everything needed for the residents in the young company town. The general store offered the inhabitants of Thurber essential foods and dry goods. The drugstore offered patent medicines, sold various other sundries, including ice cream, and filled prescriptions from the company physician. Miners patronized the hardware store to purchase blasting powder, new tools, and other items for their work; the hardware store served as a supplier for the company as well, which seemed always building anew or augmenting the old. For a few months beginning in 1891 the warehouse that housed grocery items doubled as the Catholic chapel until the company erected a Catholic church, eventually named for Saint Barbara (the patroness saint of miners), in 1892. By the end of 1889, these stores, with the mines only partially operating, had $50,000 of stock on hand and had shown net profits of between 16 and 17 percent.[21] Hunter praised the stores effusively in his company report to stockholders: "The statement made at the time of the organization of this company, that the profits from the store and rentals from the buildings would pay all interest charges, has been verified and the current year will close with a surplus for dividends."[22] Indeed, profits from the company stores were an impressive $25,825.46 for 1889, enough to cover the interest payments on the bonds the coal company sold to finance its establishment. First-year earnings from the company-operated farms and livery stable, both of which would later be components of the Texas Pacific Mercantile and Manufacturing Company, were an additional $278.85. Everyone expected profits in all departments to grow as the colliery expanded.[23]

The barbed-wire fence Hunter put around the town of Thurber might have contributed to the profit of the mercantile stores; the company's new hires certainly believed it did. Built during the first few months of Hunter's tenure, it enclosed nine hundred acres and the town itself. Presumably it was constructed to keep out labor agitators; workers assumed the fence was a way to force them to patronize only the company store. A fence was a feature not uncommon in "closed" company towns during the era, towns where management strictly controlled who could enter or exit. Opinion is divided as to whether the fence around Thurber had any real effect on employee behavior, though many Thurberites believed that it did. According to witnesses it was no mere livestock fence, as it stood six feet high, arrayed with four taut strands of barbed wire, an invention then little more than a decade old.

The design of the fence ensured that it was more of an annoyance than an impediment, as individuals could easily get through it and routinely did. Wagons and riders were another matter, as armed guards manned the gates that opened to the north, east, and west. The era of closed gates did not last long, because the company soon removed the locks on these gates after non-Thurber residents complained in court that the fence prevented them from reaching the federal post office in the town. Stories abounded that the guards kept notes on those employees who attempted to purchase goods from outside the fence, and allegations of retribution persisted even after the company removed the fence in 1903. One woman remembered her mother hiding groceries under her skirts to keep guards from seeing her contraband. Some asserted that guards followed outside peddlers and kept records on which Thurber residents purchased from them. Others, such as Roscoe Hayden Sherrill, only thirteen years of age when the fence was removed, were just as adamant that the company did not ever allow any peddlers or farmers through the gates, telling an interviewer in the 1960s: "At one time, a long time ago, the company would not allow farmers to come into the town and sell." The truth is somewhere between these extremes: the fence made it more difficult for peddlers and farmers to enter the town, but enter they certainly did.[24]

Colonel Hunter swore during an 1895 court case that the company did not compel its workers to buy at the company store, glibly acknowledging, however, that it was easier for the inhabitants to do so:

> Gordon is the nearest town to Thurber. It is certainly a fact that all the people who live, by my permission, within the enclosure there at Thurber, traded at our stores, as a general rule; that our stores are more convenient to trade at than any other stores in that country. For the purpose of supplying our employees and such, those stores were all opened and operated by our company. . . . We do not compel them to trade there. . . . A great many of them, the majority do trade there. . . . It is very true that all those stores were established there for profit and gain, and that the company expected to sell to the people who lived in there, so long as they would behave themselves and pay the money, whether they were employees or not, if they were not objectionable.[25]

As an employer struggling to entice workers to its faraway coal camp during its early years, the Texas and Pacific Coal Company could hardly afford to dismiss employees for so insignificant a reason as buying goods from outside the camp or patronizing peddlers. Surviving com-

Colonel Robert Dickie Hunter. The Colonel on his horse in Thurber. He was a self-made industrial capitalist fiercely opposed to unionism who once told labor officials: "I will run my business or run it to Hell!" Courtesy of Nita Stewart Haley Memorial Library, Midland, Texas, Miles B. Hart Collection.

pany records do not ever mention firing or evicting people who did not shop at company stores. Instead, the records indicate that company executives were distressed that profits were lost to vendors unassociated with the company. The directors sought ways to counter the peddlers by making the stores more attractive to Thurberites, not by punishing the workers. Whatever Hunter's intention in enclosing his company town within a fence, workers contended, with some credibility, that he was "forcing" them to live by his rules in what they derisively described as his "serfdom"—the Colonel was a man who once told a delegation of union officials: "I will run my business or run it to Hell!"[26] Whatever the effects on mercantile profits, until the company removed the fence after Thurber's unionization in 1903, many employees saw it as a form of company control: the thrusting of a monopoly over them in order to contribute to the profits of the colliery.

Another incident that demonstrated Hunter's efforts to control Thurber's business scene involved the first saloon on the property. When the Colonel took possession of the mines from the Johnson Coal Mining Company in November 1888, John L. Ward's lease contract remained valid under the new company. Because it was the only building not controlled directly by the company, Ward's saloon became a meeting place for the unemployed Johnson miners and labor organizers—it appears the fearsome guards at the gates allowed several unsavory characters into town. Anxious to bring the drinking-house under his control, and end any nascent labor agitation, Hunter bought out Ward's contract for $2,700, paid in installments of $150 over eighteen months. In one of Colonel Hunter's few unsure moves, he did not know if it was legal for his coal company to operate a saloon, so he leased the operation to a friend named Thomas Lawson. Lawson began operating his saloon on May 20, 1889, and was soon doing more business than any of the company's mercantile operations.[27]

After a few months had passed, with the legal issues apparently resolved and aware of the ample sums of money that the company could make if it controlled the saloon directly, Hunter decided to break his lease with Lawson. Sergeant W. John L. Sullivan of the Texas Rangers, in town at Hunter's request to protect coal company property during the lingering labor discord (McMurray left a few months before), arrested an inebriated Lawson after he shot at a miner. Hunter also claimed that Lawson was trying to break up his camp.[28] Later, Sullivan took part in "an exciting fisticuff" between Hunter and Lawson that he described in his rollicking 1909 memoir of life as a lawman:

> Lawson and his bartender, Malcolm, and Col. Hunter, all three met in a drug store. Hunter and Lawson began cursing each other, and I heard the row and rushed into the store just in time to see Hunter burst the bottom of a spittoon out over Tom Lawson's head. Hunter then threw a box of cigars at him, striking Lawson in the ear and scattering cigars all over the floor. I noticed Malcolm slipping up behind Col. Hunter, preparing to hit him in the back of the head. Just as he started to strike Hunter, however, I struck Malcolm myself, in time to stop what would have been a dreadful blow. . . . I thought I had him whipped, but when he got up he said he would fight me if I would pull my sixshooter off. . . . I removed my sixshooter. . . . He commenced beating my head, nose and eyes until my face looked like jelly. I do not know what would have become of my face if Bob Ward, the [Texas and Pacific Coal] company's lawyer, had not come to my rescue. Ward knocked Malcolm loose from me and knocked him twelve feet from where we were clinched. Tom Lawson then knocked Ward down, he falling on top of Malcolm. Hunter was pacing around after Lawson with a heavy rock, but never did get in his lick.[29]

An incensed Hunter instructed his clerks, office employees, and other white-collar employees not to enter Lawson's bar on pain of dismissal, but the miners still had access to alcohol. He stopped the delivery of water and ice to the saloon and even ordered Thurber's storekeepers to refuse service to Lawson, his employees, and their families except for essentials at the drugstore. Hunter even declined to cash the company's scrip, "coupons" or "check" the company gave to miners in lieu of cash for temporary credit, for Lawson. On August 26, 1890, Colonel Hunter levied a distress warrant on the saloon, claiming Lawson had failed to carry out the terms of his lease. He then filed suit against Lawson to have him removed from the camp and to have the lease voided, a suit that reached the Supreme Court of Texas. The justices decided in favor of Texas and Pacific Coal Company, saying the contract between Hunter and Lawson was void as being in restraint of trade. The court held that the contract created an illegal trust that closed off saloon competition in the town. Oddly, it was legal for the coal company to operate a saloon itself without competition.[30] While the case against Thomas Lawson wound its way through the courts, the coal company began operating its own saloon, which the locals soon nicknamed "the Snake." For the year 1890, although the company only managed the saloon for part of the year, the drinking house earned the company $11,216.20 in profits; the other company stores in Thurber earned $26,581.76. The saloon alone collected 42 percent of what the other stores made combined.[31]

As the 1890s dawned, with labor troubles receding from public view (the Knights of Labor having nearly disappeared and lost their nationwide influence), the Texas and Pacific Coal Company attracted hundreds of miners to Thurber. As the population increased, the tonnage of coal mined increased accordingly, and the company began turning good profits. The company continued making improvements to the town, and visitors described it as a happy, industrious village. Many of the miners were Italian, Polish, and Mexican, though many hailed from other countries. The work was hard. At 5:30 a.m. each day but Sundays and holidays, underground miners and other workers began heading toward the mines at the sound of a whistle that made itself heard all through the town. At six o'clock a train called the Black Diamond took workers to the mineshafts that lay generally west of town. Miners, dressed in their work clothes and toting their lunch buckets, took elevators down to the coal vein beneath the surface of the earth, where they had left their tools the day before. The vein at Thurber was just a few inches thick, which meant the laborer had to lie on his side to work the coal, loosening it with explosives, gathering it with picks, and loading it into empty cars. Each miner placed a tag on the car he filled, to prove how much he collected each day, and a mule and driver pulled it to the weighmaster to be weighed. Numerous other workers repaired tools, fixed cars, laid rails, monitored air shafts, and helped in other ways. In town children went to school, women did shopping and chores, accountants slaved feverishly over their ledgers, and salesmen practiced their pitch.[32] Miners continued their work until 5:30 p.m., when they boarded the trains to return to town, where dinner, revelry, and sleep commenced. A Fort Worth newspaper wrote glowingly of the town in 1896: "Here certainty of employment for the industrious render them happy. . . . Here good wages are the reward of honest toil, and the equivalent of the good things of this world is always obtainable as soon as earned."[33] As Thurber went from boom to bust, from coal to oil, and from non-union to union to non-union again, it was the Texas Pacific Mercantile and Manufacturing Company that provided these "good things" to the men and women, the workers and families, of the company town.

CHAPTER 2
A "COMPANY STORE" FOR THURBER

The Mercantile Department of the Texas and Pacific Coal Company became a substantial moneymaker for the coal company during the early 1890s. The first manager of the Mercantile Department was Frank S. Cronk, who ran it from 1889 to 1894. Under his tenure, with the heavy-handed scrutiny of Colonel Hunter and input from William K. Gordon, general manager of the mines, the company store played a role in Thurber becoming, as Hunter himself described it, "one of the most beautiful, quiet and healthy mining camps in the United States."[1] William K. Gordon played an important role in the history of Thurber, guiding the efforts of the colliery and stores as the town's general manager and superintendent, and, later, as a vice president of the coal and mercantile companies. Born in Spotsylvania County, Virginia, in 1862, Gordon studied as an engineer before surveying a rail route around Thurber, where Hunter hired him in 1889. Remembered as a Southern gentleman and "Bigga Boss," Gordon harbored a genuine paternalistic affection for the citizens of Thurber, though he was antagonistic toward labor unions. An early 1890s advertisement for the mercantile stores found in the company paper, above Cronk's imprimatur, asserted that: "We Have the Healthiest Town in Texas, and We are making it the cheapest town to live in. Hard working laborers can lay up the cold cash as an insurance account against sickness or old age, we work for the interest of those who work for us."[2] Alongside the paternalistic assertion that the company had the welfare of its workers at heart, the piece made a pecuniary pitch, claiming that the company sold the highest quality goods at the cheapest price in the state. The company always maintained that its direct access to the railroad and ability to buy in bulk with cash meant it could offer goods at low prices and still make a profit. After Cronk left the company in 1894, he was succeeded by J. M. Bass and then by Lee Simpson, both of whom served as head storekeeper for a few months each.[3]

Whether the goods were the cheapest in the state or not, customers had two options for purchases in Thurber, cash or credit. Since most newly hired workers had little money of their own, the Texas and Pacific Coal Company often paid for the transportation of miners to Thurber, a charge that was then deducted from their pay, and miners often bought their first supplies on credit. Most coal companies in the late eighteenth century extended some form of credit to their workers, enabling laborers who started with nothing to begin their work. It was an accepted part of the job "package" offered by the company to its prospective employees, luring them from one company to another. In 1892, for example, the company spent $10,496.93 on the transportation of miners to Thurber, some of which the company never recouped, as several workers left before paying their debts. For the first few months of operation in 1888, the company extended credit to employees by what was termed the commissary method: salesmen noted credit purchases, bookkeepers charged purchases to the worker, and later deducted them from earnings. As the laboring population of the town increased, this system became unwieldy as there could be multiple purchases each day and the family members of the employee often did the shopping. This created tedious and voluminous calculations, which overburdened the company accountants. To resolve these issues, Edgar L. Marston, then treasurer of the Texas and Pacific Coal Company, instituted a "scrip" system in early 1890.[4]

Many company towns used the scrip system to extend credit to laborers during the era. The company bookkeeping department issued scrip, or "check" as it was often called in Thurber, to workers who needed or requested money in between paydays. The company held the equivalent of two weeks' wages for each employee to guarantee house rent and other fixed charges like doctor fees and the train service to the mines; the miner could then withdraw any surplus secured so far during the month in scrip. The company would sometimes grant workers with a solid work record credit in excess of their earned income. The worker or one of his family members went to the check office, an appendage of the mine payroll office, and drew scrip as desired. Accountants then gave the person requesting the scrip a coupon book in values ranging from one to ten dollars, each with detachable coupons or "checks" inside with denominations from five cents to fifty cents. The purchaser then presented the scrip as payment just like cash at company-operated stores. On paydays, the worker received an envelope at the payroll office detailing what he had earned minus his scrip deductions, rent, and other fixed fees; any surplus was paid out in cash. If the miner remained in debt to the company because of an overreliance on scrip or because of slack work, the payroll office carried the debts over to the next payday. Each night, mercantile employees returned spent scrip to the payroll office, and, once a month, a bookkeeper, accompanied by an armed guard, burned the accumulated spent scrip in a company furnace. Before the town's unionization in 1903, workers believed that the company designed their monthly paydays to force them to rely on the scrip, thus keeping them in debt to the company.[5]

The "bull-pen," as detractors called the area inside Hunter's fence, and the scrip system influenced both the profits of the coal company's Mercantile Department and the grievances of the miners, who felt the company exploited them in this fashion. Profits generated by the business enterprises were indeed impressive during the first years of Thurber's existence. The mercantile department made $25,825.46 in 1889, $26,581.76 in 1890, $26,377.20 in 1891, and more than doubled this to $65,554.62 in 1892. Other components of what would become the Texas Pacific Mercantile and Manufacturing Company in 1894, like the town saloon and livery stable, whose receipts the company then tabulated separately, also made substantial sums during the early 1890s. These earnings reflected the population growth of the town and the sizable increase in the tonnage of coal mined. The population of Thurber was two hundred in 1888, but by 1892 had increased to around two thousand. The Texas and Pacific Coal Company had mined only 74,816.75 tons in 1889, but was extracting 211,097.30 tons in 1892.[6]

In 1892 Dick Naylor, a correspondent to the *Dallas Morning News,* visited Thurber, where mercantile manager Frank S. Cronk and town superintendent William K. Gordon gave him a tour of both its stores and mines. He described the business center of town, which included "a large two-story storehouse" that held the general store, post office, and Cronk's office (with Cronk doubling as the postmaster), a drugstore, and a hardware store. Meat cutters supplied Thurber with meat from the company's own slaughterhouse, "where fifteen beeves and some half dozen hogs are butchered daily." The town also sported a large warehouse, livery stable, and public hall. New additions in 1892 consisted of a library, the first in Erath County, and a reading room open to all. The company store, wrote Naylor, "Supplies its employes [*sic*] with all the necessaries and many of the luxuries of life, and at very reasonable prices." He repeated the company line that the mercantile offered its customers the best prices: "Most of the goods, such as flour, sugar, molasses, oils, paints, irons, powder, furniture, etc., are bought in car lots, and on the closest margins; thus enabling the company to sell at low figures to the miners."[7]

Thurber and its industries were not immune to the acute economic depression that struck the nation in 1893, nor the subsequent nationwide labor troubles of 1894. The Texas and Pacific Coal Company lowered wages from $1.15 to $1.00 per ton of coal mined as strikes broke out all across the United States, including the nearby mines in the Oklahoma and Indian Territories. Colonel Hunter's differences with the owners of a saloon just north of the fence that surrounded Thurber exacerbated labor frictions in the camp.[8] In 1893 an entrepreneur named Jimmie (or Jimmy) Grant opened a saloon just north of Thurber in Palo Pinto County, after Erath County officials had repeatedly raided a tavern he operated southeast of the town for illegal gambling infractions. Hunter may have instigated these law enforcement actions. Soon other businessmen established a grocery store and dry goods store near his new saloon. Locals began calling the little moneymaking settlement between Thurber and the main line of the Texas and Pacific Railroad "Grant Town" after its founding establishment. Sometime afterward, Grant sold his saloon to two men named Bruce and Stewart. Bruce and Stewart's Saloon, as patrons called it, became a safe haven where Thurber's miners could air their grievances with the Texas and Pacific Coal Company and provided a convenient place for organizers to discuss the benefits of unionism with the workers of Thurber.[9]

Colonel Hunter, determined to fight off both outside competition and any budding union trouble, closed the wagon road that ran past Bruce and Stewart's, ostensibly because it ran too close to the railroad spur track and passing trains startled horses along the route. Hunter built a new road from Thurber to the main Texas and Pacific rail line four hundred yards away from the saloon and the old road. This made it a bit more difficult for passersby to patronize Bruce and Stewart's. He also clamped down on public drunkenness that he believed emanated from the Grant Town saloon, threatening to fire any miner who arrived to work visibly affected by alcohol.[10] William K. Gordon, the superintendent of Thurber, declared that he had frequently "seen miners lying around the [Bruce and Stewart] saloon and drinking at the saloon in a state of beastly intoxication."[11] This action brought an immediate howl of protest from Bruce and Stewart, who filed suit against Hunter and the coal company for closing a public road. The local court ruled the road to be a private one owned by the Texas and Pacific Coal Company; they could move it as they pleased. Bruce and Stewart then distributed circulars all over Thurber advertising free beer and, according to the company, encouraged the incitement of a strike against Hunter. Miners were striking all around the country, and there were numerous reports of union organizers infiltrating the camp and trying to influence the workers.[12] The fliers included the phrase: "Boys drink with us; we are among you; we are one of you; we treat you right."[13]

Colonel Hunter's anti-union efforts and the supposedly monopolistic policies of the Texas and Pacific Coal Company's mercantile operations engendered strong feelings that culminated in a threat against the life of Hunter and several of his managers.[14] One of the targets of the "Avengers," as the potential killers called themselves, was the head of the company's stores, Frank S. Cronk:

> COL. R. D. HUNTER: We have started an organization of avengers to kill tyrants, and if you do not open the road to Jimmy Grant's [Bruce and Stewart's] saloon we will kill you, you son of a bitch. And we have been chosen by the goodness of God to put down all monopolies, and if you do not discharge W. K. Gordon and that son of a bitch, Bob McKeinan, and that gray haired bitch, Ben Mathews, we will kill you anyway. Open the road to Jimmy's and discharge the three sons of bitches and we will not hurt you.
> Avengers
> P.S. We are called by the Supreme Ruler to remove R. D. Hunter, F. Cronk, W. K. Gordon, Bob McKeinan, Ben Mathews and Andrew Rumage.
> Do you understand.[15]

Hunter offered a two hundred dollar reward for the arrest and conviction of the "Avengers." Eventually the Avengers, a few union organizers from out of state, were tried at the federal court in Waco for sending threats through the U.S. mail. Although the *Dallas Morning News* reported a work stoppage in early June, the presence of a company of Texas Rangers led by Captain Bill McDonald diffused any labor strife.[16] McDonald made several arrests of "outside agitators," including one person for "threatening to blow up the coal mines."[17]

It was during the labor difficulties of 1894 that company officials began considering the idea of forming a subsidiary company to operate the various mercantile enterprises of the Texas and Pacific Coal Com-

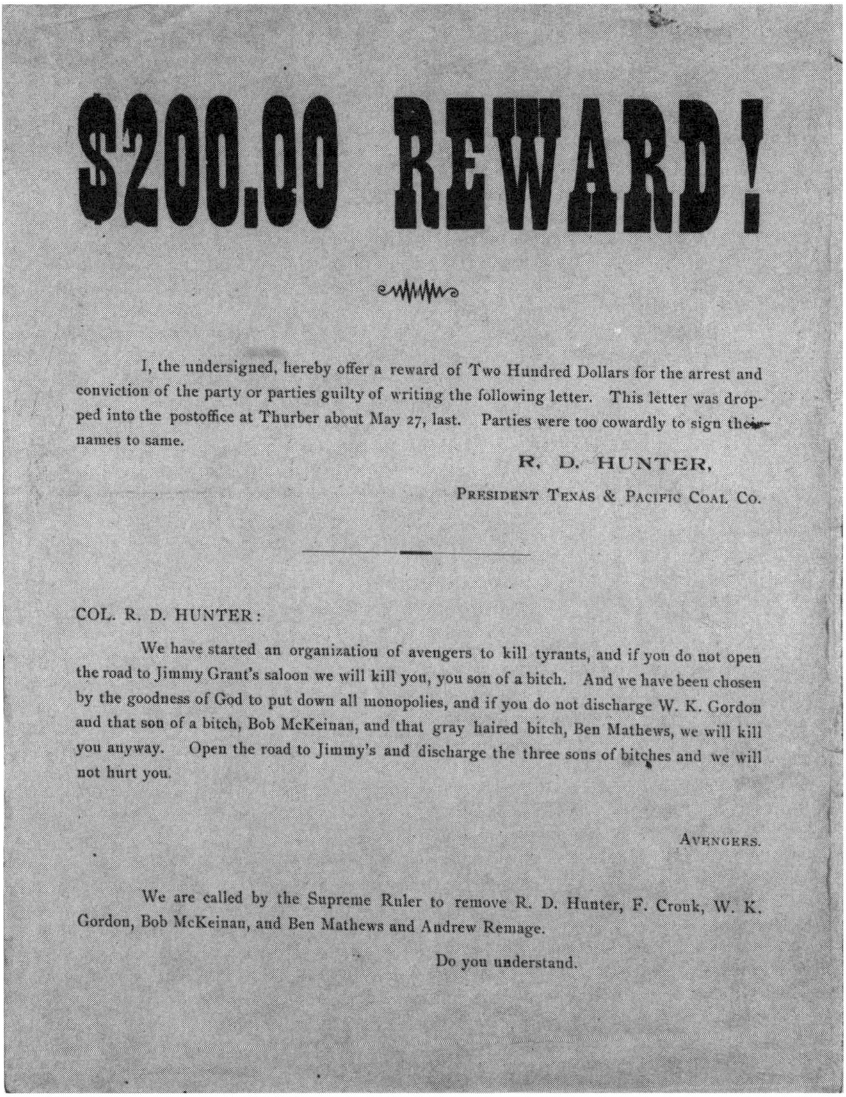

$200.00 REWARD!

I, the undersigned, hereby offer a reward of Two Hundred Dollars for the arrest and conviction of the party or parties guilty of writing the following letter. This letter was dropped into the postoffice at Thurber about May 27, last. Parties were too cowardly to sign their names to same.

R. D. HUNTER,

PRESIDENT TEXAS & PACIFIC COAL CO.

COL. R. D. HUNTER:

We have started an organization of avengers to kill tyrants, and if you do not open the road to Jimmy Grant's saloon we will kill you, you son of a bitch. And we have been chosen by the goodness of God to put down all monopolies, and if you do not discharge W. K. Gordon and that son of a bitch, Bob McKeinan, and that gray haired bitch, Ben Mathews, we will kill you anyway. Open the road to Jimmy's and discharge the three sons of bitches and we will not hurt you.

AVENGERS.

We are called by the Supreme Ruler to remove R. D. Hunter, F. Cronk, W. K. Gordon, Bob McKeinan, and Ben Mathews and Andrew Remage.

Do you understand.

Reward for the Avengers. Even under the iron hand of Colonel Hunter, labor agitation occurred at Thurber and could turn violent. This dispute centered on outside competition for the saloon dollar of Thurber's workers and threatened company store employees. Courtesy of Special Collections, University of Texas at Arlington Library, Arlington, Texas, Thurber, Texas, Collection, AR506.

pany. During a September 28, 1894, meeting held in Fort Worth, the directors and stockholders of the coal company organized the Texas Pacific Mercantile and Manufacturing Company. Colonel Hunter informed his stockholders that the new subsidiary was created "on account of our increased and diversified commercial business," but the fresh labor troubles may have been another consideration. Coal companies around the nation sometimes created subsidiaries to generate the illusion that the colliery and commissary were distinct and unconnected entities. Indeed, during further labor unrest nearly a decade later, company directors suggested that, because the company store was a perennial grievance of the miners, they operate the coal company and the mercantile company more independently of each other. Perhaps the same idea was behind the 1894 founding of TPM&M, but the record is mute on the subject. Hunter, the tight-lipped foe of unions, would probably never have admitted that he founded the auxiliary company out of fear. He would probably have conceded, however, that he wished to preemptively stifle union efforts at creating discord about the mercantile.[18]

It was easily apparent, though, that the two companies were intimately connected. The ten directors of Texas and Pacific Coal doubled as the founding directors of TPM&M. Each man held one $10 share, in trust for voting purposes, of the two thousand shares created. Colonel Robert D. Hunter held the remaining shares, amounting to $19,900, in trust for the parent coal company, allowing him to conduct the business of the subsidiary unilaterally. The directors then duly elected Hunter president, treasurer, and general manager of the new operation, while Horace K. Thurber, the town's namesake, became its first vice president. The new company was basically an arm of the coal company. Furthermore, the new Texas Pacific Mercantile and Manufacturing Company owned none of the stores it operated in or any other piece of real property, paying rent to the coal company for the buildings and acreage it used throughout its entire forty-year existence.[19]

The original 1894 charter of TPM&M delineated its primary duty: to maintain the various stores of the mercantile department. The charter charged TPM&M to do more than just operate Thurber's stores, however:

> Construct and maintain a telegraph and telephone line: the establishment and maintenance of a line [of] st[a]ges; the supply of water to the public; the manufacture and supply of light and heat to the public; the establishment and maintenance of a hotel; the purchase and sale of agricultural and farm products[,] goods, wares and merchandise and construction and maintenance of mills and gins.[20]

On the motion of Horace K. Thurber, TPM&M purchased all saloon and store merchandise, livery stable stock, and cotton gin stock from Texas and Pacific Coal with the $19,900 in TPM&M stock that Colonel Hunter held in trust. On October 1, 1894, TPM&M formally took possession of the coal company's consumer merchandise, livestock, and other wares with little fanfare. The company-operated newspaper made no official announcement of the change; editors simply replaced the advertisements reading "Mercantile Department of the Texas and Pacific Coal Company" with "Texas Pacific Mercantile and Manufacturing Company."[21]

In the first year of operation, 1894, the stores of the newly minted Texas Pacific Mercantile and Manufacturing Company earned $87,470.71 in profits. This is an impressive figure, as mining profits of the parent coal company were $98,511.41, meaning that about 47 percent of the money made in Thurber came not from the mines, but from the stores. Dividing the profits by the total gross sales at the stores, before expenses, $519,037.98, gives a profit margin of about 16.85 percent. This meant that for every dollar spent in a TPM&M store by a Thurberite in 1894, the company made almost 17 cents. Combined with the general antipathy miners had toward the company's mercantile operation, Hunter's anti-union methods, the fence surrounding Thurber, and the scrip system, these handsome profit figures led to the common assumption that the company store existed only to take advantage of the miner. Still, the mercantile did not have a monopoly, as there was growing competition from peddlers and the stores of Grant Town.[22]

A traveler to Thurber in 1894 named Larry Chittenden, who called himself the "poet ranchman of Jones County," described Thurber to a Dallas newsman. He arrived unannounced and company men gave him an impromptu tour of the town. Judging by the hyperbole in his account of the town, he was decidedly impressed:

> On my way in from Abilene I stopped off at the coal mines of Thurber, Tex., in Palo Pinto county on the Texas and Pacific railroad, and I am astonished at what I saw. I had no idea that there was any such perfect mining organization in the state. It is unique. . . . If any one had told me ten years ago, when I first visited that region, that I should find there to-day a town of 3500 people, now only six years old, with schools, churches, a hospital, a free library of 1500 volumes, several public buildings, ponds well stocked with all kinds of fish, irrigated farms and gardens, a newspaper, free ice water and a market containing the finest beef and vegetables that I have ever seen in the state I should have laughed at the idea as a fanciful dream. But I found all these things at Thurber and many more.[23]

Thurber's general store. The general store was a multipurpose building, selling dry goods and groceries. It was also a stop for Thurber's stagecoach, which until 1910 brought the company payroll in from Mingus a few miles north. Courtesy of Dick Smith Library, Tarleton State University, Stephenville, Texas, Cross Timbers Historical Images Project.

Old meat market and ice plant. The meat market and ice plant in downtown Thurber around 1900. The railroad and ready capital ensured that TPM&M served the freshest and best to its patrons. Courtesy of Nita Stewart Haley Memorial Library, Midland, Texas, Miles B. Hart Collection.

He favorably compared the mining town and miners to those in Pennsylvania, but most of his account was devoted to the extensive operations of the mercantile. Talking of the stores, Chittenden described the high quality of the goods and low prices, judging them lower than prices in Abilene and points west. He was so enamored with the stores that he envied the Palo Pinto and Erath County residents who lived within riding distance of Thurber: "Ranchmen and farmers in Palo Pinto county do nearly all their trading at the company's stores and I regret that distance alone prevents my doing the same."[24] Colonel Hunter himself sent a letter to the *Dallas Morning News* the next year to correct "some errors in the prints [newspapers]."[25] Hunter praised the various concerns of his new mercantile subsidiary: "Besides a general store, we have a hardware store, drug store, bakery, barber shop, a meat and vegetable market, with cold storage attached. . . . We have also an opera-house that will seat 700 people. We also have our own waterworks and fire department, and our own electric light plant . . . a billiard room with four tables, and a free library."[26] He described several other things that fell under the purview of TPM&M, like the machine shop, the reservoirs, farms, gardens, and the hotel.[27] These stores and service enterprises were the backbone, present already in 1895, of Thurber as a functional company town and TPM&M as a moneymaking endeavor.

Executives of the parent coal company were indeed very aware of the ample sums of money that TPM&M generated. Over the course of Thurber's existence as a working town, the directors of the Texas and Pacific Coal Company siphoned profits from TPM&M whenever needed. Colonel Hunter's successor as president of the Texas and Pacific Coal Company, and also the second president of TPM&M, Edgar L. Marston, commented to his general manager at Thurber during a period of low coal mining profits in 1916 that the dividend to be paid by the coal company could be secured from the stores.[28] Frank Martin, a clerk and later an executive for the coal company, remembers that between 1918 and 1921 "the company lost money on the mine operation, but they made it up in the 'commissaries.'"[29] Since the coal company and its directors wholly owned the mercantile company's two thousand ten-dollar shares, each time they declared a dividend for the subsidiary, Texas and Pacific Coal immediately reaped the profits. In 1908, for example, TPM&M declared a dividend of 1,200 percent and $240,000 transferred easily into the coffers of the Texas and Pacific Coal Company. During the late 1910s, when the coal mines were becoming less profitable, the company announced several TPM&M dividend payments so the coal company would remain solvent and explore for oil (which would eventually save the company and signal the end of Thurber). Another method to move money from one company to another was for the coal company to increase the amount of rent TPM&M paid for the use of the stores and buildings that housed its enterprises. Immediately preceding the First World War, Marston raised the total rents on TPM&M from $13,000 to $25,000. This sly office move meant that the government could not tax these earnings twice: once as the mercantile's profits and again once they had been transferred by dividend to the coal company. The earnings of the Texas Pacific Mercantile and Manufacturing Company for the years 1894 through 1920, from its founding until the last year the company turned a profit, were substantial, and fluctuated according to a number of factors, primarily with the town's population and any labor troubles.[30]

PROFITS AND DECLARED DIVIDENDS OF TPM&M (1894–1920)

Year	Profits	Dividend Declared (%)	Dividend to TP Coal Co.
1894	$87,470.71		
1895	$86,552.35		
1896	$76,067.18		
1897	$71,012.35		
1898	$90,837.74		
1899	$89,168.73		
1900	$92,705.62		
1901	$94,081.89		
1902	$101,968.12		
1903	$115,010.50		
1904	$73,736.09		
1905	$74,302.09		
1906	$85,009.74		
1907	$69,958.22		
1908	$78,116.71	1,200	$240,000.00
1909	$110,995.04	300 and 400	$140,000.00
1910	$94,166.03		
1911	$108,330.26		
1912	$118,286.28	250	$50,000.00
1913	$108,597.65		

1914	$94,190.82	400	$80,000.00
1915	$94,844.25	400	$80,000.00
1916	$99,294.98	400	$80,000.00
1917	$125,633.06	400	$80,000.00
1918	$151,253.71		
1919	$197,600.63		
1920	$183,060.00	400	$80,000.00
Total	$2,772,250.75		$830,000.00

Source: "Revenue and Expense Journal, 1894–1898," Ledger 637; "Revenue and Expense Journal, 1899–1903," Ledger 638; "Revenue and Expense Journal, 1904–1906," Ledger 639; "Revenue and Expense Journal, 1906–1909," Ledger 640; "Revenue and Expense Journal, 1909–1912," Ledger 641; "Revenue and Expense Journal, 1912–1914," Ledger 642; "Revenue and Expense Journal, 1915–1917," Ledger 643; "Revenue and Expense Journal, 1917–1918," Ledger 644; "Revenue and Expense Journal, 1918–1920," Ledger 645; "Revenue and Expense Journal, 1920," Ledger 646; all sources are from the Texas and Pacific Coal Company Records, S1021.1.

CHAPTER 3
THE COMMERCIAL ENTERPRISES OF THURBER

By 1900 the main business district of Thurber was located in a bustling central quadrangle residents referred to as "the square," "downtown," or, usually in company records, "the quadrangle." A large commissary, one of the original buildings constructed in the winter of 1888–89, stood on the west side of this plaza, housing both the dry goods and grocery departments. Attached to this building was a bakery that began operations in summer 1895. Across the wide street on the east side of the quadrangle stood a hardware store and the company meat market. Located south of the hardware store was the first drugstore building. The company erected a new drugstore on the north side of the square before the third and final drugstore was built on the southeast corner of the quadrangle. These were not just ordinary country stores of the era; many visitors considered them among the finest stores they had patronized. The workers were courteous and professional, and the stores operated smoothly and efficiently.[1] One visitor to the mining city commented that, "To say that [the] organization and workings of this vast camp is perfect, is but to tell the truth."[2] Another called the Texas Pacific Mercantile and Manufacturing Company "the most extensive retail mercantile institution in the state."[3]

The general store on the west side of the quadrangle was a large wooden frame structure with two stories and a basement. The central and northern sections of the building were devoted to the grocery department, described as very well stocked for a store not located in a

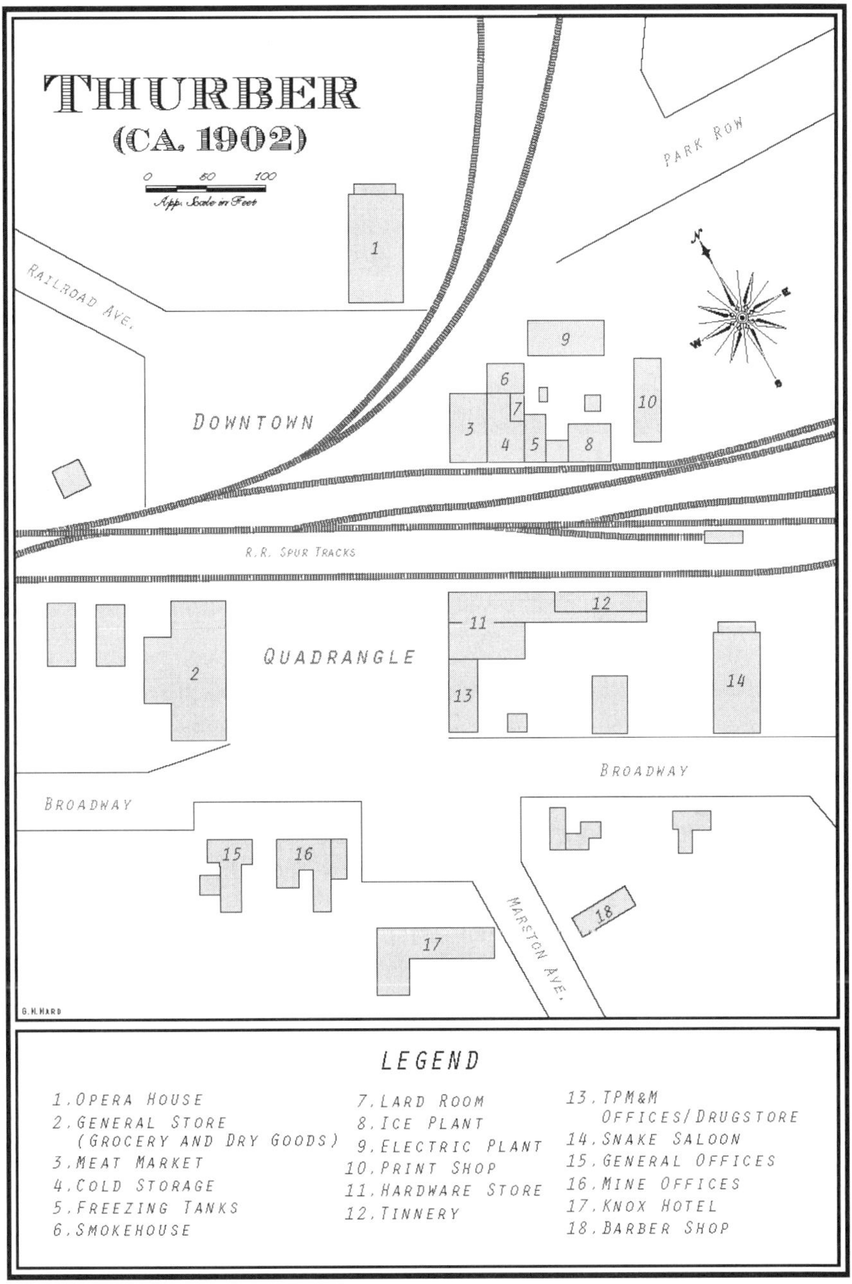
THURBER
(CA. 1902)
0 50 100
App. Scale in Feet
PARK ROW
RAILROAD AVE.
DOWNTOWN
N
E
W
S
1
2
3
4
5
6
7
8
9
10
11
12
13
14
15
16
17
18
R.R. SPUR TRACKS
QUADRANGLE
BROADWAY
BROADWAY
MARSTON AVE.
G.H.WARD
LEGEND
1. OPERA HOUSE
2. GENERAL STORE (GROCERY AND DRY GOODS)
3. MEAT MARKET
4. COLD STORAGE
5. FREEZING TANKS
6. SMOKEHOUSE
7. LARD ROOM
8. ICE PLANT
9. ELECTRIC PLANT
10. PRINT SHOP
11. HARDWARE STORE
12. TINNERY
13. TPM&M OFFICES/DRUGSTORE
14. SNAKE SALOON
15. GENERAL OFFICES
16. MINE OFFICES
17. KNOX HOTEL
18. BARBER SHOP

Downtown Thurber, ca. 1902. Map by George Ward.

Interior of the dry goods store. The dry goods store around 1900 offered a wide array of goods for sale and numerous friendly faces offering their services. Courtesy of the W. K. Gordon Center for Industrial History of Texas, Tarleton State University, Mingus, Texas, James Lorenz Collection.

large city like Fort Worth, Dallas, or Houston. Aside from staple goods found in any grocery of the period, such as sugar, flour, eggs, and potatoes, the Thurber store included harder-to-find fresh items like lemons, bananas, and grapes in season, all brought in by rail. Some other fruits and vegetables were sold in the coolers at the market. The company regularly received large shipments of grapes, which Thurber's large Italian community especially appreciated. The Italians used them to make homemade wines and grappo (or *grappa*), a form of distilled liquor flavored with the grape skins left over from winemaking. The Italians in town surely valued the hundreds of dollars worth of macaroni and other pastas the grocery received from wholesalers, such as the Houston Macaroni Company, each month. The grocery store also operated an order wagon that took requests for goods in the morning and delivered them directly to homes in the evening. This alleviated the long lines at the grocery and made it unnecessary for women with large households to make time-consuming trips to the store. The southern section of the general store building housed the dry goods department, which carried an array of cloths from broadcloth and silk to calico. Ready-made suits and dresses for men and women, as good as those in Fort Worth one reporter insisted, were also sold, as were shoes from many different national companies. Some Italian men had a fondness for the American shoes that the company sold. A reporter noted that during the 1903 strike many Italian miners bought as many as six pairs before departing town. The upper story of the building displayed and sold coffins and furniture. A newspaperman from Stephenville, the county seat of Erath County, remarked that these stores were "chock-full of the latest and best the markets afford." If customers could not find desired items on the shelves, managers offered to order them at no additional cost.[4]

This large general commissary also housed offices for the manager of the mercantile company. Perhaps the most important head store-keeper in the history of the company was Edward S. Britton of Weatherford, Texas. He served as a Texas Ranger in Thurber, along with his older brother James Magruder "Grude" Britton, during the labor disputes of late 1888 and early 1889, and he remained in the service of the Rangers until September 1889. While Britton was still a member of Texas Ranger Frontier Battalion Company B, Colonel Hunter offered him employment with the Texas and Pacific Coal Company with a starting salary of ninety dollars per month. Britton related decades later, to associate George Studdard, that this was significantly better than the seventy-five dollars a month he earned performing the dangerous job of Ranger (which required him to pay for much of his equipment out of his own pocket).[5] Britton related, "That is the first time in my life I ever knew anybody made $90 per month, and I hesitated a few seconds to make sure my voice would be normal and finally blurted out 'Colonel, you've just hired yourself a man.'"[6] He worked his way up from coal weighmaster to paymaster and then finally to general manager of TPM&M in 1895, because Hunter "recognized the rare business ability combined with sterling honesty and correct habits."[7] He ran the subsidiary company during two of its most profitable periods, from 1895 until 1904 and then again from 1915 until 1922. Britton left his mark on the TPM&M like no other manager, most of whom served short tenures, and he was well remembered by many old-time residents of Thurber. For several years TPM&M even marketed its own brand of flour under the name "Britton's Best."[8]

Satisfied with the wooden structures, company officials postponed erecting new brick buildings, but faulty electrical wiring forced their hand. Early in the morning on February 25, 1902, a fire broke out in the grocery department of the general store, apparently caused by a spark from defective wiring.[9] The Thurber newspaper described the conflagration:

Ed Britton. Texas Ranger Edward S. Britton of Weatherford, Texas, began working for the coal company in 1889 before working his way up to general manager of TPM&M. He ran Thurber's stores during two of its most profitable periods, from 1895 until 1904 and then again from 1915 until 1922. Courtesy of Dick Smith Library, Tarleton State University, Stephenville, Texas, Cross Timbers Historical Images Project.

> Vandy West discovered the "General Store" to be on fire. After firing his revolver Mr. West ran to the mine office yard and sounded the big triangle of the Thurber Fire Department. Mr. Farr ran to notify the fireman at the Ice Plant who soon turned loose the great fire alarm whistle whose multi-toned screech might awaken the Seven Sleepers. By this time the hardware and drug stores looked as if they were doomed. To the south a similar struggle was going on to save the mine office, and general office—while the big store and bakery buildings had fallen in.[10]

The blaze consumed the large commissary, bakery, and various storage rooms and did some damage to the hardware department, the town's hotel, the mining office, and the drugstore before being put out by Thurber's volunteer fire department. The cost of the damage was $13,099.97 in real estate and merchandise, with insurance reducing the company's losses to just $3,358.74.[11]

More disastrously, and of immediate importance, the fire left the town of more than five thousand people without food and supplies. All the food in the stores was burned or burning, as "all the forenoon Tuesday from the smoking heaps of canned goods one could hear a smothered explosion, a can would mount high into the air and often fall far out of the burned district."[12] The general manager of the camp, William K. Gordon, printed circulars in several languages that stated, "Our citizens could get supplies in the new warehouse by noon or a little af-

1902 general store fire. A diverse group of Thurberites mill about the smoldering remains of the general store, a victim of faulty wiring and wooden construction. The fire left a town of thousands without food and supplies, but TPM&M officials scrambled to bring essentials to Thurber in just a few hours. Courtesy of Special Collections, University of Texas at Arlington Library, Arlington, Texas, Thurber, Texas, Collection, AR88.

ter."[13] TPM&M employees gathered supplies from the surrounding towns of Gordon and Strawn by wagon, while head storekeeper Ed Britton traveled to Fort Worth where he bought thousands of dollars worth of provisions and clothing. Other TPM&M workmen converted an undamaged warehouse into a makeshift grocery and started selling goods to Thurberites by early afternoon. Britton's purchases began arriving by train later that day and early the next.[14] Soon advertisements in the Thurber newspaper declared: "Still doing business—not exactly on the same old stand . . . we are prepared to fill your every want in the Grocery Line."[15] The mercantile company's direct access to the railway and ready cash ensured that it could survive such a calamity.

Over the next two years the company replaced the burned general store on the quadrangle with a large brick dry goods building costing almost $10,000 and a separate wooden grocery store immediately across the tracks to its north. To provide storage, large warehouses stood near each building with direct access to the railroad, where workmen could easily off-load freight. The company nearly doubled the size of the

large dry goods department by extending the brick building farther south in 1908. The lower floor of the building housed the regular dry goods items, while the upper floor was dedicated to storage, furniture sales, and coffin displays. The mortician had, for a time, a small office in the building. The two-story grocery was a wooden structure that, like the dry goods department, had easy access to the railroad spur that brought in almost all sales items. The local Masonic Lodge and other fraternal organizations also had meeting space on the top floor of each building. Among the most profitable departments of TPM&M before the fire, the grocery and the dry goods stores continued to contribute to the profits of the company. In 1905, for example, patrons spent totals of about $300 a day at the grocery and about $190 a day at the dry goods store. These numbers were second and third only to the average daily take at the Snake Saloon. A new, small bakery with several ovens lay southwest of the dry goods department. The Italian families in Thurber rarely purchased from this bakery; instead they baked their own breads in small outdoor ovens they constructed themselves. Former residents of all backgrounds fondly remembered this tasty, hard-crusted Italian bread.[16]

Interior of the hardware store. Around 1900 the hardware store sold fine cutlery, china, ammunition, paint, and several other goods. Courtesy of Special Collections, University of Texas at Arlington Library, Arlington, Texas, Thurber, Texas, Collection, AR506.

The hardware store on the east side of the square carried a large stock of goods for use by laborers, from miners to homemakers. Here coal diggers purchased merchandise such as shovels, tool handles, and blasting powder. Goods for the home included heaters, ranges, pots, pans, crockery, silverware, and cutlery. Other TPM&M departments, the coal company, and the brick factory regularly requisitioned items from the hardware store, including items like hatchets, grindstones, bits, machine shop equipment, paints, brushes, and so forth. The hardware store also offered various kinds of sporting goods, guns, and ammunition. Many Thurber residents hunted in the surrounding company-owned countryside for sport and food. One story has a local doctor rushing to the home of an Italian in Thurber, where his patient was deathly ill from eating a "blackbird" he had shot while hunting. The feathers proved the "blackbird" was in fact a buzzard. Until 1913 there was a tin shop located on the north side of the building where tinsmiths constructed gutters, canisters, troughs to collect rainwater, and other metal goods for townspeople. Situated behind the building, a saddlery and harness shop sold all sorts of tack supplies, did repairs, and manufactured custom-ordered saddles. The hardware department also sold buggies and hacks. In 1905, for example, the hardware took in an average of about $135 a day in cash and scrip sales. The company replaced the stores on the east side of the square with a new spacious two-story brick building in 1913. The first floor was the new home of the meat market and hardware store, and the second story housed offices for TPM&M and the coal company.[17]

The meat market on the eastern side of the downtown plaza boasted one of the largest refrigerated storage vaults in Texas, constantly kept as close to thirty-two degrees Fahrenheit as possible. The company maintained an abattoir on the northern side of town that supplied the market with almost all of the meats it sold. Company butchers slaughtered hundreds of head of cattle each year and could hang forty sides of beef in the cold storage at a time. In addition to slaughtering beef, the meat cutters regularly prepared mutton and pork (both in demand by the European-born population). Butchers made the pork into various styles of ham, bacon, and sausages. Patrons could purchase chickens, turkeys, ducks, and geese either live or dressed. Most of these animals were raised and cared for on company lands, although many were acquired from Fort Worth stock sales or from farmers and ranchers in the immediate countryside. Drawing the animals from multiple sources helped the company to keep prices low. The company prepared meats in a variety of ways to cater to the multitude of tastes held by the multi-ethnic population of Thurber, selling such items as salami, bologna, head cheese, Polish sausage, and many other types of sausage. Employees cured these meats in a small brick smokehouse fired by pecan wood that stood behind the store. Colonel Hunter demanded the use of pecan because it was his favorite smoking wood. Salesmen also offered an array of seafood, the most popular being oysters in season, at times received in large weekly shipments. Residents remembered that Italians had an inordinate fondness for the oysters, as they did for grapes, and had several stereotypical reasons to account for that fact. Like the grocery department, the market sold fresh produce as well: onions, garlic, cabbage, tomatoes, kraut, pickles (sweet, sour, and dill), chili peppers, potatoes, and so forth. Fresh fruits like watermelons, cantaloupes, and peaches often graced the shelves of the store. The company grew many of these items in a truck garden that was irrigated from Big Lake, the town's primary water source. The company remodeled the market building, first constructed in 1889, in 1905, allowing more space for display of meats and other goods. The company marketed its own brand of lard by the bucket, produced in a lard house attached to the building.

New meat market. The new meat market around 1913 featured the latest accoutrements, friendly employees, and ubiquitous spittoons. Courtesy of Southwest Collection/Special Collections Library, Texas Tech University, Lubbock, Texas, Thurber, Texas, Photograph Collection, S1076.1.

In 1905 patrons spent an average of about $185 a day at the meat market. Around the same time, TPM&M moved into a new slaughterhouse with all the modern conveniences that was located near the machine shop on the northern edge of town. In 1913 the meat market moved into the lower floor of the new two-story brick building shared with the hardware department. Edgar Bryant, who lived in Thurber as a child in the 1920s, remembered that the meat market was spacious, sporting two marble-topped counters and staffed by half a dozen courteous employees.[18]

The first drugstore in Thurber was south of the hardware store on the east end of the quadrangle and was built early in the town's history. Like other drugstores of the time, it was more than a pharmacy, selling a variety of candies, tobacco, refreshments, jewelry, novelties, school

Old drugstore. The old drugstore did steady business, selling everything from patent medicines to refreshments to the latest magazines and books. Courtesy of Special Collections, University of Texas at Arlington Library, Arlington, Texas, Thurber, Texas, Collection, AR506.

supplies, soaps, toiletries, and other assorted items. Patent medicines were popular, including one marketed under the name of a coal company physician, "Dr. Binney's Iron Tonic." As an example of the store's earning power, customers spent an average of about $91 a day at the drugstore in 1905. In August 1904, the drugstore moved into a building on the north side of the square until the company erected a new two-story brick structure for it on the southeast corner of the plaza in 1909. The old building became Marston Hall, a dormitory for single male white-collar workers. The lower floor of the new drugstore contained the sales areas, and the upper floor was devoted to storage and an apartment for the pharmacist and his family. The front of the building showcased merchandise, sold ice cream, and boasted a soda fountain. Stationed in the rear was the pharmacist, who compounded medications from a varied stock of drugs. The company received hundreds of dollars of medicines each month, including legal narcotics like cocaine and morphine. A permanent flame burned on the front counter near the tobacco products so that customers could light cigars and cigarettes. Each year during the holiday season, the company converted the upstairs portion of the building into "Toyland," an enormous display of gifts and toys. The week before Christmas the drugstore stayed open two hours later than normal just to accommodate the trade. One former resident remembered his mother taking him to see Santa Claus there.[19]

After the large central commissary burned in 1902, the company built separate dry goods and grocery buildings on the downtown quad-

The new drugstore. The new drugstore sat in a large brick building and had the latest in furnishings. Perfumes, soda water, guitars, and cigars were all sold at this shop. Every Christmas, the storage apartment above was renamed Toyland and visited by Santa Claus. Courtesy of Special Collections, University of Texas at Arlington Library, Arlington, Texas, Thurber, Texas, Collection, AR506.

Downtown quadrangle, 1906. The downtown quadrangle of Thurber in 1906 shows the opera house in the distance, the hardware store on the right, the new brick dry goods store on the left, the long white grocery store behind it, and the town's bandstand in the center. Courtesy of Special Collections, University of Texas at Arlington Library, Arlington, Texas, Thurber, Texas, Collection, AR506.

rangle. The busiest time for these stores was after the school released pupils in the afternoon, as miners' wives often let their children do the purchasing. This was because some immigrant women did not have a confident grasp of enough English vocabulary to deal with the salesmen, who were almost all native-born white men. The mercantile developed several methods to alleviate the afternoon crowding at the stores. Most departments utilized order wagons, which would drive by the homes of established customers in the morning, take their orders, and deliver goods in the evening. To better accommodate those customers that spoke little English, the company opened a smaller auxiliary general store in 1904 on the western side of town where the greatest number of Italian and Polish miners lived. Thurberites called this building "the store on the hill," because it was located on a hill bisected by a rail track leading westward to the coal mines. Residents called this hill variously "the Hill," "Number Three Hill," or "600 Hill," but most referred to it as "Italian Hill" north of the tracks or "Polander Hill" south of the tracks. The new store, just south of the tracks, sold a limited selection of groceries, meats, and dry goods so the inhabitants on the hill did not have to make the long trek on foot to the center of town. Because Italian-speaking salesmen and, at times, Polish-speaking and Spanish-speaking ones, manned the store, the substantial immigrant population that lived nearby felt more comfortable making purchases. The store did well enough that by 1905 customers spent an average of about $139 a day in cash and scrip there.[20]

Since foreign-born workers and a saloon had been at the center of the labor trouble, 1894 also saw the company build a second smaller saloon in the western section of town to complement the Snake. Company officials wanted the workers in this section of town, predominantly Poles and Italians, to frequent the company establishment rather than competitors outside town (some Grant Town saloons were as close to Italian Hill as the Snake). Patrons soon christened this second watering hole "the Lizard."[21] The official books and ledgers of the company officially called these establishments "Saloon Number One" and "Saloon Number Two," though sometimes, because of its more limited inventory, the Lizard was called the "Beer Saloon" in company documents. But residents and visitors fondly remembered the popular names, and the bookkeepers themselves drew the reptile mascots on some of the saloon's inventory ledgers.[22] The Snake soon outgrew its original building and the company erected a new two-story brick saloon in 1897 just east of the downtown quadrangle. This new structure housed a lodge hall on the upper floor and the saloon proper on the bottom floor. A team of four or five bartenders served thirsty miners from behind an enormous horseshoe-shaped bar made of mahogany. The large horseshoe bar was so prominent that miners often simply called the Snake the "Horseshoe Bar." All of the patrons stood because the company provided no barstools or tables, believing that more men could be served in this fashion. A dozen cuspidors graced the floor at the Snake. Unlike with the typical saloon of the era, rules prohibited women from entering the bar, there was no dance floor, and gambling was strictly prohibited. A pool and billiard hall connected to the saloon building offered patrons entertainment. The company often listed the amusement hall and the Snake on the same inventory and put them under the same management in 1899. This amusement hall contained three pool tables and a billiard table with all the attendant cues, cue racks, triangles, and balls, including a set of expensive ivory billiard balls. For its part, the Lizard had three domino tables and fifteen chairs.[23]

In February 1901 the company opened a combination restaurant and saloon, named Saloon Number Three in the company ledgers, in the town growing up just north of the coal camp, where the spur to Thurber met the Texas and Pacific Railroad. Locals called the area just north of Thurber's fence Grant Town, and the community just north of that around the junction Thurber Junction, Mingus, or "the Y," for the shape the spur track made as it met the main line there. An inventory of this Thurber Junction saloon listed just twenty-four beer glasses, twenty-

The horseshoe bar of the Snake Saloon. This is the only known photograph of the Snake Saloon's large horseshoe-shaped bar, around 1904. The bar had no stools, no tables, and did not allow gambling. Miners often stopped by to fill their pails with beer to take home. Courtesy of Southwest Collection/Special Collections Library, Texas Tech University, Lubbock, Texas, Thurber, Texas, Photograph Collection, SWCPC 209.

The Lizard Saloon. The smaller Lizard Saloon offered beer, liquor, and cigars, catering to the workers on the western side of the city. Courtesy of Special Collections, University of Texas at Arlington Library, Arlington, Texas, Thurber, Texas, Collection, AR88.

four beer mugs, twenty-four whiskey glasses, twenty-four toddy glasses, three wine glasses, twenty-one water glasses, twelve cocktail glasses, twelve lemonade glasses, and two sets of dominoes. The company also purchased and closed a competing saloon in the same town. Unlike the primary two drinking establishments in Thurber, this one made only hundreds of dollars a month—the others made thousands a month—and was closed in August of 1907.[24]

The Snake, on the other hand, served its customers a wide variety of alcohol. One saloon ledger from 1898 lists many different wines, including port, Malaga, and Madeira; brandies traditional and apple- or peach-flavored; rum both domestic and Jamaican; multiple types and brands of whiskey; sherries; gins; and ciders. Even with this selection, the most popular beverage among the workers of Thurber was beer, which both the Snake and the Lizard served in abundance. TPM&M bought beer from the Dallas Brewing Company early in its existence, switching to the Texas Brewing Company of Fort Worth and adding the Milwaukee Beer Company later. Beer arrived by the carload in casks, barrels, half barrels, and quarter barrels. Thousands of dollars worth of alcohol arrived at the saloons each month. Before the unionization of Thurber in 1903, the company regularly traded carloads of "nut-sized" coal to the brewery for carloads of beer. This angered miners because the company did not pay them for this coal, yet they had to pay for the beer that the company got for that coal—it was one of labor's demands that this practice be ended. Champagne and imported beers like Bass's Pale Ale and Dublin Stout also sold by the bottle. Prices ranged from five cents a pint and ten cents a schooner to four dollars for a keg. Miners often pooled money to purchase a keg and drink it outside or at home; some even took beer home in their lunch buckets after work. Many Italians had company-built "beer iceboxes" constructed on the outside of their homes.[25]

Most beer was consumed off the premises, as a 1900 Snake Saloon inventory listed only forty beer glasses, forty-six water glasses, eighty-six whiskey glasses, two toddy glasses, thirty cocktail glasses, and sixteen ginger ale glasses—hardly enough vessels to slake the thirst of hundreds of Thurber miners each night. The same inventory lists the Lizard as having seventy-four beer glasses, twenty-four water glasses, thirty-six whiskey glasses, seven toddy glasses, four cider glasses, and five cocktail glasses—because it primarily served beer by the glass. Superintendent William K. Gordon suggested that the company build small arbors or sheds around the Snake and Lizard in 1899. Similar to European beer gardens with tables and benches, these structures allowed patrons to congregate and drink in the company of others. Thurber residents remembered that the foreign population tended to congregate outdoors in these drinking sheds, while Anglo-Americans as well as black Americans, preferred to imbibe indoors at the bar. The bartenders also sold cigars and other tobacco products, and after 1894 they offered quick lunches and light snacks. The saloons opened at 5:30 a.m. and closed at 10:00 p.m. Monday through Friday, closing at midnight on Saturday. They were closed on Sundays and holidays.[26]

The bars did steady and profitable business for the company. In 1900, three years before the unionization of Thurber, drinkers spent $40,256.76 in cash and scrip at the Snake Saloon, while $33,435.55 went into the coffers at the Lizard Saloon. Together the two saloons grossed $73,692.31, second only to the gross sales at the grocery store. That same year, patrons bought $43,530.05 of this alcohol, 59 percent of it, on company credit. Although workers may have thought otherwise, the company kept prices fairly low, as this translated to net profits of only $4,467.96 at the Snake and $1,345.48 at the Lizard—the company earned only about 7.8 percent on every dollar spent. The average profit margin at several other TPM&M outlets could be considerably higher.[27] Even if the profit margins of the saloons were not very impressive when compared to those of the mines and brickworks, or even the grocery, these drinking institutions were needed because without them the miners might opt to find work elsewhere, or drink in establishments outside company control, increasing the chances of rowdiness or drunkenness on the job. Even the head of TPM&M and its parent company, Edgar L. Marston, who was the son of a teetotalling Baptist minister, recognized this.[28] Drunkenness could hurt mine output; one coal train operator remembered that the Texas and Pacific Coal Company had three crews of miners: "One working, while one was drinking, and another one was sobering up."[29] Drinking affected more than the miners, as Marston threatened to summarily fire any TPM&M employee found to be intoxicated on the job.[30]

Though most residents did not generally remember the saloons as evil places, the barrooms often saw more than their fair share of fisticuffs and arrests for drunkenness.[31] A 1900 newspaper article from the *Fort Worth Register* included a fanciful account of a black newsroom galley boy's visit to the Snake and Lizard written in the stereotyped black dialect of the day: "Say, de Lizard is a corker. De bar is six hundred feet long and you can't see de other end. De Snaik is full 'o tanglefoot o' de Parrydise ally kind, and de micks and chinks an' niggers go dere to cool off after de daygo women t'row vitrified bricks at 'em."[32]

The criminal docket generated in Thurber at the time included citations for profanity, assault, disturbing the peace, and carrying concealed weapons, charges that often arose from indulgence at the saloons. In a move apparently made to increase efficiency, the company even made the manager of the Snake, A. T. Albright, the constable of Thurber. This did not prevent Albright himself from being charged with using profane language in public. In most cases this charge would lead to a five-dollar fine, but in this instance the Erath county attorney dismissed the case.[33]

Prohibition in Erath County often threatened to close the saloons, a fact that caused trepidation for company officials. For years these local option elections turned on voters in Thurber. In 1902 the Commissioners' Court of Erath County excluded the Thurber precinct from voting, and declared the rest of the county "dry"—Thurber remained "wet." Superintendent William K. Gordon of Thurber surreptitiously engineered this odd arrangement with two Erath county commissioners, over the protestations of one other commissioner—a judge later declared it illegal.[34] Two years later in 1904 county officials attempted a countywide ban on the sale of alcohol. A bitter campaign ensued before the June election, centered on the supposedly evil influence that Thurber and its saloons had on the rest of the county.[35] One handbill writer from Stephenville, the county seat, intoned that allowing Thurber, which he called "a foreign city of dagoes," to serve liquor while the rest of the county was dry meant that Thurber would "rule supreme in commercial power and will absolutely control the business of over one-half the citizenship of Erath County."[36] In fact, the frequent elections over prohibition spurred many foreigners, "dagoes" included, to become citizens, pay their poll taxes, and exercise their right to vote.[37] The handbill further asked the voters why they should send their money to "a rich syndicate [at Thurber] and destroy the commerce of their own happy village [of Stephenville]."[38] A letter in the Stephenville newspaper, *The Empire,* advocated voting for countywide prohibition over the machinations of those residing in Thurber, warning that "the whiskey business is deception from beginning to end."[39]

The colliery wanted to ensure that its miners could continue to slake their thirst, and the mercantile would continue reaping profits. In previous elections on the local option, company officials donated money to antiprohibition causes, and the company-controlled newspaper printed articles attacking prohibition.[40] Even as early as 1895, a campaign piece in the Thurber newspaper, the *Texas Miner,* ran an editorial making the company position abundantly clear:

> Voters, do you wish to return to the Blue Laws of the Puritans, long since ridiculed and condemned? They prohibited the drinking of rum, but they did not stop at prohibiting liquor—they went further, and prohibited spitting in public, and prohibited the wearing of jewels, then enforced attendance at church, prohibited a husband kissing his wife on Sunday, prohibited witchcraft, and hanged and burned several innocent old women as witches, and drove old Roger Williams, the founder of the Baptist church, out of the colony. You have no guarantee that the fanatics of to-day will be any more moderate or reasonable than Puritans. See to it that your ballot reads "Against Prohibition."[41]

In that 1895 election the county remained wet, with 1,503 votes against prohibition; 702 of that number were cast by the denizens of Thurber. The editors of the *Texas Miner* duly congratulated the populace of Thurber.[42]

In the June 1904 election the voters of Erath County finally managed to bring prohibition to the entire county by a vote of 1,026 for and 642 against, even though Thurber voted against prohibition 269 votes to 21.[43] The company closed the Snake and the Lizard in July 1904 and fulfilled its threat to build a saloon a quarter mile north of downtown Thurber, just across the county line in wet Palo Pinto County. The new

The new Snake Saloon. After Erath County went dry in 1904, the company moved its lucrative saloon north into Palo Pinto County. The new establishment lacked the horseshoe bar, but served men from behind a counter said to be two train cars long. Courtesy of Special Collections, University of Texas at Arlington Library, Arlington, Texas, Thurber, Texas, Collection, AR88.

saloon was one hundred feet long and forty feet wide, and also christened the "Snake." The saloon boasted a straight bar that was said to be as long as two train cars and could handle hundreds of men at a time. The new accoutrements included hundreds of glasses, a hundred-dollar icebox, a safe, stove, and a Winchester rifle. The last item might have been useful in bringing the frequent fistfights to an end.[44] The safe, however, was not safe enough, as one industrious robber opened it with a hatchet in 1910, making off with $980 in cash.[45] Outside this building, like the old Snake, arbors and benches were built so foreign-born miners could enjoy their beer outdoors, often sharing the price of a keg, lunch, and camaraderie. Luckily for the drinkers, fields of soft grass surrounded the saloon; one former resident remembered that "if they [the patrons] got too drunk to go home they would lie down in the grass and sleep until they sobered up enough to go home."[46]

Famed Texas historian Walter Prescott Webb spent the summer of 1911 in Thurber selling stereoscopic slides and boarding with a miner. He thought the town was unique and the saloon one of the largest, and wildest, he had ever seen.[47] He wrote a poem about Thurber on returning to Austin for his junior year at the University of Texas, part of which read:

There's nothing here but booze and beer,
Except an occasional fight.
Life is cheap and talk is dear,
For in this place might is right.

Men spend their nights at the saloon,
The women at the ball,
And in the final reckoning,
Hell will claim them all.[48]

Rules again prevented women from entering the premises, but a bartender minded a back door where women could fill lunch pails with beer or order kegs to go. For a time the company even offered free home delivery of beer with the purchase of a barrel. A railway spur track ran to a refrigerated warehouse that stood next to the saloon, where workers could roll barrels by a ramp from railcars directly into the warehouse. When bartenders needed more beer, they could roll the kegs from the warehouse directly into the saloon, making a noise one resident said "growled like distant thunder."[49]

In the first six months of operation at the new site, the saloon took in $34,815.38, earning $2707.49 in profit, and making about 7.8 percent profit on each dollar brought in, similar to the previous profit margins earned at the old Snake and Lizard. In 1905, two years after unionization of Thurber, the new Snake grossed $93,906.20 in cash and scrip. Workers seemed to be in a slightly better position because of the increased pay after unionization and the expanded coal output, as Thurberites bought only 50 percent of this alcohol on credit. Beer again was the most popular beverage choice. Between 1910 and 1914, the Texas Pacific Mercantile and Manufacturing Company purchased more than 52,000 barrels of beer from the Texas Brewing Company of Fort Worth and almost 3,500 casks of beer from the Milwaukee Beer Company. It took 753 train cars to deliver this brew, costing the company $384,660.25. Between 1901 and 1907 the company also operated a small combination restaurant and saloon in Thurber Junction that did less business than the Thurber establishments, dispensing only one carload of beer a week.[50]

Proponents of prohibition continued their efforts around Thurber and throughout the state. Beginning in 1905 dry advocates forced numerous local option elections in Palo Pinto County, where the new Snake Saloon in Thurber lay, but efforts to turn the county dry failed. The saloon move also prompted a new survey of the boundary line between Erath County and Palo Pinto County to reassure officials the bar was indeed on wet territory.[51] There were several people in favor of prohibition in Thurber, particularly a number of the Baptists. A group of temperance advocates formed a lodge of the Independent Order of Good Templars, an international organization advocating temperance and prohibition. The Good Templars of Thurber during the first decade of the twentieth century included as many as 97 to 118 dues-paying members in good standing at any time. Members from lodges all across Texas met in Thurber in 1907 for the annual statewide conference of the Independent Order of Good Templars.[52] "Pros," as advocates of prohibition were called (those against prohibition were called "antis"), also engineered statewide prohibition elections in 1908 and 1911. These campaigns failed, but an increasing number of counties went dry by local option, in the northern and western sections of Texas especially.[53] Pros called for another local option election for Palo Pinto County, and Superintendent William K. Gordon wrote from Thurber to President Edgar L. Marston in New York City:

> A county prohibition election is called for the 26th instant; I have visited Mineral Wells [the largest city in Palo Pinto County] where the Antis have their organization and headquarters; a desperate fight will be made throughout the county to carry it wet, and I agreed to contribute five hundred dollars to the cause at Mineral Wells; in the vicinity of Thurber we are also making every possible effort to carry the county wet; you will recall that in two previous elections the county went wet by a very close margin, at one time by two and at another time by three votes.[54]

The county remained wet by about seventy votes, no doubt helped by the efforts of company officials at Thurber. In late 1914 another local option election was scheduled. For unknown reasons the pros and antis conducted this campaign quietly, and, after eighteen years as a wet county, Palo Pinto finally voted to enforce local prohibition. Extant financial records fail to indicate whether the company contributed to the 1914 prohibition election campaign.[55]

On January 8, 1915, Thurber officially became a dry town after nearly twenty-nine years.[56] Many researchers have incorrectly stated that the Snake Saloon closed in 1918 when Texas ratified the Eighteenth Amendment prohibiting alcohol or when the Eighteenth Amendment came into force with the Volstead Act in January 1920.[57] Even the official state historical marker at the site of the Snake Saloon incorrectly states that it closed in January 1920 with the institution of national prohibition.[58] However, the Snake Saloon officially closed its doors in 1915; one ledger simply reads: "Saloon closed on Jany. 8th 1915."[59] The company moved the cash register from the saloon to the drugstore and salvaged other items for use in other departments.[60] Although the company no longer operated drinking-houses, consumption of alcoholic beverages continued in Thurber. Until Texas passed statewide prohibition in 1919, the residents of Thurber ordered alcohol from liquor dealers in Fort Worth and received it via railway express. Sadie M. Plummer, a postal assistant in Thurber during this time, remembered that it was not unusual for her to process 250 orders for kegs each week, which would arrive by refrigerated railcar just in time for the weekend. Railroad employees of the day recalled that two express cars full of liquor would arrive before holidays. Due to the regularity of these shipments and the demand, some railway men ordered several packages of liquor to sell in Thurber as a secondary source of income.[61]

Most of the alcohol that flowed in Thurber after the closing of the saloons in 1915 was of the bootleg variety. Even before prohibition the Italians of Thurber were known for their homemade beers, wines, and grappo. Since the 1890s the Italian community at Thurber had made good use of the regular and large shipments of grapes that TPM&M ordered. County law enforcement even arrested one Thurber resident in 1900 for transporting twenty-six barrels of what he swore was just "grape juice."[62] Once a year TPM&M would order a few boxcars of red and white grapes and put them on a side track in Mingus. A witness recalled:

> The wine makers of Thurber would drive teams of mules or horses to Mingus and buy as many cases of grapes each needed and papa was no exception. It was indeed a be[e]hive of activity, as wagon after wagon would line up waiting to get their wagon loaded, and you know what, you guessed it, the greatest majority were Italians. Papa would dump a few boxes of grapes in a wine barrel he had cut in half and we kids would get in barefooted and stomp the grapes. . . . He always made at least three barrels of wine.[63]

As Thurber gained a reputation for homemade alcohol, after the beginning of statewide prohibition in 1919 the area became a mecca for people seeking illegal liquor. Observers remembered that Italian families often built makeshift cellars beneath their homes to store, and hide, their alcohol (as well as keep meats and cheeses cool).[64] The grappo, made in large copper pots, was said to be about 170 proof.[65] One drinker thought, however, that it was "about 200 proof," which would be 100 percent pure alcohol, because it was "smooth as silk" and "it'd just make everybody drunker than everything."[66]

The illegal trade in liquor still managed to bring money into the coffers of TPM&M. Local Thurber-Mingus bootleggers preferred to use ice from the Thurber ice plant for their booze-making, because the water used to make the ice was distilled and pure. In the 1920s, two bootleggers came into Thurber to purchase a dozen or so huge blocks of ice, which ran to a couple of tons. The manager of the ice plant refused to sell such a suspiciously large amount of ice to the two characters, saying: "I know what it's for. It's for bootleggers. And bootlegging is against the law." The two men then went to see Thurber's general manager, William K. Gordon. Gordon then called the ice plant manager, telling him: "Please understand that all ice we make is for sale to anybody, and it's none of our business what it's used for."[67] Still, company president Marston considered bootlegging such a problem in Thurber that, from faraway New York City, he asked the head of Thurber's stores, Ed Britton, if there was any way of "curing the boot-legging business."[68] Marston probably did not know that several of Thurber's white-collar workers drank the illegal alcohol. During the 1920s several workers bought liquor in the Thurber area and sold it for a profit to the oil workers in the boomtown of Ranger several miles away.[69] One Thurber resident recalled that: "My dad used to go to meetings, where they'd have a big safety meeting, you know, at the hotel, and they'd be having punch, and they'd go by and dump a pint of grappo in that punch, and everybody in that damn place would be drunk."[70]

TPM&M earned a large share of its profits from sales in the grocery, dry goods store, drugstore, hardware store, meat market, and saloons. The great volume of business at these large and prominent buildings ensured that these enterprises featured prominently in company documents and the remembrances of Thurber residents, who encountered or avoided them on a daily basis.

CHAPTER 4
MORE THAN JUST STORES: SERVICES FOR THE TOWN

The 1894 charter of the Texas Pacific Mercantile and Manufacturing Company called for more than operation of retail commercial outlets like stores and saloons. The mercantile company offered numerous other services to the residents of Thurber that made life easier, ensured that the town operated smoothly, and secured profits for the company. TPM&M provided Thurber with electrical power, water, and ice. Company gardens, ranches, dairies, and farms produced meat, produce, and other goods for Thurber markets. Sidelines and accoutrements deemed necessary to the operation of a city of the time, like a livery stable, a print shop, carpentry service, amusements, hotels, restaurants, and so forth, were all operated or leased out by TPM&M. Though less profitable than the commercial stores and saloons, the services furnished by the mercantile company were nevertheless essential to the operation of the company town, and made it more hospitable to the people who lived there.

One of the responsibilities of TPM&M, according to its 1894 charter, was to supply water to the public. With no nearby permanent sources of water (the few nearby creeks were intermittent in nature), the company could not provide water for the townspeople or its industrial operations. Before 1891 the Texas and Pacific Railway Company delivered water in railroad tank cars to the town at an enormous cost of four hundred to five hundred dollars per month, a cost that was then passed on to the inhabitants of Thurber, who purchased water by the barrel for all of their uses. To provide the town and the mines with an independent supply of water, the company built a substantial dam, designed by Thurber general manager William K. Gordon, also a director of TPM&M, on the southern edge of town. The dam, which stopped a small creek, soon filled the depression behind it with rainwater. Workers constructed two water tanks and a steam pumping plant next to the dam that piped water from the reservoir into a series of storage tanks throughout town. By 1896 the increasing population of Thurber necessitated a new water source, and the company again called upon Gordon to plan and build a new reservoir. Dubbed "Big Lake," it covered more than one hundred acres and provided water to the town for the remainder of its existence. The company built two new water tanks on the hill at the northern edge of town, and the company began pumping water to stores and residences, although many people still received home water deliveries by wagon rather than pay extra for the luxury of running water. Costs for water delivery began at ten cents per barrel. The initial construction of Big Lake cost the coal company over $20,000, with various further improvements made over the years. As with rent payments, Thurber residents who chose to have water pumped directly to their home had a "water charge" deducted from their pay. This charge began as one dollar and fifty cents a month per house, later increasing to two dollars. Although the charter for TPM&M mandated that it operate the water system, the money earned by the waterworks went into the coffers of the coal company, though TPM&M workers maintained the system. Thurberites called the old reservoir "Little Lake," and the population enjoyed it for fishing, swimming, and recreation.[1] These reservoirs still exist and retain water today.

In 1895, the year after the founding of TPM&M, company machinists built a small electric light plant from scratch that supplied electricity to essential store buildings, the opera house, and some executives' homes, making Thurber one of the first cities in West Texas to have an electric light plant. In 1899 the coal company transferred operation of this electric plant to TPM&M. To meet the growing needs of the town, a large direct current generator replaced the homemade dynamo in 1901. Nearby in the same block as the electric generator was the ice plant. Before 1896 the company purchased ice and had it shipped in by rail, stored in a cold storage room, and delivered by saloon employees. In that year, the company constructed a new ice plant and state-of-the-art cold storage vault for the meat market at a cost of $20,619.01. Coal boilers provided steam for the highly polished eighty-horsepower engine that was capable of producing up to thirty-five tons of ice each day. This new ice house produced all the ice for the residents of Thurber who wanted to purchase ice for their own needs. TPM&M entities like the cold storage vault, the markets, and the saloons needed the ice to keep their commodities cool. The company sold any surplus to surrounding communities and to the Texas and Pacific Railway for its ice cars. In 1903 a 100-pound block of ice sold for just fifty cents and could be picked up or delivered. In 1908 and 1909, the company totally renovated the ice plant and the attendant electric light plant, now identified in some company documents as a combined power plant. The ice plant received new coal boilers, stokers, and a brick smokestack 148 feet high that is still standing today. The company installed a new and larger engine for ice production in 1912 at a cost of $15,750, paid in installments. In 1915 further renovations to both the electric and ice plants allowed the boilers to be fired with local sources of natural gas instead of coal. Around this time the electric plant saw the addition of an alternating current generator, and Thurber homes and businesses ran on two types of current, alternating and direct. Thurber residents remembered living with and using both "day current" and "night current." The alternating current generator powered the town from 8:00 a.m. until 4:00 p.m., when workers turned on the direct current generator. Those tenants who chose to have electricity in their home paid only for each light fixture installed in the house, twenty-five cents per fixture. The company deducted the amount from the worker's pay. The power plant also housed the official time clock and steam whistle, the loud shriek of which governed the work days in town.[2]

A livery stable, the largest in the surrounding countryside and at times employing as many as thirty people, existed in Thurber since the inception of the town and was an important component of TPM&M until the 1920s, when the automobile made it an anachronism. The livery lay east of the main downtown quadrangle and experienced various expansions and modernizations over the life of the company. As with many of the services offered under TPM&M, a substantial portion of the income for this department came not from paying customers, but from transfers to other TPM&M departments or requisitions by the coal and brick companies. Until 1910, when the mines were electrified and the company switched to electric coal cars, the Texas and Pacific Coal Company used a number of mules below ground in the mines to haul coal, and teams of horses and other draft animals above ground for numerous jobs. Workers at the Thurber Brick Company also employed animals for much of their work. When the horses, mules, and donkeys

The livery stable. The livery stable provided horses, mules, and wagons to the citizens of Thurber for trips and excursions, and work animals for the mines until the underground mules were replaced by electric coal cars. The automobile hurt the profits of the department in the 1920s. Courtesy of the W. K. Gordon Center for Industrial History of Texas, Tarleton State University, Mingus, Texas, James Lorenz Collection.

that belonged to these companies needed to be replaced, they requested new animals from the livery. The various delivery and order wagons used by the grocery, meat, saloon, and ice departments of TPM&M and the animals to pull them were from the stables of the subsidiary. The livery also operated a four-horse Concord stagecoach that ferried up to fourteen people and mail from the main Texas and Pacific Railroad line at Thurber Junction to Thurber. Four Percheron horses, a breed of powerful draft animals, pulled the stage. The company phased out the stagecoach around 1910 when a large-capacity automobile took its place. The stage (and later the automobile), under a heavy armed guard, also transported the cash payroll from the depot at Thurber Junction to the Thurber pay office.[3]

The liverymen also rented saddle horses and surreys to the local inhabitants, who made them popular items on weekends. One Thurber resident remembers that men often hired a buggy to "take [their] sweetheart[s] out for a Sunday afternoon ride in the country side."[4] Another recalled hiring a horse for day trips to the nearby town of Strawn. For a time the stable sported a sign that proffered some apparently much needed advice: "You like something to drink in hot weather? So does your horse. The whip is merely used as an ornament and not to be used on our horses and don't drive to kill, you may want to hire him again some day."[5] A 1900 inventory listed twelve saddles, two side-saddles, a stagecoach, two single-horse buggies, five double-horse buggies, six three-seated hacks, two water wagons, and various other delivery wagons. Thirty-eight mules with names like Kit, Red, Pete, and Bill and seventy-seven horses with names like Mart, Lum, Tops, Charlie, Gordon, and Mack appeared on the inventory. Workers presumably named Gordon for the town's general manager.[6] A Fort Worth reporter related in 1896 that workers named one mine-working mule for Colonel Hunter:

> Each mule has a separate stall labeled with the name of the occupant, and the first one is occupied by the "Colonel," a particularly prosperous-appearing animal, which is said to be the veteran of the mines, having served continuously for seven years in the various pits. In this connection an amusing story is told by Colonel Hunter himself . . . on one occasion [in the mines], as he stood in a recess to allow an approaching cart to pass, he was astonished to hear the burly negro driver shout: "Colonel, you — — — —, what are you doing there? Get along out of that — quick." As soon as he was able to choke down his indignation sufficiently to enable him to articulate he approached the driver with fist doubled up and demanded an explanation. It is said the negro nearly turned white through skin and coal dust, as he tremblingly explained: "Why, Kunnel, Ise torking to de mewl—de mewl's name is Kunnel." The explanation satisfied and pleased the autocrat of the mines. . . . The colonel rarely comes to the bottom of mine no. 7 without demanding to see the other Colonel.[7]

Even if workers dearly appreciated and fondly remembered the animals, the electrification of the coal cars and the rise of the automobile in American society cut heavily into the profits of the livery stable.

The Texas and Pacific Coal Company wholly owned all the real estate, company buildings, and houses in Thurber, yet TPM&M carpenters provided all the maintenance and construction for the town. A team of painters worked for the mercantile as well. During busy building periods the company employed about a dozen carpenters and ten painters. In the early days of the town, the carpenters chose where to build homes, leading to a jumbled layout in which the front door of one house sometimes opened on the back door of the next one. With the passage of time, the arrangement of the town grew more ordered and the houses became more complex and varied in design. Most of the first homes were of simple design and made of wood, but beginning around 1900 the company erected brick homes for executives on Marston and Lakeview Streets near the downtown quadrangle. These bungalow-styled homes featured brick exteriors, finished interiors, electricity, indoor plumbing, and other modern conveniences. Along Church Street, TPM&M built a few hacienda-styled square homes with flat roofs. The majority of dwellings were built for workers, and were composed of two, three, or four fourteen- by fourteen-foot rooms with closets and cupboards built diagonally across the corners of each room. The carpenters typically used one-by-twelve pine boards for exterior and interior walls and installed either wooden shingles or corrugated iron as roofing. The occupants often covered the drafty interior walls with newspaper, as most found wallpaper an expensive luxury. The interior of the dwellings could either be ceiled, for a higher monthly rent, or unceiled. Painters applied standardized red, green, or gray paint to the houses; later houses also had painted white trim, perhaps to break the monotony. In the early era, some householders built their own fences with used barrel staves provided by TPM&M. Later, company carpenters built these. TPM&M builders added porches, and later garages, to homes as requested by renters. They also erected outhouses and washhouses behind the dwellings that did not have indoor plumbing. When a tenant needed any repairs or maintenance, company officials informed the superintendent of carpenters, who dispatched workers to jobs in priority order. The improvements added value to the homes, so the company duly increased rents commensurately. TPM&M even built more mundane items for tenants, like sheds or chicken coops, if they wished. The majority of homes cost the coal company about $150 to erect, with the rent depending on the size, number of improvements in, and the age of the house. In 1910, for example, house number 243 with two ceiled rooms rented for five dollars a month, and house 509 with four rooms, two of which were ceiled, and a porch cost eight dollars per month. Company officials placed families in homes based on their needs and requests as they built new homes or old ones became open. Many single workingmen boarded with families, paying the householder around sixteen dollars a month for room and board.[8]

The carpenter's shop sat next to the lumberyard in Thurber, east of the town square and just north of the livery stable. The lumberyard, opened in 1899, furnished the carpenters with a majority of the raw materials they utilized in their many building efforts. The yard lay between two rail spurs to facilitate loading and unloading of wood and

A typical Thurber street. A Thurber street in the early 1900s showing the typical homes built and maintained by TPM&M carpenters and painters. Courtesy of the W. K. Gordon Center for Industrial History of Texas, Tarleton State University, Mingus, Texas, James Lorenz Collection.

other materials that the company ordered by the carload. Most of the employees here worked part-time. A substantial majority of the profits the "splinter and knothole" department earned came from requisitions by company carpenters, the coal company, and the brickworks. TPM&M operated a blacksmith shop between the lumberyard and livery stable. Most of the company blacksmiths, however, worked at the entrances to the mines. Here they sharpened and repaired tools for the miners, shoed work mules, and performed maintenance on mine equipment. The colliery deducted a blacksmithing charge of one dollar per month from each miner's paycheck. The smiths in town provided similar repair work and also served as farriers for the livery stable. The money earned by the blacksmiths belonged to the coal company, though they worked under the management of TPM&M. A team of blacksmiths and machinists also worked in a machine shop and foundry on the north side of town adjacent to a spur track. Here workers repaired mine equipment, manufactured coal cars, and made many other things needed in the camp. Although the machine shop was paid

Blacksmith shop at the mines. A group of miners pose for a photograph in the early 1900s, beside one of the blacksmith shops at the entrance to one of the mines. Courtesy of Special Collections, University of Texas at Arlington Library, Arlington, Texas, Thurber, Texas, Collection, AR88.

TPM&M machine shop. TPM&M machinists take a break from repairing mine equipment, building coal cars, and manufacturing anything else the town needed. Courtesy of the W. K. Gordon Center for Industrial History of Texas, Tarleton State University, Mingus, Texas, James Lorenz Collection.

through TPM&M, the coal company managed the shop until 1917, when President Marston transferred management to the mercantile.[9]

A cotton gin, for removing seeds and impurities from picked cotton, stood north of the brick yards on the eastern edge of town. The company built a state-of-the-art cotton gin in the fall of 1894, and the company newspaper immediately advertised for business from the surrounding farmers:

> Our Cotton Gin is now complete, and is the most complete system of gin machinery in this country. We feel sure you will get better ginning at our gin than anywhere. We have a complete Munger gin system, which has gained a world renowned reputation for making the best sample and cleaning the seed better than any other system made. We are going to gin your cotton as cheap as any one, and will put your bagging and ties in at first cost. Remember this. We respectfully solicit your patronage.[10]

An adjacent machine then pressed the cotton into bales. A later note in the paper assured readers that the gin had been well received by area farmers. For years during ginning season, the company ginned cotton, purchased baled cotton from farmers, and sold bales. TPM&M easily shipped cotton out to larger markets, as a railroad spur track ran to the gin. During planting season the mercantile offered area farmers high-quality cotton seed for sale. In 1908 the company upgraded the engine and erected a new stack. Over the next decade profits declined as many local farmers stopped raising cotton and opted to convert their farmland to ranchland and grow other crops. TPM&M ceased operation of the gin by 1920. The gin complex also had the ability to process other farm products. As early as 1900 the gin house included a corn sheller worth $150, while a grain mill for grinding animal feeds shared space with the gin by the 1910s. The company also ground its own animal feed using these machines, taking the crops from company lands, processing them, and feeding them to company animals.[11]

The coal company established a dairy east of town in 1895 to provide milk to residents of the community. Less than a year later, a barn fire killed over thirty cows and destroyed the buildings. This incident and the creation of Big Lake in 1896, the waters of which submerged the old location, forced construction of a new dairy north of the previous site. Four or five men worked the thirty-five registered Holstein cows at the rebuilt dairy. The large new stable included cement flooring, was well cleaned, and had all the modern accoutrements for the operation of a good-sized dairy. Consumers in Thurber bought milk and cream with cash or scrip at the grocery. The dairymen also produced butter,

TPM&M dairy. TPM&M operated a dairy on the eastern side of town that provided milk to the town for decades. Courtesy of Special Collections, University of Texas at Arlington Library, Arlington, Texas, Thurber, Texas, Collection, AR506.

ice cream, and other products that sold in the market, grocery, and drugstore. In 1903 milk sold for five cents a pint, buttermilk cost ten cents per pint, and the price for a pound of butter was twenty-five cents. In 1899 the coal company transferred operation of the dairy, which earned thousand of dollars in profit each year until the mid-1910s, to TPM&M. TPM&M officials believed that competition from stores in nearby towns and mismanagement made the dairy less profitable by 1916. Management proposed closing the dairy, although President Marston was loath to see that happen. Newly rehired mercantile company director Ed Britton managed to make the enterprise successful again for a few more years.[12]

Colonel Hunter, a former cattleman, established ranches and farms on the many thousands of acres owned by the Texas and Pacific Coal Company. By 1895 Hunter put between six hundred and eight hundred head of cattle to pasture on twenty thousand acres of grassland and raised the same number of hogs. Farmers renting company land planted as much as fifteen hundred acres in corn and oats for feed. Most of the livestock eventually ended up in the meat market on the quadrangle. The Texas and Pacific Coal Company rented the ranch and farmland but built and owned the various ranch and farm houses, barns, and fences on the coal lands.[13] Advertisements in the newspaper at

TPM&M farmland. TPM&M tried to achieve a measure of self-sufficiency by growing food for company livestock and store shelves on the thousands of acres that surrounded the town. This field was several miles north and east of the town; the hill in the distance was the source of much of the clay used to make bricks in Thurber. Courtesy of Nita Stewart Haley Memorial Library, Midland, Texas, Miles B. Hart Collection.

Thurber called for farmers: "Farms! The right kind of men that want Land on Favorable Terms should apply at the office of the T. and P. Coal Co."[14] The company rented the farmland and ranchland until about 1913, when TPM&M operated them itself in an attempt to maximize profits. Earnings did not justify the time and money expended, so beginning in 1918 the company once again leased farmland out. Most renters were native-born white men with otherwise no connection to Thurber, but some were foreign-born individuals from the mines with names like Bonilla, Rosetti, and Zalenski. Jake Galik, a prominent Italian miner who played a leading role in the 1903 unionization of Thurber, rented a company farm for 1919 and 1920. TPM&M gave these farmers credit at the mercantile stores in return for their future produce. TPM&M also leased grazing land from the coal company for the animals it owned. The public could rent pasture land as well. The mercantile store operated a garden near the slaughterhouse before moving it to the space below the dam of Big Lake in 1896. Water from the reservoir provided an excellent source of irrigation for the various vegetables that found their way into the commercial stores of TPM&M. The grocery and market purchased produce from the company garden at low prices and then sold it to the inhabitants of Thurber for higher prices. The garden itself rarely earned much money, but it helped other TPM&M departments to keep costs low and turn handsome profits.[15]

To provide wholesome entertainment to Thurber residents, the coal company constructed a large wood-framed opera house in 1896 on the north side of the downtown quadrangle. Fifty feet wide and one hundred feet long, the building could seat almost seven hundred people and featured electric lights and power, steam heat, and ceiling fans. The interior of the opera house contained a spacious lobby, general seating, private boxes, and a balcony. Black patrons, as known from the only recorded instance of official company segregation, sat in the balcony derisively called "Negro heaven." The entertainment facilities included a large stage, a place for a band, a large loft from which backdrops could be lowered onto the floor, and three dressing rooms. Removable seats in the floor allowed it to be converted into a dance floor. Traveling acting troupes performed theatrical pieces such as *Brown's in Town, Plunger,* and *Kentucky Colonel* at the opera house. Traveling opera troupes played the venue, and the Italian inhabitants of Thurber especially enjoyed the performances, as many of the compositions were performed in Italian. Minstrel shows or vaudeville acts also occasionally played the opera house. Pupils from Thurber schools presented class plays and held graduation ceremonies there. TPM&M held some department meetings at the opera house, and coal company executives met with miners there during the 1903 strike. By 1910 a company employee named Cyrus Mowers ran a moving picture show in the theater. Around 1915 workers installed a permanent silent movie projection system in the building and began showing films. Westerns and comedies proved to be the most popular genres. Ticket prices ranged from thirty-five cents to a dollar. The opera house, though remembered as the cultural and entertainment center of Thurber, never earned much money for TPM&M.[16] Recognizing its social impact, however, company president Marston decided against closing the venue, stating, "I suppose we should take into consideration the fact that we are receiving $75.00 rent for the building and something for light and heat."[17]

Colonel Robert D. Hunter decided that Thurber, to be a proper town, needed a newspaper and bought the necessary printing equipment in late 1893. Coal company employees printed the first issue of the *Texas Miner* on Saturday, January 20, 1894. Described as a high-class weekly journal, the paper could be picked up free by town residents, was sold for five cents a copy to outsiders, or could be ordered and delivered by subscription for one dollar a year. The coal company transferred operation of the newspaper to TPM&M after its founding in the fall of 1894.

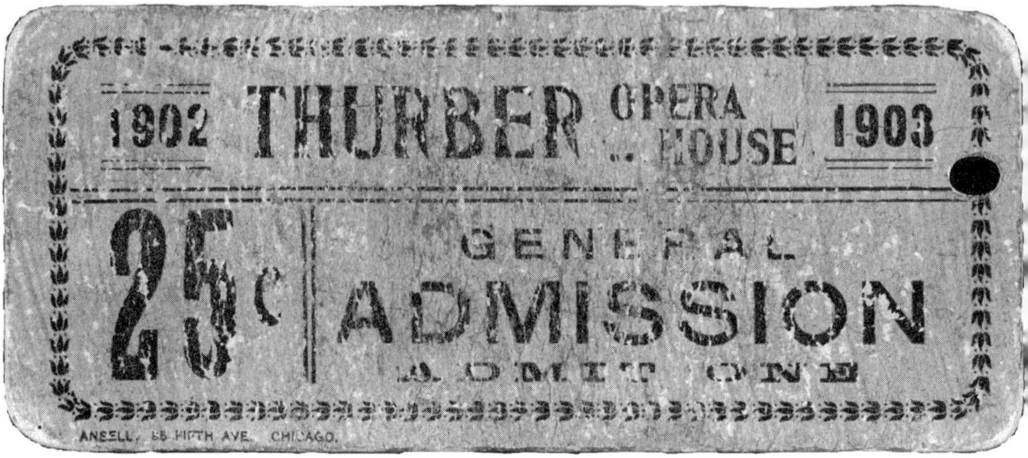

Opera house ticket from the 1902–1903 season. Thurber's opera house provided wholesome entertainment to the town for decades, including plays, Italian operas, and, later, silent movies. Residents remember this as the only public company building that was racially segregated. Courtesy of Special Collections, University of Texas at Arlington Library, Arlington, Texas, Thurber, Texas, Collection, AR506.

A typical issue in the 1890s was twenty pages long, and contained international and national news, political opinion, local news items, and ten or more pages of advertisements. The first editor, Walter B. McAdams, solicited advertisements from merchants whose goods were sold in the company stores. The editors strongly supported local and national Republican candidates in a state and region generally controlled by Democrats, these being sentiments that mirrored those of company executives. Society columns chronicled the marriages, births, deaths, and other events of the native-born white population, particularly the white-collar families, but were largely silent about the lives of foreign-born residents, who made up much of the blue-collar population.[18] Occasional articles appeared in Italian or Polish, including an article entitled "Thurber E La Colonia Italiana" that grandiosely compared Colonel Hunter and Horace K. Thurber to Cavour and Garibaldi, the heroes of Italy's nineteenth-century unification: "Uomini questi di onore, sagacita e generosita" (these men of honor and sagacity and generosity).[19]

The newspaper offered an inexpensive form of advertisement for TPM&M and had a hand in increasing sales. An article proclaimed that "cash sales have increased in the company stores since the TEXAS MINER was born."[20] Still, town superintendent William K. Gordon suggested that the company "wind up the paper" and simply print adver-

Thurber print shop. The Thurber print shop printed the company newspaper, advertisements, and much of the paperwork for the office staff. Courtesy of Dick Smith Library, Tarleton State University, Stephenville, Texas, Cross Timbers Historical Images Project.

tisements: "I do not think the paper a particle of value to the Mercantile Department here as an advertiser. The better way to attract country trade is by hand bills distributed throughout the neighborhood."[21] Though the newspaper made little profit, TPM&M continued to issue the publication, which became the rather grandiosely titled *Texas Mining and Trade Journal* in 1897 before changing permanently to the *Thurber Journal* in 1902. In addition to producing the newspaper, the print shop offered job printing and created many of the forms used in company offices. The enterprise moved into the old library building east of the quadrangle in 1908. President Edgar L. Marston sent a copy of the *Thurber Journal* to fellow industrialist John D. Rockefeller, Jr., praising the operation of the town and obviously taking pride in the first-class paper. TPM&M maintained the newspaper until early 1918, when the publication was suspended. The print shop continued to create office ledgers, forms, and stationary for Thurber and take the occasional order from the public.[22]

The coal company owned a succession of hotels in Thurber and nearby Thurber Junction that TPM&M either managed or leased out during the history of the town. Hotel Knox, named for John J. Knox of New York, a coal company director, opened its doors to the public on June 3, 1894. After an addition in 1895, the hotel contained twenty-six rooms, a dining room, a parlor, and a kitchen with modern conveniences such as electric lighting and hot water. The dining room contained ten tables and more than thirty chairs and locals described it as serving good food. A mineral water well flowed in the front yard of the hotel until it dried up in 1901. Rooms rented for $2.00 or $2.50 a day and lodged travelers as well as many unmarried male white-collar workers. The hotel also hosted social events such as dinners and grand balls. TPM&M operated the establishment, advertised as the "Best Hotel West of Fort Worth" and described as "a first-class city inn," under its own auspices but made little profit from it. In 1898 the company began leasing the hotel to outsiders who managed the property. These hotel managers paid the company rent for the building and reaped the profits, but the company retained ownership of the property, furniture, and fixtures. For many years around the turn of the century, a Chinese man named Quong managed the property and employed several Chinese cooks and other workers. One former Thurber resident remembered that the "Chinamen" served good American apple pie. Fire destroyed the Knox Hotel on April 25, 1907, and a new building named the Plummer Hotel replaced it southwest of the downtown plaza. The company also leased this new hotel to outside managers. Beginning in 1894, the company occasionally owned and leased a smaller hotel and restaurant in Thurber Junction on the main rail line as a convenience to train travelers who could not make it to Thurber.[23]

As with the hotels it leased out, TPM&M did not operate every commercial enterprise in Thurber. The Texas and Pacific Coal Company rented many buildings in the town to businessmen unaffiliated with the company. The physicians in Thurber were coal company employees and worked rent free in a small infirmary during the early years before moving into a doctor's office south of the newly built drugstore in 1909. In 1913 the company erected a new brick building on the east side of the quadrangle between the hardware department and the drugstore. This location housed the new doctor's office on the second floor, above the barber shop. The company usually kept between two and four physicians on staff at any one time. Well-remembered doctors included Charles Binney, a nephew of Hunter's, Pettigrew, and Dorsey.[24] One doctor had the unfortunate name of Killar and didn't believe in the efficacy of the germ theory, writing in a journal called *The Medical Brief* that "knowledge of the germ theory would avail [a patient] naught";

the patient, he said, would still die.[25] The coal company took a fee of fifty cents each month for the doctors. These funds paid the doctors, but any surplus could also be given as TPM&M scrip to sick workers and their families to buy food, drugs, and supplies, or coffins, if the need arose.[26] A new brick post office constructed in 1915 also included living quarters for doctors on the second floor. Dentists occasionally rented buildings in town but never remained long. The first barber shop stood southwest of the quadrangle until 1909, when the new drugstore forced it to another location south of the square. The barbers moved into their third location with the doctor's office in 1913.[27]

A photographer opened a shop just southeast of the square before moving to a building adjacent to the second barbershop. During the early 1910s a shoe repair business lay east of the quadrangle and then moved into a shop west of the bakery and dry goods building between the late 1910s and early 1920s. The 1910 U.S. census lists a Robert Ayers as proprietor of a confectionery on rented company property. For a time the town boasted a tailor shop and a laundry managed by Chinese immigrants. In addition to the restaurants operated by the hotelkeepers in Thurber, a diner known as the Modern Café stood on the north side of the quadrangle next to the opera house in an old wooden-framed building that had once been the post office. A proprietor named Reyes Gomez ran a Mexican food eatery well remembered by the children of Thurber because he offered them free samples. Another Thurber resident remembered a duo named Ruiz and Magger that managed another Mexican restaurant near the grocery. A 1924 inventory of the "Old Mexican Restaurant" listed $170.50 worth of items in the empty old building, including plates, cutlery, chili bowls, and pictures on the walls. These restaurants catered to both the sizable Mexican population and the rest of the inhabitants.[28]

Although the charter for TPM&M tasked it to maintain a telegraph and telephone system for the town, it was the Texas and Pacific Coal Company that erected, operated, and repaired these lines. The operators of the telephone switchboard and telegraph worked for the coal company, not TPM&M, as most calls, directives, and orders routed to the mines. The mercantile company did employ half a dozen night watchmen to watch over the town during evening hours. The company also paid janitors for cleaning store and office buildings. Most former residents of Thurber remembered or wrote little about these workers, who, though their service may have seemed mundane, contributed importantly to the growth and vitality of Thurber.[29]

CHAPTER 5
THE COMPANY STORE AND THE WORKERS

The miners and their families in Thurber generally harbored suspicions and grievances against Texas Pacific Mercantile and Manufacturing, especially before the 1903 strike that made Thurber a union camp. There were numerous reasons for this. Union propaganda played a role, stoking resentment between the coal company, and its subsidiary arms, and the worker. Miners across the United States generally believed that the company store profited to their detriment: forcing purchases, instituting credit systems geared to engendering debt, and selling at inflated prices. Unions exploited these feelings, and Thurber was no exception. The blue-collar employees of the mines and brick plant also moved in decidedly different social circles and hailed from disparate ethnic groups, nations, and classes. Though company officials insisted that TPM&M operated for the benefit of the townsfolk, the workers usually contended that the mercantile exploited them. Labor-held grievances toward TPM&M played a significant part in the 1903 unionization of Thurber, and labor animosity toward the company store would depress its profits. The company's efforts to increase profits, encourage business in town, and attract outside trade aided in Thurber's continued survival but only seemed like proof to the common laborers that the mercantile was meant to take money from the workers.

Ethnicity was one of the factors that separated the coal diggers from the employees of the mercantile company. A majority of the miners were foreign-born, representing more than twenty different nationalities and ethnic groups. The remainder were native-born white and black citizens of the United States. On the other hand, the people who held jobs with TPM&M, in both white-collar and blue-collar positions, were predominantly native-born white men. In 1900 approximately 66 percent of the mining population of Thurber was foreign-born, while a scant 13.27 percent of TPM&M employees—only thirteen people—were immigrants. The other blue-collar workers in Thurber, the employees of the brick plant, were, unlike the coal diggers, but like TPM&M employees, mostly native-born white men, although a number of black and Mexican men worked for the brick company at times. While the average miner was a foreigner or recently naturalized immigrant, almost every TPM&M employee these miners met was a white American citizen. Nine of the thirteen immigrant workers for TPM&M in 1900 came from western Europe: four Scots, three Germans, one Irishman, and one Englishman; another TPM&M worker was a Canadian. All of these men undoubtedly found assimilation and acceptance into white, native-born society relatively easy. Just three TPM&M employees were from eastern and southern Europe: two hailed from Italy and one originated from Poland. All mercantile employees, regardless of their origin, spoke fluent English, while many coal workers and their families spoke little, if any, English.[1]

According to the 1900 census, the mercantile company employed eleven men in the grocery and three in the dry goods department, all American-born. Only one salesman at the dry goods was a foreigner. Of the five employees at the meat market, the manager hailed from Canada, one meat cutter emigrated from Germany, and the rest were born in the United States. At the drugstore, the pharmacist and clerk were both native-born citizens. The bartenders listed in the 1900 census at the Thurber saloons, the Snake and the Lizard, included three foreign-born men, one from Scotland and two from Italy; two others were American-born men. TPM&M employed eleven blacksmiths: eight were U.S. nationals, three were immigrants. Only five of the remaining sixty indefinable TPM&M employees, who worked in service jobs such as liverymen, wagon drivers, machinists, painters, carpenters, and plasterers, hailed from foreign nations. Over the years, the makeup of TPM&M employees was similar: most were white, native-born, and spoke fluent English. The company did employee Italian-, Polish-, and Spanish-speakers in the saloons and in the general store on the hill. A few black men held jobs with TPM&M, usually as porters and janitors. The mercantile also employed women in the dry goods store to assist women with their purchases.[2]

The company had no specific segregation policy, but the nationalities in Thurber tended to group together, which suggests that people could choose the general area they wanted to live and company officials obliged. Most of the Italians lived on Italian Hill north of the railroad tracks leading west to the mines, the Poles on Polander Hill south of the same tracks, the Mexicans on Stump Hill just south of the Poles, the Irish below and east of Stump Hill in an area called "the Flat," the blacks just north and east of Little Lake, and the whites near downtown. These neighborhoods were not distinct and were, in fact, often mixed. Following state law, separate schools existed for blacks and whites; there was a Catholic school as well. William K. Gordon, Jr., son of Thurber's longtime general manager, remembered that blacks and Mexicans probably faced more discrimination than other groups, but probably less so than elsewhere in that time period and locale, Jim Crow era Texas. One Thurber resident, Lillie Ivey Gibson, recalled that nobody balked at the company not segregating any of the stores—only the opera house had a designated section for blacks. The language barrier between much of the mining population and mercantile employees affected trade, as many immigrants felt uncomfortable buying from clerks who did not speak their language. In 1904 TPM&M opened a general store on Polander Hill staffed with Italian-, Polish-, and Spanish-speaking employees in an attempt to generate higher sales among the immigrant workers, a tactic that succeeded. Over time TPM&M even began to employ more foreign-born and black workers, though the black workers mainly served as porters or laborers. Still, the overwhelming majority of TPM&M store employees remained white American-born males.[3]

Economic and social distinctions separated the blue-collar workers in the mines and brick plant from the primarily white-collar TPM&M employees. Mercantile company employees generally earned more money than coal company laborers. Before the 1903 unionization of Thurber, miners grossed, before deductions, an average of about $43 per month, and that increased to about $48 per month in the few years after 1903. Brick workers earned similar sums for their labors. Before and after Thurber became a union town, TPM&M salesmen, clerks, managers, and other employees generally earned, before deductions, between $50 and $125 each month. Also, almost all TPM&M employees were salaried, while a miner's earnings depended on the amount of clean coal he brought to the surface. Sickness, slack days, injuries, broken tools, and several other occurrences could reduce the monthly pay of a miner or brick worker; TPM&M employees earned their pay even if sales were slow or inventories were slack. Religion also separated the workers. Many of the coal diggers and their families were of southern

(top) R. D. Hunter Fishing and Boating Club. Only management and white-collar Thurberites could belong to the members-only R. D. Hunter Fishing and Boating Club on the shores of Thurber's Big Lake. The laboring classes of Thurber had to content themselves with the inexclusivity of Little Lake. Courtesy of Dick Smith Library, Tarleton State University, Stephenville, Texas, Cross Timbers Historical Images Project. (bottom) Blue-collar Thurberites picnic. Working-class Thurber residents often imbibed in the open air at Little Lake. Courtesy of Dick Smith Library, Tarleton State University, Stephenville, Texas, Cross Timbers Historical Images

European, eastern European, Mexican, and Irish extraction and practiced Roman Catholicism, while the native-born white families of Thurber generally belonged to Protestant denominations. Methodist, Baptist, Church of Christ, and Pentecostal churches all met in Thurber over its history. The black families had their own segregated Protestant churches. Social life was also stratified. The company-controlled newspaper regularly printed society columns detailing the activities and lives of the U.S.-born white inhabitants of Thurber, most associated with TPM&M, but rarely discussed members of the foreign-born, working-class population in the same ways. The infrequent articles in Italian or Polish were usually either advertisements for company stores or editorials effusively delineating the positive aspects of Thurber. The white-collar workers also had access to recreational facilities unavailable to the men who worked the mines. Everyone in Thurber could fish or swim in Little Lake, hunt in the surrounding countryside, or attend dances and performances at the opera house, but only the company executives, office staff, and TPM&M store clerks and their families could hunt, fish, and relax at the members-only R. D. Hunter Fishing and Boating Club on the shore of Big Lake. The bylaws of the organization forbade most nonmembers from entering the premises or acreage and even limited the duties that black or white servants of members could perform while on the grounds.[4]

Both blue-collar and white-collar workers found jobs for family members. Many of the foreign miners in town, especially the Italians, urged their relatives to immigrate and take up jobs at the mines. The employees of TPM&M also maneuvered their family members into positions within the company. The brothers of General Manager Ed Britton of TPM&M, Joe, James, and John, all worked for the mercantile company at one time or another. James Magruder "Grude" Britton was, for several years, one of the chief bartenders at the Snake Saloon. His past as a Texas Ranger surely helped him to forestall any rowdiness from getting out of hand. Another general manager in the mid-1910s, Thomas R. Tennant, got his brother a job in the dry goods department. Robert Terbet, a blacksmith, worked with two of his sons in the blacksmith shop; his brother was a machinist, and his wife served as a saleslady at the dry goods store. Employees and managers in every department of the mercantile company practiced nepotism. Even the second president of the Texas and Pacific Coal Company and TPM&M, Edgar L. Marston, hired his brother, A. B. "Bert" Marston, as a clerk in Thurber. He was quickly promoted to assistant general manager of TPM&M under Ed Britton in 1900. With support from the company, voters even elected A. B. Marston county commissioner for the Thurber precinct in 1902. His ascent in the company ended rather abruptly just a few months later. On December 8, 1902, Marston died under mysterious circumstances in Pittsburg, Kansas. Sent to the state to recruit black miners for Thurber, Marston suddenly and inexplicably collapsed and died in the Hotel Stilwell after playing billiards. As he was healthy and not suicidal, doctors on the scene believed that someone had murdered him using arsenic poison, a finding supported by the coroner's initial cursory examination of Marston's stomach. A month after the incident, an analysis of Marston's stomach by a Kansas state chemist found that he in fact had not been poisoned and the death was declared natural. The precise cause of his death, however, was never determined. Thurber's company paper printed effusive eulogies for A. B. Marston.[5]

The perception miners held of TPM&M before the unionization of Thurber in 1903 was generally negative. Many residents viewed the barbed-wire fence that surrounded the town as an exploitative form of company control, allowing the mercantile company to charge monopolistic prices at its stores. In the first few years of Thurber's existence, the nearest town with competing merchants was Gordon, eight miles to the northeast, or Strawn a bit farther than that to the northwest. Although Colonel Hunter insisted that the residents of his town could shop anywhere they wished, the fence kept most people from leaving or entering the town, whether it was the guards or fear of the guards that stopped them. Likewise, the distance to Gordon and Strawn discouraged travel there, unless someone owned or could afford to hire a horse, mule, or wagon. Despite the fence, some farmers and peddlers regularly entered and sold their wares. The town's newspaper, for instance, regularly noted when area farmers came into town to both buy and sell. Stories abounded that company guards kept notes on those employees who attempted to purchase goods from these outsiders; some believed that guards followed peddlers and kept notes on which Thurber residents bought from them. But the Texas and Pacific Coal Company could hardly afford to dismiss employees for such an insignificant reason as buying goods from outside the camp or patronizing peddlers.[6] Workers were hard to come by and hard to keep.

Surviving discussions on the subject by TPM&M officials show they never considered punishing inhabitants who purchased goods from outside sources, but in fact brainstormed ideas on how to lure in new customers and keep them buying in company stores. In 1905, the general manager of TPM&M, Thomas R. Tennant, described the situation to his retail employees: "You are aware that our camp is invaded with peddlers of wares of every descry[i]ption, that we must redouble our efforts to overcome this competition by showing our people that we have better goods at less prices."[7] The TPM&M workers constantly promoted the quality of their goods, which were fresh, comparing them to the less-than-fresh goods of the peddlers. The workers noted the shady practices of outside vendors too. John Vietti, the manager of the general store, recounted an incident illustrating the methods of the peddlers:

> A few days ago a peddler who sells quite a good deal of goods on the [Italian] hill, came into my department and ask[ed] me for $5.00 worth of sugar. I, of course, sold him the sugar. After I had sold him the sugar, he ask[ed] me for some small sacks. I refused to give him the sacks, but he then purchased them from me. He put $5.00 worth of sugar up in six separate sacks, then out of these six packages he took enough sugar to make a 50¢ package, stating that he could make the 50¢ bale out of the other packages and the customers would never know the difference.[8]

The record of the meeting indicates that "quite a discussion followed Mr. Vietti's talk, all showing a tendency of the peddler toward short weights in order to make up for some of the [low] prices which they make."[9] The salesmen and managers suggested various methods to counteract the peddlers, including price reductions, drawings, and going door-to-door to ask working families how they could be served better.[10] However, for workers predisposed to mistrust "company men," the latter tactic may have seemed like an act of intimidation, no matter how kindly done.

By 1890 a string of businesses had sprung up just north of company property at the junction of the main Texas and Pacific railway line and the spur track that ran southward to Thurber. Businesses, saloons, and peddlers soon made Grant Town, just north of the fence, and Thurber Junction, usually called Mingus, their base of operations. Peddlers regularly entered Thurber, while the stores in Gordon and Mingus sent order wagons into Thurber, returning later in the day or the next day with their goods.[11] Company reports dating before unionization and removal of the fence complained about the effects of competition; TPM&M was hardly operating a monopoly. In 1897 the company noted, "The percentage of profits did not come up to our monthly estimates, owing to strong competition we were forced to reduce prices on all articles, especially staples."[12] The 1899 annual report told the stockholders of the company:

> It is proper that your attention should be called to the building up of a town at Thurber Junction, two miles north of Thurber, where stores and saloons have been started and every inducement is made to our miners to

attract and gain their trade, and it will only be by economical management and close attention, and using advantages which we have in buying our goods that we can expect to realize in the future the profits of the past.[13]

Loss of TPM&M profits to competition also featured in company reports in 1900 and 1902. By this time Thurber Junction had a number of bars, hotels, and a drugstore. The 1900 census lists four combination saloon and grocery stores operated by Italians Mazzano, Ronchetti, Sealfi, and Corona that lay just across the company fence in Grant Town. In 1899 two TPM&M employees even considered opening a general store at Thurber Junction in opposition to the commercial enterprises in Thurber. In 1903 one of these employees, Robert Loflin, opened a general store named the Loflin Mercantile Company at Mingus that was a fixture in the area for decades.[14]

The September 1903 strike that made Thurber a union camp centered on the issues of the working miner in the pits. The primary disputes involved wages, fees deducted from pay, the screening of coal, and the right to join a union. The official list of miner demands sent to William K. Gordon, drawn up by Peter Hanraty, president of District 21 of the United Mine Workers of America (UMWA), C. W. Woodman, secretary and treasurer of the Texas State Federation of Labor, and William Wardjon, chief organizer of the UMWA, included the following:

1. Price of mining to be $1.35 per ton of 2000 pounds of coal to be mined on the same basis as heretofore. Cross entries $1.50 per yard, corner entries $1.50 per yard
2. The inside day wage to be as follows: Timber men $2.50 per day, tracklayers $2.50 per day, airmen or ventilators $1.50 per day, driver $2.35 per day, motor drivers $2.35 per day, cagers $2.35 per day, greasers and praggers $1.50 per day, trappers $1.20 per day.
3. Outside Day Work Scale—Car trimmers and slate dumpers $2.00 per day, slate pickers $1.50 per day, blacksmiths $2.75 per day, firemen $2.00 per day, engineers same as agreed to and paid in Arkansas and Indian Territory.
4. Eight hours to constitute a day's work.
5. That we be paid in full every two weeks.
6. We demand the right to organize into the United Mine Workers of America organization, and respectfully ask the Texas and Pacific Coal Company of Thurber to recognize said organization.[15]

None of the written demands refers to anything directly related to the company stores, but accompanying oral demands mention the guards,

Management-Labor meeting, 1903. The meeting between coal company officials and the UMWA in the Worth Hotel, Fort Worth, that made Thurber a completely unionized city. General Manager Gordon (labeled 1) stands along the wall to the left; president Edgar L. Marston (labeled 2) sits at the conference table. To his left is future labor leader John L. Lewis. Courtesy of the W. K. Gordon Center for Industrial History of Texas, Tarleton State University, Mingus, Texas, James Lorenz Collection.

the wire fence, and the prices at the stores. "There is no reference in the written demands to the subject of guards," a reporter related. "Mr. Wardjon says, however, that one of the demands is that the company shall cease having guards around the mines."[16] Another report a few days later expanded on this mention:

> The ex-employes [*sic*] of the coal company speak of many things not mentioned in their written demand as grievances. One of them is that the company put a wire fence around its properties except at the public thoroughfares. For the first time a reason was heard assigned today for this objection. It was that the fence made it difficult for the farmers to come to Thurber with produce and that the miners in consequence paid higher prices.[17]

The fence and the prices in the stores almost seem to be an afterthought to the union's demands, but the official organ of the United Mine Workers painted a far grimmer picture of conditions at Thurber, with TPM&M a prime component.

In the midst of the strike the *United Mine Workers' Journal* flatly called Thurber a "tyranny":

> To appreciate the situation at Thurber one must go there and visit the miners in their homes, talk with the miners' wives, see the hovels they are compelled to live in, and hear the women tell of their experiences. One can hardly believe having visited the village that peddlers were followed into the grounds by the guards, and the names of patrons of the peddlers taken and reported to management, with the inevitable result that the patron was told never to repeat the offense under penalty of being compelled to pack up and leave.[18]

The union newspaper described the evils of the "scrip" or "check" system rather inaccurately:

> But, perhaps, what worked the greatest hardship was the check system—the issuing of scrip in lieu of money. There being but one pay day a month, and miners barely making a living, hardly a week would pass after pay day until all cash had been spent, and then to do business, to purchase anything, scrip must be obtained, and this scrip was discounted by the company at 20 per cent.[19]

The UMWA, of course, had reasons to stoke resentment between the laborers and the company—every reason to portray the company as bad and the union as good. After one pro-union speech during the 1903 strike, a black miner was heard to exclaim: "We are going to have everything 'union' after this, union 'lasses, union battercakes, union steaks—everything will be union."[20] Many labor historians have echoed the fears and accusations of the miners and the unions. David Corbin, in his work on miners in southern West Virginia, gives an often quoted summary of the store-as-monopoly view of company towns:

> If a coal miner survived a month of work in the mines, he was paid not in U.S. currency but in metals and paper (called coal scrip), which was printed by the coal company. Because only the company that printed the coal scrip honored it, or would redeem it, the coal miner had to purchase all his goods—his food, clothing, and tools—from the company store. Hence, the miner paid monopolistic prices for his goods. Journalists and U.S. senato-

rial investigating committees repeatedly revealed that the region's coal company store prices were substantially higher, sometimes three times higher, than the local trade stores. . . . To miners, it meant, as they later sang, that they "owed their souls to the company store." For some miners, it meant being held in peonage.[21]

Some historians of Thurber follow this line. William P. Powers wrote in his 1989 master's thesis on Thurber that, "Throughout the years 1900 to 1902, the phenomenon of miner indebtedness to the company was played out time and again. . . . While the average Thurber miner was earning his pittance, the Texas & Pacific coal company was becoming increasingly profitable."[22] Local chronicler Leo Bielinski, who has lived in the Thurber area since childhood and written several works on the town, repeated the prevailing point of view in his 1993 historical novel *The Back Road to Thurber:*

The T.P.M. and M. Co. was in business to make a profit, and in this respect they were assisted by the barbed wire fence and company guards. The fence kept people from going outside to buy, and it kept peddlers from selling inside. Horse-mounted guards patrolled the fence line, and there were guards at the gates. . . . The company promoted script for use as money. These coupons resembled theater tickets, were called "check" and were good at all company stores. An employee could borrow "check" against his wages, but once enmeshed in this system, it was difficult to catch up and get back on a cash basis.[23]

In fact, coal company towns were generally not the bleak, monopolistic tyrannies the unions described. The 1911 report of the U.S. Immigration Commission, chaired by Senator William Dillingham of Vermont, found the following generally applied to coal company stores:

In isolated communities, where the "company store" is the only available place for the employee to make his purchases, it has been charged that the prices at the store were too high and that stock of an inferior quality was carried. In the majority of cases, however, the reverse is true, the employee being able to secure from the company store as good, if not better, articles for the same or a less price than would be charged by an independent store.[24]

The commission further found that because these companies could buy in bulk, they could keep prices low. This is just what the operators of TPM&M had always contended:

> Many company stores handle first-class goods throughout and charge prices no higher than in the best-managed town and city stores. They buy in very large quantities, thereby receiving unusually favorable quotations. They have few or no bad debts and consequently are able to make more than the average profit at moderate prices. These prices are maintained fairly, although the store enjoys a practical monopoly of trade and might exact higher prices.[25]

Some economic historians, such as Price V. Fishback, have analyzed statistical data at several mining camps, finding that companies could not charge monopolistic prices because they had to compete for geographically mobile miners in a labor market offering hundreds of possibilities.[26] Thurber drew its miners from all over the world, particularly the United States, Mexico, and Europe. These miners could work in several fields in the United States, including several bituminous mining sites in the immediate vicinity of Thurber, including nearby Strawn, Lyra, and Mineral City, all of which unionized years before Thurber did in 1903.

The fence and the guards may have been more symbolic deterrents to trade than actual ones. Indeed, a closer reading of the record indicates that many miners resented the very idea of being guarded more than they felt any fear of buying from outsiders. William Wardjon told striking miners that "the miners were peaceable and law-abiding and resented the presence of guards."[27] Confusion or union propaganda may have contributed to some memories of company control and issues like the fence in pre-union days. During the 1903 strike, for instance, a woman interviewed by a reporter made a number of striking assertions:

> The first signs of dissatisfaction I ever noticed among the miners was when W. K. Gordon, the general manager of the company, issued orders prohibiting merchants and peddlers from Gordon and the surrounding towns from coming to Thurber and selling their wares. That was about one year ago, and previous to that time merchants from Gordon came to Thurber daily and delivered groceries and general merchandise to their trade, and in all cases they sold their stuff a great deal cheaper than it could be bought at the company's stores in Thurber.[28]

This woman claimed erroneously that General Manager W. K. Gordon erected the fence only in 1901 or 1902 and that only then did he prohibit peddlers from entering town. In fact, the company erected the fence in the winter of 1888 under the direction of Colonel Hunter, and in late 1901 William K. Gordon instituted a strong quarantine guard between Thurber and Mingus to prevent an outbreak of smallpox from spreading into the coal camp.[29] The ease with which a temporary quarantine guard could be confused with a permanent action against peddlers highlights the animosity and mistrust that existed between laboring families and management policies. It is also noteworthy that, though she insisted prices were high in Thurber, the interviewee admitted peddlers were a common sight in town.

Besides their recollections of the objectionable fence, many town residents remembered company store prices being higher than those of outside competition. One woman interviewed during the 1903 strike stated that outside peddlers and stores *always* had lower prices than the stores of TPM&M. Another woman told reporter James Hays Quarles of Fort Worth that her husband was unable to make enough money because of low wages and high store prices. Quarles then listed common retail goods like lard, salted meats, and cheese and noted their respective prices; he commented that they seemed reasonable. Another newspaperman reported that some miners believed the company made higher profits from the mercantile than from the selling of coal, which was untrue. Many former residents of Thurber, especially those who were miners or the children of miners, remarked that prices offered in Mingus or by peddlers were lower than those in Thurber.[30]

Some scattered evidence does indicate that TPM&M and its parent company did utilize fixed profit percentages. In a 1908 letter from William K. Gordon in Thurber to Edgar L. Marston in New York, the vice president and president of TPM&M respectively, Gordon noted: "As far as requisition supplies are concerned, regardless of what the goods cost, the Mercantile Department gets its five (5%) and seven and half (7-1/2%) per cent profit, the smaller profit on supplies in quantities of one hundred ($100) dollars or more, the larger on amounts of less than one hundred dollars."[31] Gordon then recounted, with some bewildered displeasure, an instance from a few years earlier when TPM&M head Ed S. Britton sold corn at eighty cents per bushel while peddlers in town sold it for just sixty-five cents. Gordon reported that Britton had argued "that the corn had to be sold at eighty cents to enable him to get cost and seven and half per cent profit out of it."[32] Gordon was not averse to using the company store to generate revenue, just not in Thurber. In 1902 the Texas and Pacific Coal Company bought the Rock Creek coal mines of the Texas Coal and Fuel Company in nearby Parker County, Texas. Gordon, in charge of both the Thurber and Rock Creek concerns, noted that the company store at Rock Creek charged higher prices than the store in Thurber for the same goods. In order to make these Rock Creek mines more profitable, he decided to keep the "considerably higher" prices in effect.[33] Knowledge of these practices, or just rumors of them, may have prompted some Thurber residents to smuggle goods past guards at the fence into the enclosure in fear of being fired or asked to leave the town. Catalog sales, especially through Sears, Roebuck and Company, thrived in Thurber because the company could not legally stop mail delivery. The miners generally resented the *apparent* company stranglehold on business.[34]

On the other hand, many other former residents of Thurber remembered prices that were either reasonable or cheaper than elsewhere. In the mid-1890s, prices for goods at Thurber stores were often lower than or equal to most prices offered by outside businesses. In 1896 a pound of sugar cost five cents a pound in both Thurber and Stephenville, the county seat of Erath County and the nearest large town for which records survive. For example, fifty pounds of flour retailed for $1.00 in both towns; other prices were similar, especially on staples. Both towns had large businesses and ready access to the railroad. Visitors passing through Thurber often mentioned that goods sold for less in Thurber than in their hometown.[35] One wrote: "Everything is sold at the company's stores. They buy for cash in large quantities, sell for cash, and I was much interested in getting at the prices for which goods are sold. I figure that they are about 25 to 40 per cent less than what I have to pay for supplies in Abilene country."[36] Advertisements in the company newspaper, of course, touted their lower prices. In contrast to the small stores in the vicinity with little access to capital, the departments at Thurber each received multiple carloads of goods every week. Such bulk cash purchases allowed TPM&M to sell at lower prices than its competitors, competitors so cash-strapped they often bought and sold goods on credit.[37] This applied to the saloons in Mingus as well. When the saloon of George Scalfi lost its five thousand dollar liquor dealer's bond after selling alcohol to a minor in 1901, Scalfi had to close his drinking house until he could recoup his losses and repay his Baltimore, Maryland, bond dealer.[38] TPM&M could have easily absorbed any such loss, or hired a team of lawyers to fight the charges.

In stark contrast to the memories of some miners and the claims of the union in 1903, businessmen from surrounding areas often complained that the ability of TPM&M to offer lower prices unfairly hurt their trade. A handbill in Erath County grumbled that the mercantile company at Thurber offered "necessaries and their hardware at cheaper rates than Stephenville or Dublin ever did or ever will."[39] Another Stephenville resident remembered that "the company was accused by the stores in Mingus, Strawn and Stephenville, Texas, of selling for less and being guilty of unfair competition and unsuccessfully taken to court a time or two on this score. The company contended because they bought on a large scale for cheaper prices, they could sell for less and still make a good profit."[40] The ever-present issue of liquor and prohibition in the surrounding predominantly dry counties reared its head as well, because the saloons of TPM&M were open to the public in addition to Thurberites, selling beer "by the schooner and the bottle some cheaper, and by the keg and the barrel much cheaper."[41] The miners and area storekeepers could not both be right. Were prices in Thurber high due to monopolistic pricing and the fence? Or were prices cheaper due to "unfair" purchasing power? Of course, the answer lies in between these two extremes. On certain goods and at certain times, sometimes the peddler or the Grant Town store had lower prices, and sometimes TPM&M had the lower price.

Miners also complained about the scrip system during the 1903 strike. Payday occurred only once a month, and the workingmen contended that this forced them to obtain scrip, or check as they called it in Thurber, between paydays. Borrowing against future earnings compelled many miners to become indebted to the company and forced them to continue purchasing from only the company store. In the years before the strike, workers in Thurber took home well below half of their pay in cash after deductions. In 1900 employees received only an average of 41.14 percent of their net earnings in cash on paydays. The average had increased to 44.48 percent the year of the strike. The rest of the miner's pay had already been spent in scrip or deducted for rent, utilities, and other service costs, such as for doctors or blacksmithing. As time passed, workers tended to earn more in cash and owe less to the company. This tendency continued during the years after unionization. As a comparison, miners in Thurber took home more of their earnings in cash than most miners in Appalachian mining camps during the same period. The amount workers were indebted to the Texas and Pacific Coal Company and TPM&M fell during this period as well. Company policies by the late 1890s made the labor force more content and stable than before, and made it easier to save earnings. The payroll office even offered miners passbooks to account for their scrip spending. Some employees in Thurber even made and saved substantial amounts of money before the strike.[42] No true chartered bank ever operated in Thurber, and a bank was not established in nearby Thurber Junction until 1907, but the Texas and Pacific Coal Company held savings for its employees. An 1897 newspaper article noted that "the books of the company now show on deposit with it over $20,000 in savings of the miners, so perfect is the confidence and esteem in which the management is held by its employe[e]s. It was only a short time ago that one party of six left for the old country with $5000 of savings earned there."[43] A small note in the 1902 annual report of the coal company recorded the purchase of $25,000 in bonds from a railroad company "to off-set the deposits made by our Employees," suggesting savings were at least stable enough to make this substantial investment.[44] A reporter from Stephenville during the strike in 1903 reported that one Italian miner withdrew $1,500 in savings from "the company's bank," quite a sum considering the average monthly income for miners in Thurber.[45] This hardly reflects the image of miners in debt peonage to the company, or as the UMWA said of Thurber before unionization: "To sum it all up in a few words, for fourteen years there was a reign of terror at Thurber, and the miners were compelled to obey blindly the rules of the company."[46] The company hardly held people in "debt bondage," as miners often left town of their own accord while deep in debt to the company, both before and after unionization.[47]

Amount Paid and Deducted from Payrolls in Thurber (1900–1910)

	1900	1903	1904	1910
Paid in Cash	$237,237.22	$309,671.95	$341,862.81	$567,294.88
	41.14%	44.48%	46.83%	49.25%
Paid in Scrip	$244,665.06	$287,795.66	$270,335.38	$386,442.81
	42.42%	41.34%	37.03%	33.55%
Other Deductions	$94,812.02	$98,661.93	$117,795.46	$198,155.32
	16.44%	14.17%	16.14%	17.20%
Total Deductions	$339,477.08	$386,457.59	$388,130.84	$584,598.13
(Including scrip)	58.86%	55.52%	53.17%	50.75%

Sources: "Payroll Book, Mine, 1900–1902," Ledger 121; "Payroll Book, Mine, 1903," Ledger 122; "Payroll Book, Mine, 1904–1905," Ledger 123; "Payroll Book, Mine, 1910," Ledger 128; the previous four sources are from the Texas and Pacific Coal Company Records, S1021.1; computer analysis of records by the author.

Union propaganda may have played a role in some of the misinformation miners held about the company. In the September 24, 1903, article entitled "Thurber on Strike" in the *United Mine Workers' Journal,* the official journal of the union, the writer claimed that company scrip was discounted 20 percent on issuance to workers. This would mean that for every dollar issued in "check" to a Thurber miner, the company kept twenty cents. The United Mine Workers of America union often used misinformation or propaganda to make its pro-labor point. No contemporary record substantiates the claim, nor do company payroll records indicate any such penalty. Reporters from several newspapers in Dallas and Fort Worth covered the strike at Thurber, and though they recorded several grievances of the miners, none mentioned the discounting of scrip as one of them.[48] One newspaper even asserted that "there does not appear to be the objection to the check system at Thurber as is the case at other camps."[49] Surely an onerous 20 percent discount would raise such objections. As with the claims about the quarantine guard and the company fence, the claim that the company discounted scrip 20 percent before issuance could have resulted from conflation with another company service. Around 1909 a Polish traveler from Chicago named Stefan Nesterowicz mentioned that a miner could exchange his scrip for cash at the "company bank" with a discount of 10 percent.[50] Aside from the *United Mine Workers' Journal,* evidence indicates that the company did not discount scrip when issued or when spent at the stores, but did so when exchanged for cash.

When the Texas and Pacific Coal Company, led by Edgar L. Marston, agreed to recognize unions in late September 1903, the company removed the fence and acknowledged (in Marston's mind, reiterated) that miners did not have to purchase at the stores in Thurber. The scrip system remained in effect. Although portrayed as solely a miners' affair in some historical accounts, the town's brick workers unionized as well. During the strike, reporters noted that the liverymen quit working and joined a union, as did one of the bartenders. Eventually, the blacksmiths, machinists, bartenders, ice plant workers, salesmen, and retail clerks who did not have management positions all joined unions. A female union organizer named Emma Lanphere brought many of the white-collar employees into the clerks' union.[51] Edgar L. Marston commented after the strike that "the question of 'Company Stores' having been discussed by the Union miners in their Union meetings and by members of the State Legislature, it has been thought best to have the Coal Company and the Mercantile Company more independent of each other than heretofore."[52] The two companies remained intimately linked, however, as the coal company continued to own and operate

TPM&M. Miners and other workers in Thurber could now freely and without fear purchase goods from outside vendors and stores. The institution of two paydays a month allowed employees to take home more cash than before; by 1910 they earned nearly 50 percent of their pay in cash. By 1913, the year the miners at Thurber extracted the most coal from the earth and unionism had been firmly entrenched for a decade, employees began taking home a majority of their pay in cash. By this time, many miners lived and shopped off company grounds, and competition for their dollars had grown significantly. Before 1903 the customers in Thurber purchased a significant portion of their goods at the five major retail departments of TPM&M—the grocery, dry goods, hardware, drugstore, and meat market—with scrip instead of cash. After unionization at these same departments, scrip sales fell sharply but still constituted a major portion of sales. The use of scrip remained high in the grocery and meat market, presumably because people needed food daily and would spend more scrip in those places when there was little or no cash between paydays, and because fresh food goods here were often of higher quality than could be offered by peddlers or Thurber Junction stores.[53]

Grant Town and Thurber Junction boomed as never before in the years after unionization, as many workers from Thurber and surrounding areas bought goods there. There was the Loflin dry goods store in Thurber Junction, and a Lebanese peddler named Joe Abraham Habib, remembered simply as Joe Abraham, opened his combination dry goods and grocery store in 1903. Abraham, like many other store owners in Thurber Junction, delivered groceries directly into Thurber. Angelo Taramino operated a saloon in 1903, and Angelo Castaldo opened a grocery store around 1905; both were Italian immigrants. These stores made excellent money that may have, at times, rivaled the take at the TPM&M stores. Joe Abraham boasted that if he failed to take ten thousand dollars in orders from his Thurber customers on the first and fifteenth of every month, then business was slow. A 1908 Thurber Junction telephone directory showed seven general stores, two meat markets, and many other businesses with telephones in the town. Peddlers based in Thurber Junction sold goods all over the coal town, sometimes at prices lower than TPM&M.[54]

The managers of TPM&M in Thurber recognized the effect of nearby competition and sought ways to counter it. For example, when a miners' cooperative store opened at Thurber Junction in 1911 and accepted scrip from TPM&M in lieu of cash, General Manager William K. Gordon wrote to company President Edgar L. Marston: "An effort will be made to have us cash these checks [scrip], possibly at a small discount,

Labor Day parade, about 1907. The downtown square hosted several Labor Day parades after unionization in 1903. In the background, the northern addition to the dry goods store is being built. Courtesy of the W. K. Gordon Center for Industrial History of Texas, Tarleton State University, Mingus, Texas, Raymond Thomas Collection.

but of course we shall refuse to do this."[55] TPM&M refused to cash $400 in scrip presented by the managers of the cooperative store. The county attorney of Palo Pinto County considered an investigation into the matter but decided against it. The miners' cooperative store, like other stores in Thurber Junction with little access to working capital, presumably suffered after the loss of $400 in goods; company records do not mention the store again. Despite the hostility of TPM&M to the businesses north of town, Thurber Junction–Mingus thrived. In the late 1910s and early 1920s the town boasted a state bank, a flour mill, four dry goods stores, seven grocery and meat markets, a drugstore, two restaurants, two garages, and a handful of saloons. Italian and Lebanese merchants owned and operated many of these businesses, and they catered to the foreign population at Thurber.[56]

The management of TPM&M sought to combat, as one company official called it, "the evil of the peddlers who are overrunning the camp."[57] Operators of many of the boarding houses in the camp, buildings owned by the coal company and run by private individuals, patronized peddlers. A Mrs. Reasoner bought all her goods from the nearby town of Gordon direct, including delivery of a wagonload of meat daily. Another boarding-house keeper, a Mrs. Roberts, purchased all her goods from Thurber Junction peddlers, even financially backing one peddler who lived in her house and used it as a base of operations. One Mrs. Alexander regularly received a carload of goods from Chicago and Fort Worth and kept "a small dry goods store at the boarding house."[58] Instead of evicting these women, which the company had the power to do, and other companies might have done, the managers of various TPM&M departments visited them and offered special discounts and lower prices. Management also asked company doctors to keep track of who bought goods from outside town so salesmen could persuade them to buy from TPM&M stores. The questioning by company doctors could have been intimidating to the workers and their families, but these tactics seemed to reduce the effect of peddlers. It was not just the company that advocated buying from TPM&M stores. The union organizations of Thurber recommended that their members patronize the union men who worked in the businesses of TPM&M instead of the peddlers. The blue-collar workers in Thurber were not the only ones who did not loyally shop at company stores. A 1905 meeting of TPM&M department heads noted that even some coal company office personnel and TPM&M employees patronized outside vendors. In the first few years after the 1903 strike, the profits of the mercantile company fell dramatically but soon thereafter began to recover. By 1909 changes in company policies and an increasing population helped TPM&M reach profits greater than pre-strike levels.[59]

Outside peddlers and stores were not the only competition for the dollars of Thurber's population. Though no existing books, articles, interviews, or remembrances concerning Thurber mention prostitution, there most assuredly were ladies of less than stellar repute operating in and around the town. In 1900, more than half of the miners were single men, and women willing to ply their sexual wares would not pass up a town of Thurber's size in a relatively isolated, but still easily accessible area. Extant company records and criminal dockets do not mention prostitution, but one criminal appeal in a theft case offers some insight into the practice at Thurber. In 1906 a white man named Handy accused a black woman named Willie Thomas of stealing about sixty-five dollars from his pocket purse during the act of sexual intercourse. The trial transcript offers the following exchange, after Handy admitted Thomas was a prostitute and that he entered her home:

> [Court:] Tell what you did there.
> Witness to the Court: Must I answer that question?
> Court: Yes, sir; it is proper.
> A. I was just having carnal intercourse with her. We got on the bed. She got on the bed first. She laid down on the bed. She got on the bed on her back.
> Q. What did you do.
> A. That is not a fair question. Well, I just got on the bed and had carnal in-

tercourse with her, and she put her hand in my pocket. She put her left hand in my right-hand pocket. My purse was in that pocket; that is, the purse I had in the pocket. I had $66.10 in it at that time. She slipped her hand in my pocket, and I put my hand on that pocket, and my purse was about half way out of the pocket, and she jerked her hand out when I put my hand on my pocket, and put it in her apron pocket. And she says, "I ain't going to get your money." and held up her empty hand, and in a few minutes I went to the blacksmith shop, and the blacksmith told me to pay the stable manager for fixing my wagon, and when I went there to pay him I run my hand in my pocket and pulled out my purse, and it was open, and the $65 was gone. The purse was just unsnapped. I paid that woman $1 for that act of intercourse. I suppose I had gone between one-half and one mile from her house before I missed my money. I had never seen this defendant before that time.[60]

It is worth pointing out that the Erath County district attorneys prosecuted Willie Thomas for theft, not prostitution; nor was Handy prosecuted for patronizing a prostitute. Interestingly, the activity of this woman of easy virtue cut into the profits of the wagon-menders at the blacksmith shop.

The perception that laborers had of TPM&M changed for the better after the 1903 unionization of Thurber. The easy access Thurberites had to the stores of TPM&M ensured that most of their purchases would be there, even with the unfettered ability to purchase outside the limits of the company town. William K. Gordon, Jr., the son of longtime General Manager William K. Gordon, estimated that miners made 95 percent of their purchases at the stores in Thurber. He also emphatically stated that his father would not have permitted exploitation of the workers and that "the profit margin at the company store was held to an acceptable figure."[61] Lawrence Santi, a union leader in Thurber during the 1910s and 1920s, and not one predisposed to toeing the company line, claimed that the mining population did not complain much about the stores since there was access to outside purchases. He too agreed that most of the money made in Thurber returned swiftly to the company coffers. TPM&M, Santi maintained, "were making substantial profits, I wouldn't say excessive."[62] Sometime during the 1910s, the union reached an agreement with the company that allowed TPM&M scrip to be accepted by outside stores and redeemed by the company. Still, Thurberites spent at least 90 percent of the scrip at TPM&M entities. In 1910 the miners at Thurber and surrounding minor coal camps went on a two-month strike for higher wages. In 1903 the coal company had

Downtown quadrangle, 1910. This postcard shows the downtown Thurber quadrangle in 1910. The long brick store on the left is the dry goods store; above that is the long grocery store. The building on the north side of the square is the old drugstore, and the building to the right of it is the opera house. The large building in the foreground is the hardware store and associated buildings. In the center of the square is the bandstand. On the right is the power plant smokestack built in 1908. Courtesy of the W. K. Gordon Center for Industrial History of Texas, Tarleton State University, Mingus, Texas, Eugene Proctor Collection.

threatened to evict striking miners, but in 1910 it allowed the miners to remain in their homes. Scrip sales fell dramatically at TPM&M stores during the eight-week work stoppage, and cash sales dipped as well in every department but the grocery. Miners presumably continued to buy much-needed food from TPM&M during the strike with savings or union-provided funds, and the mercantile company allowed them to shop. In other company-controlled towns during the same era, strike trouble led some companies to evict troublemakers from housing and to prohibit them from patronizing stores.[63]

Though relations between TPM&M and the unionized inhabitants of Thurber were less strained after 1903 than before, the deep-seated mistrust and suspicion that workingmen and their families harbored toward companies, perhaps instilled in them by union pronouncements, remained. Surviving interviews with Thurber inhabitants generally show that blue-collar workers and their children remembered that the company stores had high prices, whereas white-collar workers and their children usually recalled reasonable or low prices at the stores. Across the country, laborers often held similar notions about the "company store." Many old miners especially recalled that their experience mirrored the refrain to the popular song "Sixteen Tons," written by Merle Travis and popularized by Tennessee Ernie Ford: "I owe my soul to the company store."[64] Historian Richard Clyne, in his study of the coal towns of the Colorado Fuel and Iron Company, recorded the words of a company president during this era: "Most of our mines are near enough to some town so that once a week or so the men can go to town and trade . . . it does not look like we are forcing our men to make all their purchases at our stores."[65] Clyne concluded that "the company store in southern Colorado, then, was more of a necessary service to employees than a weapon for corporate control."[66] The same was true of Thurber.

The company store provided a vital service: bringing foods, goods, and services to remote areas. The oft-maligned scrip system was used in most company towns as a way of extending credit. Companies that paid miners only in scrip were never common, and "debt peonage" or "debt bondage" appears not to have been prevalent. In fact, management stated that the scrip system kept laborers from descending into deep debt. Still, the laboring classes in America, including those in Thurber, could not shake the feeling that their company store could only profit to their detriment. Indeed, the Texas and Pacific Coal Company needed the profits of TPM&M to sustain itself in the 1910s as the wages of workers increased and coal was slowly being replaced by oil as a source of energy throughout the country.[67] One miner named Joe Marchioni believed that the company increased sales prices after every raise the miners received.[68] He was correct in that belief. A 1917 letter from company President Edgar L. Marston to the head of TPM&M at Thurber, Ed Britton, baldly declared: "In view of increased wage[s]. I would think there is justification for increased price of goods, especially [at] the [meat] market."[69]

CHAPTER 6
A WITHERING TOWN WITH DWINDLING BUSINESS

General Manager William K. Gordon of the Texas and Pacific Coal Company began searching for oil on land in the vicinity of the coal fields in 1915. In that year he and his men discovered small amounts of petroleum a few miles northwest of Thurber. As the Great War raged in Europe, Gordon and company president Edgar L. Marston desperately believed that the company needed to find significant amounts of oil to remain profitable. The three-week strike by the miners of Thurber in 1916 led to higher wages and put the company in financial straits.[1] That year Marston, in a letter to industrialist John D. Rockefeller, Jr., predicted that any more significant pay raises would force an increase in coal prices. Marston also believed that the Texas and Pacific Railway, the primary customer of the coal company, would probably convert its steam engines to run on oil if coal prices continued to rise. This, he said, would "thereby wipe out a town [Thurber] of seven thousand people."[2] Marston realized that oil would enable the company to survive as consumer demand for coal decreased. He directed his general manager to continue the search for petroleum while mining coal and making money through the Texas Pacific Mercantile and Manufacturing Company (TPM&M). Marston told Gordon, "If we can keep our mines running and make our dividend out of our stores and have a surplus equal to our dividends," then the Texas and Pacific Coal Company could wait for the oil and gas situation to improve.[3]

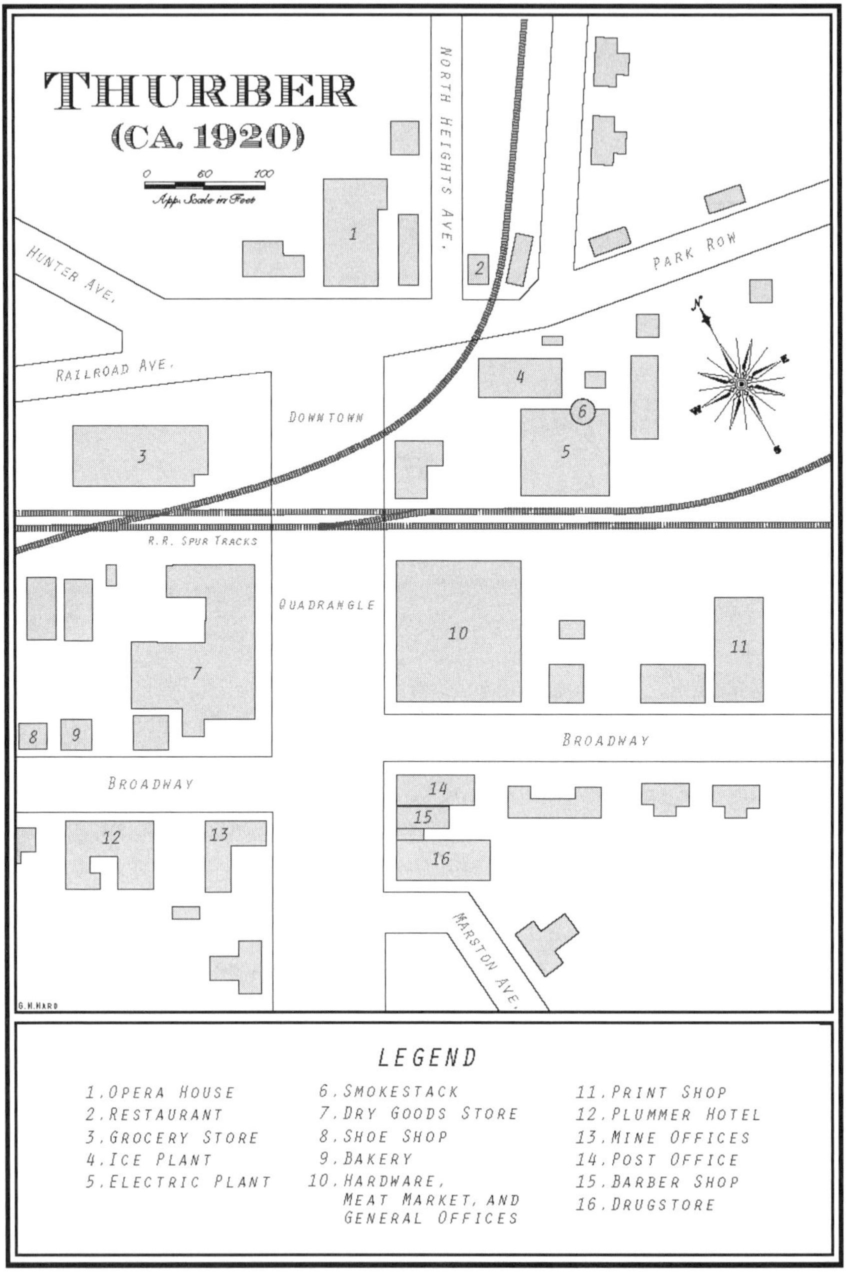
THURBER
(CA. 1920)
0 60 100
App. Scale in Feet
NORTH HEIGHTS AVE.
HUNTER AVE.
PARK ROW
RAILROAD AVE.
DOWNTOWN
R.R. SPUR TRACKS
QUADRANGLE
BROADWAY
BROADWAY
MARSTON AVE.
N
E
W
S
1
2
3
4
5
6
7
8
9
10
11
12
13
14
15
16
G.H.WARD
LEGEND
1. OPERA HOUSE
2. RESTAURANT
3. GROCERY STORE
4. ICE PLANT
5. ELECTRIC PLANT
6. SMOKESTACK
7. DRY GOODS STORE
8. SHOE SHOP
9. BAKERY
10. HARDWARE, MEAT MARKET, AND GENERAL OFFICES
11. PRINT SHOP
12. PLUMMER HOTEL
13. MINE OFFICES
14. POST OFFICE
15. BARBER SHOP
16. DRUGSTORE

Downtown Thurber, ca. 1920. Map by George Ward.

In 1916 and 1917 Marston and the directors of TPM&M declared two 400 percent dividends and transferred $160,000 in badly needed funds to the coal company. The rent TPM&M paid to the Texas and Pacific Coal Company for use of buildings in Thurber increased as well. These infusions of money helped the coal company offset the thousands of dollars it spent each year on purchasing oil leases and exploratory drilling. By the fall of 1917, Gordon had found only small amounts of crude petroleum, and professional geologists hired by Marston believed that the company would discover no more. Marston asked Gordon to cease exploratory drilling, but Gordon nevertheless persisted. On October 22, 1917, the J. H. McCleskey No. 1, a well drilled by Gordon and his men on the J. H. McCleskey farm near Ranger, Texas, struck oil and produced more than a thousand barrels a day. Other wells followed, and soon the coal company was earning millions of dollars in profits from petroleum while making less than half a million dollars from coal. Gordon's find for the coal company also opened up the Ranger oil field, and was the first significant West Texas oil strike, altering the economy of Texas forever.[4]

In recognition of the company's new efforts, on April 17, 1918, the Texas and Pacific Coal Company changed its name to the Texas Pacific Coal and Oil Company. The company-owned town of Thurber became not just a coal camp but an oil field staging area. The company sent several executives from New York City to Thurber, and TPM&M carpenters built more than thirty large modern homes for them on a hill on the south side of town. These homes cost around $8,000 each to build. Since many of these new employees transferred from New York City, Thurberites named the hill "New York Hill," a name it carries today. Carpenters and workmen connected many of these residences to the phone system operated by the company and brought electricity and running water to them and to an increasing number of homes throughout the town. The new white-collar workers played golf, so the company built a nine-hole golf course behind Little Lake for them. President Marston also considered erecting a new hotel in Thurber on New York Hill to accommodate now frequent visitors from the Northeast. He declared that the Plummer Hotel then in use was a disgrace to the company, but the company never built the planned hotel.[5]

After the discovery of oil, the amount of coal mined and shipped from Thurber fell drastically. But since the Texas Pacific Coal and Oil Company chose to use Thurber as its base of operations for West Texas oil discovery and production, the population of the town increased

Thurber downtown on parade day. Cars fill Thurber's downtown quadrangle in the 1920s for a parade. The brick building on the left housed the hardware store, meat market, and general offices; the brick building farther away housed the post office; and the last brick building in the distance was the large, modern drugstore. Courtesy of Southwest Collection/Special Collections Library, Texas Tech University, Lubbock, Texas, Thurber, Texas, Photograph Collection, SWCPC 209.

Texas & Pacific filling station. The modern filling station built on the south end of the square in the 1920s signaled that oil was replacing coal as Thurber's primary reason for existence. Courtesy of Southwest Collection/Special Collections Library, Texas Tech University, Lubbock, Texas, Thurber, Texas, Photograph Collection, S1076.1.

during the last few years of the 1910s. In 1919 the company built a modern water filtration plant adjacent to the ice plant to purify water from Big Lake. By 1920 the population neared ten thousand as the town filled up with workers associated with the burgeoning petroleum industry. These employees commuted daily between Thurber and Ranger in a fleet of company-owned vehicles, mainly Model T Fords. In 1918 the company constructed a large wooden garage east of the hardware store to perform maintenance on these automobiles. Here a half-dozen TPM&M mechanics repaired cars and trucks, drawing from a stock of machine bolts, side boards, rollers, and numerous other parts on hand. Around this time the company made additions to the filling station that it had built on the side of the hardware store in 1915. TPM&M servicemen used funnels to pour gasoline from five-gallon buckets directly into gas tanks, checked oil, and performed other routine maintenance.[6]

Although coal shipments and profits were falling during the oil boom, profits for TPM&M increased from below $100,000 in 1916 to about $125,000 in 1917. This was probably due to the growth of Thurber in this period and an increase in the number of non-unionized workers that would not shy away from the company stores. In 1919 the earnings of the mercantile company reached their highest level yet, $197,600.63. TPM&M again earned high profits in 1920, making $183,060.00. But the town's days as a coal camp were numbered, when, as Marston suspected, the Texas and Pacific Railway, the chief customer of Thurber's coal, began using oil-burning locomotives in West Texas in 1919 and then in 1920 abandoned the use of the old coal-burning steam engines altogether. This drastically reduced the demand for coal from the Texas Pacific Coal and Oil Company. Miners removed less coal from the ground in 1919 and 1920 than in any year since 1907. Faced with increased wages demanded by the unions between 1918 and 1920, the coal company sold its coal at cost on the open market to make ends meet. With the increased wages, however, Thurberites during this period were using more cash than scrip to purchase goods at every major department of TPM&M for the first time. This continued the trend toward more cash sales and fewer scrip sales that began before unionization and was accelerated by increases in wages after 1903. Even purchases made at the grocery and meat markets were now mostly in cash.[7] Frank Martin, a clerk in Thurber and later an executive for the oil company, remembered that between 1918 and 1921 "the company lost money on the mine operation, but they made it up in the 'commissaries.'"[8]

Cash and Scrip Sales at Five TPM&M Departments in 1915, 1920, and 1925

	1915		1920		1925	
TPM&M Department	Cash Sales (%)	Scrip Sales (%)	Cash Sales (%)	Scrip Sales (%)	Cash Sales (%)	Scrip Sales (%)
Grocery	29.86	70.14	52.87	47.13	36.95	63.05
Dry Goods	50.22	49.78	78.01	21.99	71.99	28.01
Hardware	49.01	50.99	74.05	25.95	54.13	45.87
Drugstore	62.45	37.55	80.65	19.35	78.49	21.51
Meat Market	34.38	65.62	54.54	45.46	44.31	55.69

Source: "Cash and Check Sales Record, 1914–1927," Ledger 608, pp. 10–43, from the Texas and Pacific Coal Company Records, S1021.1; "Cash and Check Sales Record, 1914–1927," Ledger 608, pp. 10–43, from the Texas and Pacific Coal Company Records, S1021.1; computer analysis of records by the author.

During this period Marston and Gordon attempted to reduce costs and make extra money to justify Thurber's continued existence and retain as many miners as possible. In 1917, trying to save money on feed grain, builders erected two large silos near the dairy on Big Lake to furnish silage for the cattle of TPM&M. Gordon hired an expert dry land farmer and put hundreds of acres of soil into crops, but only ever filled one silo. After two years of droughts and poor harvests, TPM&M considered the project a failure and abandoned the silos. To reduce expenses, in 1917 Marston suspended use of the delivery wagons utilized by various departments of TPM&M. In 1918 the firm suspended publication of the company newspaper, the *Thurber Journal,* because it rarely turned a profit. The general store on Polander Hill that catered to the foreign-born townspeople on the western edge of Thurber closed at the end of June 1920. Still, residents of Thurber and nearby Thurber Junction, now usually called Mingus by its inhabitants, remained optimistic about the future of the area as the Texas Pacific Coal and Oil Company and the Thurber Brick Company continued to earn millions in the Ranger and Thurber areas.[9]

Despite the rosy outlook of area residents, in 1921 the Texas Pacific Coal and Oil Company proposed a reduction in wages for coal miners in order to remain profitable in the mining business. The unionized miners at Thurber countered with a proposal for a smaller reduction, but the company refused. On May 1, 1921, the management closed the mines to union workers even though it still had coal contracts to fill and an agreement with the United Mine Workers of America that lasted until 1922. Observers have called this action variously a lockout, a strike, a defensive strike, or a "strike/lockout." The majority of the miners refused to work, and company officials refused to pay union wages. In September the company evicted all miners and their families who had not paid rent or utility bills from company housing. Many of these families moved into "Tent City," an encampment of tents funded by the miners' union just north of Thurber near Grant Town. During the next year many of these families left for other jobs all across the country. The Texas Pacific Coal and Oil Company continued to work the mines with a handful of non-union laborers that stayed on after 1921, mainly black miners who had been with the company for many years. The mercantile company allowed these men ready access to scrip, perhaps because of their loyalty after the 1921 labor action. The company did import some additional Mexican workingmen to work for the low non-union wages. TPM&M gave these miners credit at the company store to cover the cost of tools, clothing, housing, food, and other items. But because there was little demand for coal, these miners rarely worked full-time. Customers now purchased most of their all-important food at the grocery and meat market with company scrip. Gross income fell in each department during this period. After 1921 the town that had been a mining camp since 1886 became a town of office workers, brick workers, and only a few miners.[10]

The loss of thousands of people in 1921 changed the role TPM&M played in the history of Thurber. It ceased being a profitable subsidiary; instead it became just a necessary component of life in the town. For the first time since its founding, the mercantile company failed to turn a profit. Sales at company stores fell by almost 50 percent in 1921 compared to the year before. TPM&M lost $64,796.40 in 1921 and operated at a deepening loss until the demise of the company in 1934. In 1920 Edgar L. Marston resigned as president of both the Texas Pacific Coal and Oil Company and TPM&M. John Roby Penn, an experienced oil company executive from Pennsylvania, became the third president of both companies. On December 31, 1922, William K. Gordon resigned his post as vice president and general manager of the company, although he remained on the board of directors. Ed Britton, head of TPM&M, succeeded him as general manager of Thurber for 1923 and part of 1924 until his final retirement from the company. The population dropped from almost ten thousand to only several hundred. Company-owned homes that once housed immigrant miners of several nationalities now stood empty and bare. TPM&M carpenters removed all doors, hinges, windows, and light fixtures from the houses and stored them in warehouses for possible future use. The homes did see new uses, as one Thurber resident remembered that children played and roller-skated in the remaining empty dwellings. Area farmers and others purchased many of these homes intact at very low prices, or the company demolished them and sold the scrap lumber.[11]

Although the coal mines operated only part-time in the early 1920s, the Thurber Brick Company made record sales during the same period as many communities and paving contractors bought vitrified paving bricks to pave streets and roads all across Texas and the Southwest. The town also remained a staging area for oil exploration and was home to pipe yards and other oil field equipment. The general clerical offices of the company were at Thurber as well, located in the buildings on the south side of the downtown quadrangle and on the second floor of the hardware and meat market building. TPM&M carpenters kept busy in this era installing garages and porches and upgrading the remaining occupied homes with running water, ceilings, and telephones. The commercial stores such as the grocery, meat market, and dry goods department continued to do steady business, though considerably less than before. Area farmers that had once always peddled in Thurber did so only infrequently. Other services in town, like the lumberyard and livery stable, made less money as time passed. The livery stable, which patrons once utilized daily, saw customers visit perhaps only once a week by 1925, as many Thurberites now had access to automobiles. The dairy, founded in 1895, closed in 1921. Milk and other dairy goods sold in the TPM&M stores now came in by train from outside sources. In 1924 the service station next to the hardware store was revamped and upgraded. The print shop still printed most of the forms and ledgers for the company offices in Thurber and elsewhere. For many years the ice plant continued to do good business, providing ice not only to the inhabitants of Thurber and Mingus, including bootleggers, but to the Texas and Pacific Railway. The power plant persisted in delivering power to the town. Its manager, J. E. S. Lee, saved money by pressing all the wiping rags until they drained oil, filtering and reusing the oil again and again.[12]

The few miners that remained in Thurber by 1926 worked part-time and rarely made enough money to cover their monthly expenses. Accordingly, the Texas Pacific Coal and Oil Company ceased coal mining operations after May 1927. The now jobless miners who stayed in town, mostly black men, transferred to the Thurber Brick Company, worked as janitors or porters for TPM&M, labored in the oil company pipe yards, or took odd jobs around town such as gardening for the few white families that could afford to pay them. Many of their wives supplemented their meager income by working as personal housekeepers. The company even allowed a handful of the former miners to live rent free in their homes. TPM&M discontinued the use of company scrip, because it cost too much to print, but they still gave the employees in town ready access to buy on credit, which accountants directly handled.[13]

In the summer of 1926, TPM&M spent over $20,000 on a new electric cotton gin and associated buildings. The company hired an experienced local gin operator named Bill Rigsby, built or repaired roads into town, and spent large amounts of money on publicity in the surrounding countryside. Although the company expended thousands on the gin, which turned out cleaner cotton than any other in the area, it was not a success. By 1926 much of the cotton production in Texas had shifted to the plains area around Lubbock and surrounding counties.[14] Local antipathy toward TPM&M and Thurber also contributed to the failure of the gin. Charlie Wilkins, a sociologist writing his 1929 master's thesis on the town then in decline, stated that: "All of them [the area cotton farmers] realize that when they sell a dozen eggs or buy a sack of flour they are dealing with a ten million dollar concern, and they cannot help but feel that this economic inequality may in some mysterious way be to their disadvantage."[15] The gin continued to operate at a loss into the 1930s.

With the advent of motion pictures with sound in the late 1920s, a new film projector was set up in the Presbyterian church, leaving the opera house to school programs and occasional plays or dances. In March 1930 the Thurber print shop again began issuing another newspaper. Dubbed the *Thurber Tiny Journal,* the diminutive publication was a little more than six inches by seven inches with just four pages per issue. Like its predecessors, the paper reported on local news items and served as a platform to advertise TPM&M goods. A typical issue contained advertisements for the grocery, hardware, and dry goods departments, listing items for sale and stating prices. At times other departments received some ink, like the garage or the movie house. The editors, as before, even tried "to advocate a little more home loyalty" in the buying of goods from TPM&M stores.[16]

By the late 1920s the Texas Pacific Coal and Oil Company no longer mined coal, and low oil prices nationwide hurt corporate profits. Led by the new president of the company, Edgar J. Marston, son of Edgar L. Marston, the Texas Pacific Coal and Oil Company began what William K. Gordon deemed an ill-advised and expensive attempt at refining and marketing petroleum products at its own line of filling stations. One of these new stations, selling TP Aero brand gasoline, opened in Thurber in 1929 on the downtown quadrangle. The Thurber Brick Company idled its plant due to a lack of brick orders for increasingly longer periods of time nearly every year from 1924 onward. It idled the brick plant for much of 1931 and finally closed it for good at the end of the year. At the end of 1930, the first full year of the Great Depression, the Texas Pacific Coal and Oil Company posted net losses amounting to $970,272.68.[17] All of the companies that built Thurber were hurting.

In the early morning hours of September 14, 1930, the large brick hardware and meat market building, which housed the general office department on the second floor, caught fire. Firefighters and volunteers called the three fire trucks of Thurber into action and asked for assistance from the towns of Strawn and Ranger. With reams of office paper acting as fuel and the shaft of a freight elevator acting as a flue, fire consumed the building very quickly. Embers from the fire threatened other buildings in the town and even damaged the roof of the opera house. After several hours firefighters finally brought the flames under control. Reporters estimated the loss to the company at about $250,000. The fire destroyed any official papers not in the fireproof storage vault; this included the records of the credit department.[18] Witness and office worker George Studdard remembered that while the fire was in progress, one Obie Merritt, hoping the records of his debt were destroyed, jokingly asked the credit manager, W. A. "Wiltie" Creswell: "Hey, Wiltie, do you remember how much my account is?"[19] After the fire, the company indeed wrote off many of the credit sales. Other business was lost through confusion and delay. TPM&M shuffled around many of its departments after the fire. The large dry goods building became the general office building, and the dry goods department was combined with the hardware department and moved into the drugstore building. The drugstore set up shop in the barber shop building adjacent to the post office. The meat market moved into the grocery building.[20]

The Texas Pacific Coal and Oil Company and TPM&M surreptitiously recouped $121,621.62 of the losses incurred by the fire from insur-

Office building fire, 1930. In the early morning hours of September 14, 1930, the large brick hardware and meat market building, which housed the general office department on the second floor, caught fire. Though the company clandestinely recouped its monetary losses, the building was never rebuilt. Courtesy of the W. K. Gordon Center for Industrial History of Texas, Tarleton State University, Mingus, Texas, Ruby J. Schmidt Collection.

ance policies held by yet another subsidiary company. On April 13, 1929, three men unconnected to the Texas Pacific Coal and Oil Company or any of its subsidiary companies, Clarence Wightman, Clarence C. Dean, and R. W. Wingo, had met in Fort Worth and invested $200,000 to form an insurance company named the Texas Pacific Fidelity and Surety Company. After receiving the right to operate an insurance business in the state of Texas from the proper authorities, the three men sold all the stock of the firm for just "one dollar, lawful money of the United States" to the Texas Pacific Coal and Oil Company of Delaware, another subsidiary company chaired by Edgar J. Marston. This new insurance company, the Texas Pacific Fidelity and Surety Company, insured much of the property owned by the oil company, including the entire town of Thurber. The firm held reinsurance policies with several concerns in London and New York. Thus when the company asked for reimbursements worth $121,621.62 for the Thurber fire, these policies paid for most of the damages. The Texas Pacific Fidelity and Surety Company paid the remainder, just $25,000, from the surpluses it had earned through investment. Thus the damage to the town of Thurber was paid for at no loss to the insurance company.[21]

In a special Texas Pacific Fidelity and Surety Company board meeting held soon after the Thurber fire, "a discussion of considerable length" took place on whether to dissolve the insurance company due to "comparative inactiveness." The board members placed a special note in the official minutes of the meeting that stressed the move to disband the company had been contemplated some time before the September fire: "It was suggested that this reference be inserted in the minutes so as to avoid any impression that the conclusion to dissolve was influenced by the fire loss [at Thurber]." The Texas Pacific Fidelity and Surety Company was duly dissolved and broken up within a few months. The directors had no reason to fear the prying eyes of the curious as officials deemed the fire at Thurber an accident and neither lawmen nor scholars have ever investigated the suspicious dealings of the Texas Pacific Fidelity and Surety Company.[22]

TPM&M continued streamlining its operations. The mercantile company sold $300 in bakery equipment, and the nearby town of Gordon bought some old news printing equipment. The Texas Pacific Coal and Oil Company absorbed $25,453.58 in equipment and other losses incurred by TPM&M in 1930. When the brick plant closed for good in 1931, Thurber became a mere office town of just 270 families. The company allowed the out-of-work brickmakers to live rent free in their houses. TPM&M also gave each family from ten to thirty dollars free credit each month at the mercantile for food and other goods. Many of the families that remained never repaid the company for its generosity and still owed TPM&M money when they found new jobs or when Thurber was abandoned. Some people were in debt to the company for thousands of dollars by 1933. In the last four months of 1930, a small percentage of employees living in Thurber earned a little more than $18,000 in cash, combined; most other employees collectively owed the company more than $40,000 in unpaid debts. With such a small population, the town of Thurber with all of its facilities and utilities now cost more money to operate than it generated. Still TPM&M showed kindness to the families still in town by sending them Christmas baskets every year filled with Brazil nuts, almonds, pecans, candy, apples, and oranges. In 1931 and 1932, with the country in a depression, the Texas Pacific Coal and Oil Company and associated companies lost money and continued to owe money on loans with high interest rates. The company sought drastic ways to avoid bankruptcy.[23]

In 1932 Edgar J. Marston resigned as president of the Texas Pacific

Coal and Oil Company, citing ill health. His son Robert C. Marston claimed that the board planned to fire his father, making him the "'fall guy' responsible for the poor corporate financial position."[24] In 1933 the board of directors hired a firm from New York, Crandall and Osmond, to suggest ways to save money. Crandall and Osmond recommended that the company dispose itself of all assets not directly related to oil production. The operations of four Texas Pacific Coal and Oil Company subsidiary companies, TPM&M, the Thurber Brick Company, the Thurber Tank Line Company, and the Thurber Construction Company, were discontinued and their assets sold. This included the town of Thurber.[25]

In June 1933 the executive department decreed that on the first of July they would transfer all office personnel in Thurber to Fort Worth, moving into offices on two floors of the Fort Worth National Bank Building. The executives also decreed that all goods in the stores must be sold if possible. The print shop distributed flyers announcing a clearance sale for June 15, 1933. Prices for goods at all TPM&M stores were reduced 50 percent.[26] Mary Jane Gentry described the sale at the dry goods department in her 1946 study of the town:

> On the morning of the sale, great crowds of people thronged outside the doors, most of them from outside Thurber. They were people who had always taken a great delight in condemning Thurber as a company town, and as a general rule, they would buy nothing in Thurber. When the clerks opened the doors, they were almost trampled under foot by the crowd. People grabbed, pushed, and shoved. Women would seize bolts of cloth and share with no one.[27]

Witnesses recounted that people took goods and left without paying; women changed into new dresses in fitting rooms and exited the store; others put on new shoes and left their old ones in the shoe boxes. Still, the company made hundreds of dollars on the first day of their clearance sale. The rest of the month showed a large increase in gross income. Soon the shelves were practically empty. On July 1, 1933, TPM&M officially ceased operations in Thurber. The oil company transferred many of the last mercantile company employees—twelve salesmen, three night watchmen, two carpenters, one printer, three printer's helpers, and two janitors—to other departments and other jobs in other towns.[28]

The Texas Pacific Coal and Oil Company continued to dispose of the infrastructure of Thurber. After July 1933, the empty homes built by

ANNOUNCEMENT

Big Sale at Dry Goods to Last Another Two Weeks

To the People of Thurber and Surrounding Country:

The T. P. M. & M. Co. wishes to thank the people for their generous response and splendid co-operation during our final Close Out Sale.

This sale far exceeded our expectations, but even so, we find we still have several thousand dollars worth of merchandise yet to dispose of, and since we had rather let the public have what is left of this stock at still further reductions, we have decided to continue our Close Out Sale for two weeks extending to

JULY 15th

Remember the Big Sale at the Dry Goods Store will be continued another two weeks, with PRICES MUCH LOWER on the remainder of the stock in order that we may be able to dispose of everything to the bare walls.

Last Big Chance

We still have quite a stock of men's women's and children's winter underwear, and it will be to your advantage to lay in your winter supply at less than wholesale prices.

Nothing Reserved—Everything Must be Closed Out

Prices will be smashed beyond comparison. Come in at once and let us save you much money on your purchases. Don't spend a cent anywhere else until you have looked at our Final Close Out Stock.

Last Call before T. P. M. & M. Co. Closes Its Doors in Thurber

Texas Pacific Mercantile & Mfg. Co.

Thurber, Texas

TPM&M closes its doors. In 1933, the Texas Pacific Coal and Oil Company decided to abandon Thurber to save money, and TPM&M closed the doors of its stores forever, after decades of catering to Thurber's population. Courtesy of Special Collections, University of Texas at Arlington Library, Arlington, Texas, Thurber, Texas, Collection, AR506.

TPM&M carpenters were sold intact and moved to nearby communities or demolished for scrap lumber. One Henry Zweifel purchased the electric cotton gin built in Thurber in 1926 for $19,733. The motion picture equipment in town sold cheaply for just $50. Shelving units from the grocery store sold for $600. Mose M. Miller rented the wooden grocery store and purchased the remaining stock. He attempted to operate the store for the next few months but closed it due to a lack of business. The grocery store building sold for $378.78 in September 1934 and moved to the small community of Hannibal south of Thurber. A salvage company dug up water and gas pipes and resold them. The company even sold toilets from the dry goods building to whoever had cash. The high school closed in 1933, and the elementary followed suit in 1935. The Thurber Masonic Lodge held its last meeting in 1935. On November 30, 1936, the Thurber Post Office closed. A few buildings escaped the wrecking crews. The home of the superintendent, where William K. Gordon lived during the heyday of Thurber, and the home of the assistant superintendent remained standing. The water filtration plant functioned for the next few years and the building still stands. The drugstore and dry goods buildings remained standing on the square.[29]

On April 18, 1934, TPM&M directors held a meeting in Thurber and voted to reduce the capital stock of the company from $20,000 to $5,000 and changed its official place of business, for legal purposes, from Thurber to Fort Worth. The mercantile company, which had not turned a profit since 1920 and was rarely mentioned in company documents after the discovery of the Ranger oil field in 1917, ceased to exist as a viable company. Every resident of Thurber—whether a miner, a brickmaker, a common laborer, or a white-collar worker—came into contact with or felt the influence of the enterprises and services of TPM&M. Thurberites lived in TPM&M-constructed homes, shopped in or avoided TPM&M stores, and utilized TPM&M services like electricity and the livery stable. The mercantile stores of Thurber ensured that a town of thousands remained fed, supplied with tools, and comfortable in their homes. In written accounts of Thurber's history, TPM&M plays an ancillary role. It is a sideline to the mining, it is a nuisance in the labor struggle, it is a subsidiary in every sense of the word. TPM&M set the stage where the drama of Thurber's history played out. It built the sets, it provided the props, it staged the scenes. The stores and services of TPM&M were the most visible symbols of the company's power. After unionization, miners negotiated the rates by which they worked in the pits, but they could never set the prices at the company store. The wives of Thurber's miners never viewed the underground where their husbands toiled, but most of them lived in homes erected by TPM&M carpenters and painted by TPM&M painters. The water that flowed into their basins was provided by TPM&M, as was the electricity that lit their rooms. Thurberites attended dances in TPM&M's opera house or purchased beer in TPM&M's saloons. Even if fear of company skullduggery convinced a resident to buy from outside peddlers or stores, he was still going out of his way to ignore the presence of TPM&M. From 1894 to 1934, a span of forty years that saw its parent company go from coal mining to oil drilling, the Texas Pacific Mercantile and Manufacturing Company operated and managed various commercial and service enterprises that were essential to the life and history of Thurber. With the death of Thurber as a viable working town, what had once been called "the most extensive retail mercantile institution in the state" passed into the pages of history.[30]

EPILOGUE
THE AFTERLIFE OF A GHOST TOWN

The Texas Pacific Mercantile and Manufacturing Company played a significant role in Thurber's nearly fifty-year existence as a company town. Thurber, where miners, brickmakers, and laborers struggled to make a living from the dirt of Texas, did not completely disappear from the landscape like numerous other industrial ghost towns in the state, nor did memories of it fade completely. Though the Texas Pacific Coal and Oil Company destroyed most of the town, it also made a concerted effort to preserve some of it, and, since the company remained a viable oil producer in petroleum-rich Texas, the records of its coal-mining and brickmaking days survived to one day greet the prying eyes of historians. A large number of Thurber's inhabitants remained near to the town and had fond enough remembrances of the place to keep it alive through various historical associations. The physical remains of TPM&M buildings in Thurber mark the location of the most important ghost town in Texas.

After the Texas Pacific Coal and Oil Company directed that Thurber be abandoned on July 1, 1933, Thurber's remaining workers transferred to Fort Worth, Ranger, or West Texas. With their near absolute power, the corporate owners sold most of the physical property of the town. Homes were sold intact for as little as twenty-five dollars a room. The buyer could haul it away intact, tear it down and rebuild it later, or sell the scrap lumber. Area house movers were in high demand. The young son of one professional remembered that his father worked nearly every day for six or seven years straight moving homes throughout the local area, one ending up as far away as Midland. The nearby city of Stephenville has several surviving examples of the handiwork of TPM&M housebuilders on its lots. The large wooden TPM&M grocery store building has stood in the little community of Hannibal since 1934, serving as a general store and restaurant down to the present. Even Thurber's bandstand, which once sat in the downtown quadrangle, was walled to become a home in the Erath County community of Duffau. In 1937 St. Barbara's, the company-owned Catholic church that had seen thousands of worshippers in its day, was moved three miles north to Mingus. By 1940, all but a few of the buildings where thousands of people from all parts of the globe had lived, worked, or shopped had been removed from Thurber.[1] Around this time, a vehicle with Arizona plates drove up to the filling station, and the couple inside looked around in astonishment. "What in the world has happened? . . . Where are all the houses?" the woman asked the attendant. "You been here before?" he replied. While brushing aside her tears she said, "We were married here in 1901. . . . This is our first trip back."[2]

The wholesale abandonment of Thurber extended to more than just the people and their homes. The company sold much of the remaining mining equipment to various salvage firms hired to aid in the dismantling of the town. By 1935 the ice plant, state-of-the-art electric-powered cotton gin, and the sound motion picture equipment sold for far below their actual values. The public school building was moved to the local community of Bluff Dale, and the Thurber High School library was sold to the nearby Huckabay School. In 1936 salvage firms bought the water pipes from the extensive Thurber water system, which TPM&M used to pump water to many of the homes in town. The company sold them in the ground, and the salvagers removed and resold them. Southern Methodist University in Dallas used some of these pipes in the construction of its Fondren Library. Various crews hired by the oil company recovered the underground equipment, which had been left in the mines in the vain hope that coal mining would someday resume. Some of the scrap metal was shipped to Mussolini's Italy. These salvage jobs were dangerous, resulting in at least one death from natural gas that had seeped into the mines. Most of the salvage work was completed by 1940.[3]

The most spectacular incident in the Texas and Pacific Coal and Oil Company's demolishment of Thurber led to the founding of the first association concerned with preserving Thurber's history. By 1937 all that remained after the methodical leveling of the brick plant was its 160-foot smokestack chimney built in 1897. On March 29, 1937, workers

Thurber brick plant smokestack demolished. In 1937 all that remained of the Thurber brick plant was its 160-foot smokestack chimney built in 1897. Thousands, many of them former residents, watched as forty sticks of dynamite felled the giant. Today the remaining smokestack at the site was once part of the ice plant. Courtesy of Southwest Collection/Special Collections Library, Texas Tech University, Lubbock, Texas, Thurber, Texas, Photograph Collection, S1076.1.

placed forty sticks of dynamite under the smokestack.[4] Reporters from Fort Worth described the scene: "Ba-loom! Forty sticks of dynamite thundered," then "the base of the great chimney shot out with a dull roar, ballooning red dust. The giant shook, tilted and crumbled."[5] Thousands of spectators were on hand for the widely publicized event; many who had lived in Thurber "watched the spectacle through tear-filled eyes."[6] Others ran to the rubble and collected handfuls of bricks as souvenirs.

Several of those who viewed the destruction of the brick plant stack made plans for a reunion of former inhabitants on July 4, 1937. Two thousand people attended this first reunion, which was held beside the remaining brick buildings of TPM&M in what was once downtown Thurber. The reunion-goers honored William K. Gordon, Sr., who as general manager had made Thurber into a productive settlement and was responsible for the Ranger oil strike, and celebrated Thurber's fiftieth year "jubilee" and the twentieth anniversary of the Ranger boom.

The Thurber Old Settlers Association was formed at this meeting, and the reunion was made an annual event to be held each Labor Day beginning in 1938. The homecomings were large, important affairs, with thousands coming from Texas and from across the nation.[7] The September 4, 1939, crowd numbered nearly five thousand of all nationalities. A Dallas reporter noted: "Because the Texas and Pacific Coal Company's mines had recruited workers from the far corners of the world, Monday's reunion saw a cross section of all Europe fraternizing here as happy Americans while their homeland nationals were embarking on a devastating war."[8]

The Texas Pacific Coal and Oil Company did not destroy all the buildings in Thurber and retained ownership of the townsite and thousands of acres surrounding it. The company used the large brick dry goods building as a storage facility and housed company records there in a large interior vault for decades. Several times a year company employees from Fort Worth came to work in the makeshift archive. The company also continued to grant access to this building for the annual reunions through the 1960s. Former Thurberite Billy Boyd leased the 1909 brick drugstore structure and converted it into a service station and café. The company retained a few houses as well, using the old superintendent's home as a company retreat for executives. Thousands of acres were leased to ranchers, who lived in a few remaining homes with their families and hands. The company permitted a few black families who had been loyal to the company for many years to remain as semi-official town caretakers, including Albert Whitehead, a former miner who had worked there for several decades. William K. Gordon himself, now on the board of directors of the oil company, requested that the 150-foot powerhouse smokestack be allowed to remain as a sort of monument to Thurber. One reporter called it "Thurber's Tombstone." The company maintained the members-only R. D. Hunter Fishing and Boating Club on the shores of Big Lake as a private club for Texas Pacific Coal and Oil Company employees. The lake garnered a reputation as one of the best bass fishing spots in Texas.[9]

The Thurber Old Settlers Association continued to hold its annual meeting on Labor Day, until switching it to Independence Day by 1952. Crowds that had numbered in the thousands in the late 1930s had dwindled to less than five hundred each year. The restaurant in TPM&M's old drugstore went through various lessees and was renamed the Ghost Town Café in an effort to draw in tourists. In 1960 the Texas Pacific Coal and Oil Company erected a plaque at the base of the smokestack memorializing the history of the town. This era also saw

The Whitehead family at Thurber, 1950s. After Thurber was abandoned, the company permitted a few black families who had been loyal to the company for many years to remain as semi-official caretakers, such as Albert Whitehead, a former miner who had worked there for several decades. In 1953 a passing motorist photographed Albert and his wife, Liza, gathering wood on the northern outskirts of Thurber. The hill on the left was the source of much of the clay used to make bricks in Thurber. Courtesy of the Charles W. Cushman Collection, Indian University Archives, Indiana University, Bloomington, Indiana, P6944.

some of the first both scholarly and informal writings about Thurber and its importance to the history of Texas and the region. Following a few cursory theses and booklets about the town, the most important examination was a thesis entitled "Thurber: The Life and Death of a Texas Town," written by Mary Jane Gentry under the direction of noted historian Walter Prescott Webb. Gentry became the town's "unofficial historian," even speaking at the April 1940 meeting of the Texas State Historical Association.[10] In 2008, a dozen years after her death, her thesis was published in book form as *The Birth of a Texas Ghost Town: Thurber, 1886–1933.*

In 1961 a new historical association named the Thurber Ex-Students and Teachers Association instituted two-day reunions beginning on the second Saturday of June. The town's two historical associations, scholarly investigations, and the easy access provided by Highway 80 ensured that Thurber remained in the public eye. On November 1, 1963, Joseph E. Seagram and Sons purchased the Texas Pacific Coal and Oil Company and merged it with their other oil interests under the name Texas Pacific Oil Company. The new concern continued to allow the reunions to be staged in the old dry goods building and continued to lease out the drugstore as an eatery and filling station. The new president of Texas Pacific Oil Company, Carrol M. Bennett, became enchanted with the property and bought most of it from his employer as a tax write-off in 1966. The company retained the area around the 100-acre Big Lake, now simply called Thurber Lake, and continued to utilize it as a vacation getaway for its employees. The company built recreational facilities, offering six air-conditioned family cabins and a bachelors' lodge, along with camping and picnic areas, stone barbecue pits, and fishing boats.[11]

With most of the old townsite now in private hands, the twin historical associations hoped that a museum could be built in the ghost town. The Texas Pacific Oil Company offered to help build something dignified and solicited the donation of artifacts.[12] The Ex-Students and Teachers Association contacted various museum and historical professionals, including Dr. William Curry Holden and his wife Frances Mayhugh Holden of Texas Tech and Charles Woodburn of the Texas State Historical Survey Committee for suggestions. Dr. Holden was impressed with the site, stating that he had "seen nothing like it this side of Carson, Nevada. . . . I have never seen so many people show as much dedication and love for a hometown as this group shows for Thurber."[13] The members of the Ex-Students and Teachers Association decided to merge with the Old Settlers Association and combine their reunions. On February 27, 1969, the state of Texas granted incorporation to the Thurber Historical Association, which survives and holds reunions at the townsite to this day.[14]

The plans for a museum continued apace as the Texas State Historical Survey Committee dedicated a historical marker at the base of the smokestack on June 7, 1969. William K. Gordon, Jr., and William K. Gordon, III, son and grandson of the late William K. Gordon, who died in 1949, unveiled the marker that provided a brief history of the town, focusing primarily on the coal industry. The Thurber Historical Association hired Fritz A. and Emilie Toepperwein, noted historical consultants from the San Antonio area, to create plans for their coveted museum. The resulting document included plans and drawings for numerous wax exhibits, a roadside park, and a reproduction light rail train. Much to the distress of members of the Historical Association, these museum plans were never brought to fruition, probably because of a lack of funds and the Bennett family's objections to the scheme.[15]

In early 1970, the Texas Pacific Oil Company began constructing a larger and more modern lodge with a training room, kitchen, dining room, and recreational facilities at Thurber Lake. Workers built a three-hole golf course around the ponds near the highway entrance. The facility, christened the Carrol M. Bennett Training Center, opened in early 1971 and was used by the company for the rest of the decade. During this time, Thurber was home to the Bennett family, the occasional vacationing Texas Pacific employee, and motoring tourists. A few miles from town was the American Soul Clinic, a 400-acre ranch owned by televangelist Fred Jordan of Los Angeles. In 1970 he allowed members of the Children of God, a Jesus movement group (which some have called a cult), to establish a commune at the ranch. Well remembered for their unique lifestyle by area residents, the communal "religious hippies" painted their shacks vibrant colors, performed physical labor, and raised their own food. Jordan evicted them from his property in October 1971 after a well-publicized dispute concerning the sexual "recruiting" of the group's female members. Around the same time the federal government enlarged Highway 80, turning it into Interstate 20. The expansion of the road resulted in the demolition of two original buildings, which had served as TPM&M warehouses, and cut a swath through what had been the center of Thurber. In 1972 Humble Oil of Houston erected a new filling station just east of the drugstore in the form of an old mining tipple, leasing the property from the Bennetts. It operated until the 1990s. The drugstore Ghost Town Café was remodeled and went through several name changes and lessees before settling on the "Smokestack Restaurant," highlighting Thurber's most visible landmark. In 1978 the Texas Pacific Oil Company donated a treasure trove of Thurber-related manuscript material to the Southwest Collection at Texas Tech University. These records included financial, payroll, and various other documents, allowing scholars to utilize company records for the first time. In 1979 Thurber was placed on the National Register of Historic Places.[16]

In October 1979, Randy Bennett, son and heir of the late Carrol Bennett, leased thirty-three hundred acres of his ranch property south of the Thurber townsite to Texas Industries for the purpose of coal mining. Over the next three years, Texas Industries strip-mined over 100,000 tons of coal and employed around twenty individuals, who commuted to the site. Falling energy prices in the early 1980s and expansion of other mines outside Mount Pleasant, Texas, doomed the project. In 1980 Seagrams sold its oil subsidiary, Texas Pacific Oil Company, to Dallas-based Sun Oil. The last property in the area that the company owned, the recreational training facility at Thurber Lake, was sold to private individuals, who turned it into a family resort. During the 1980s, the Thurber Historical Association continued to hold its annual meetings, now reduced from two-day affairs to a single Saturday in June, and attendance continued to fall to little more than one hundred at each meeting. Association members continued to be strong advocates for turning the ghost town into a state park, a dream that was never realized. The association did, however, develop a video documentary entitled *Thurber, Texas: Boom Town to Ghost Town.* Replete with interviews, rare motion pictures, and a theme song written by Texas country music artist Larry Joe Taylor, the documentary has been televised across the nation.[17]

In 1989 a new restaurant was built south of Interstate 20 on historic New York Hill, housing memorabilia donated by Thurber Historical Association members. In 1992 a grease fire destroyed the Smokestack Restaurant in TPM&M's old drugstore building, but the Bennett family reopened the restaurant in the remodeled dry goods building later that year. In 1993 the Thurber Historical Association was very busy. In June the group dedicated a monument at the Thurber cemetery, designated a Historic Texas Cemetery, to those people lying in unmarked graves. In August the association helped move the 90-ton, 101-year-old Catholic church back to Thurber, placing it at the base of New York Hill. The association refurbished an old miner's house and railway car at the same site, opening a little historical park for tourists. The Historical Association was instrumental in the placement and dedication of eight new historical markers in Thurber on October 12, 1995, the most unveiled for an individual site in a single ceremony. Mr. and Mrs. W. K. Gordon helped donate funds for a bronze plaque and overlook constructed on New York Hill, giving tourists both an excellent view of the ghost town and helping them interpret the nearly vanished geography of the town. Two of the historical markers detail the history of TPM&M establishments, one marking the site of the dairy by Big Lake and another the Snake Saloon.[18]

In 1995 Dallas–Fort Worth Metroplex businessman Jack Daugherty began building a medieval-style castle on a hill just southeast of the townsite as an expensive hunter's lodge. He sold his interest in the venture, and by 1997 the new owners opened Greystone Castle to visitors, offering hunting, fishing, and plush accommodations. The incongruous sight of a castle on the Thurber skyline elicits many questions from passersby, who are just as shocked to hear a huge mining town once dominated the landscape. Efforts to better preserve Thurber's history continued, concentrated less in the Thurber Historical Association and more in Tarleton State University in nearby Stephenville, Texas. Planning began in 1997 and moved ahead in 1999 when Mrs. W. K. Gordon, Jr., daughter-in-law of the town's noted general manager, offered to donate considerable money to support a Tarleton-managed venture. With multimillion-dollar endowments from Mrs. Gordon and substantial funds provided by the state and the Tarleton State University Foundation, groundbreaking ceremonies began in 2001 and the W. K. Gordon Center for Industrial History of Texas opened to the public on November 1, 2002. Under the direction of Dr. T. Lindsay Baker, a noted historian of Texas industry and ghost towns, the Gordon Center tells the story of Thurber through re-creations of buildings, a life-sized representation of a miner digging coal, and many other smart, state-of-the-art exhibits. The Gordon Center, built to resemble TPM&M's brick drugstore, also houses a growing collection of archival material and Thurber artifacts, manuscript records, and other documents.[19]

The afterlife of Thurber has allowed scholars to look at a large company town through several lenses. Thurber was an extensive and relatively long-lived company town with a large dependent population. Unlike with most mining camps in the United States, the inhabitants of Thurber were less transient and many stayed in the general area after the closing of the town. Those that moved farther away could easily reach the town via the highways that split the town. The company that operated Thurber also remained a solvent corporation, and, although it demolished the physical property, it made a conscious effort to preserve certain buildings and the extensive records of the town. An early historical society, founded in 1937, and a handful of books and scholarly accounts of the town's history helped keep the community in a position of prominence. These surviving remembrances and, especially, the extensive records of the Texas Pacific Mercantile and Manufacturing Company allow the mercantile concern to be seen as not just an adjunct to life in the coal town, but a central player in the life of Thurber, touching and influencing every person connected to the city.

NOTES

Chapter 1

1. *Thurber Journal,* May 22, 1902, quoted in Mary Jane Gentry, *The Birth of a Texas Ghost Town: Thurber, 1886–1933* (College Station: Texas A&M University Press, 2008), 97.
2. Edgar L. Marston, New York, New York, to John D. Rockefeller, Jr., New York, New York, September 6, 1916, typewritten letter signed, letterpress copy, Correspondence Files, Vol. 1, February 1, 1916 to January 12, 1917, p. 447, Series VI, A, Miles B. Hart Collection, Nita Stewart Haley Memorial Library, Midland, Texas, hereafter cited as Miles B. Hart Collection.
3. "Mining Town Fades into Past," *Fort Worth Star-Telegram,* August 20, 1964.
4. Larry Lane Smith, *Historic Coal Mines in Texas: An Annotated Bibliography* (Austin: Railroad Commission of Texas, 1980), 5, 7; Mary Jane Gentry, "Thurber: The Life and Death of a Texas Town" (master's thesis, University of Texas, 1946), 6–7; George G. Shumard, *A Partial Report on the Geology of Western Texas Consisting of a General Geological Report and a Journal of Geological Observations along the Routes Traveled by the Expedition between Indianola, Texas, and the Valley of the Mimbres, New Mexico, During the Years 1855 and 1856* (Austin: State Printing Office, 1886), 40; Willie M. Floyd, "Thurber, Texas: An Abandoned Coal Field Town" (master's thesis, Southern Methodist University, 1939), 20; Ruth A. Allen, *Chapters in the History of Organized Labor in Texas* (Austin: University of Texas, 1941), 91; Weldon B. Hardman, *Fire in a Hole!* (Gordon, TX: Thurber Historical Association, 1975), 8; John S. Spratt, Sr., *Thurber, Texas: The Life and Death of a Company Coal Town,* ed. Harwood P. Hinton (1986; repr., Abilene, TX: State House Press, 2005), xvi; Marilyn D. Rhinehart, *A Way of Work and a Way of Life:*

Coal Mining in Thurber, Texas, 1888–1926 (College Station: Texas A&M University Press, 1992), 72.

5. Robert William Spoede, "William Whipple Johnson: An Enterprising Man" (master's thesis, Hardin-Simmons University, 1968), 48–52, 54; Michael Q. Hooks, "Thurber: A Unique Texas Community," *Panhandle-Plains Historical Review* 56 (1983): 1; Thomas R. Hall, "Data Submitted by Thos. R. Hall, Cashier and Paymaster, for the Texas & Pacific Coal Company's Twenty-fifth Anniversary Souvenir, Thurber, Texas, July 30, 1913," in *Life of the Texas Pacific Coal & Oil Co.: 1888–1963,* by George B. Studdard (Fort Worth: privately printed, 1992), 41; Rhinehart, *A Way of Work,* 5–6; Don Woodard, *Black Diamonds! Black Gold! The Saga of Texas Pacific Coal and Oil Company* (Lubbock: Texas Tech University Press, 1998), 5–12. For more information on the Johnson brothers and their various enterprises, see the William Whipple Johnson Papers and the Robert W. Spoede Papers, both located at the Southwest Collection, Texas Tech University, Lubbock, Texas.
6. Gomer Gower to Mary J. Gentry, August 14, 1944, in Gentry, "Thurber," 228; Woodard, *Black Diamonds! Black Gold!* 13; Floyd, "Thurber, Texas," 23; Hall, "Data Submitted by Thos. R. Hall," 41–42; Smith, *Historic Coal Mines in Texas,* 5; Spoede, "William Whipple Johnson," 60.
7. Jimmy M. Skaggs, "To Build a Barony: Colonel Robert D. Hunter," *Arizona and the West* 15 (Autumn 1973): 245–53; Spoede, "William Whipple Johnson," 55–56, 60; Hall, "Data Submitted by Thos. R. Hall," 42; Rhinehart, *A Way of Work,* 6; the quotation is from Hall, "Data Submitted by Thos. R. Hall," 42.
8. John C. Brown, to Johnson Coal Mining Company, March 24, 1888, typewritten letter signed, Correspondence, 1870–1897, box 1, folder 8, William Whipple Johnson Papers, S496.1, Southwest Collection, Texas Tech University Libraries, Texas Tech University, Lubbock, Texas; Spoede, "William Whipple Johnson," 57, 61–64; Rhinehart, *A Way of Work,* 6.
9. Spoede, "William Whipple Johnson," 59–68; Skaggs, "To Build a Barony," 253.
10. "Directors and Stockholders, 1888–1909," Ledger 440, pp. 1–10, Texas and Pacific Coal Company Records, S1021.1, Southwest Collection, Texas Tech University Libraries, Texas Tech University, Lubbock, Texas, hereafter cited as Texas and Pacific Coal Company Records S1021.1; "Texas and Pacific Coal Company, Stockholders and Directors Meetings Minutes, 1888–1904," Series VI, B, 4, Miles B. Hart Collection; "May Be Organized," *Dallas Morning News,* September 20, 1903, p. 4, Skaggs, "To Build a Barony," 253; Gentry, "Thurber," 10; "Death List of a Day," *New York Times,* July 22, 1899, p. 7.
11. "Annual Report of the Texas and Pacific Coal Company to the Stockholders for the Year Ending December 31, 1889," box 1, folder 3, unpaged, Texas and Pacific Coal Company Records, S1021.2, Southwest Collection, Texas Tech University

Libraries, Texas Tech University, Lubbock, Texas, hereafter cited as Texas and Pacific Coal Company Records S1021.2; Rhinehart, *A Way of Work*, 74, 78–79; Gentry, "Thurber," 229–32; Brad Crawford, "Black Diamonds: A Researcher Shines Light on African-American Coal Miners' Invisible Lives," *Family Tree Magazine*, February 2006, 8–9; "A Strange Case," *Fort Worth Weekly Gazette*, November 6, 1899; Albert Alcorn household, 1910 U.S. Census, Erath County, Texas, population schedule, Justice Precinct Thurber, enumeration district 30, supervisor's district 12, page 23, sheet 23a, dwelling 243, family 415, National Archives micropublication T624, roll 1551; "Rent Book, 1910," Ledger 325, Texas and Pacific Coal Company Records, S1021.1.

12. Hardy Green, *The Company Town: The Industrial Edens and Satanic Mills That Shaped the American Economy* (New York: Basic Books, 2010), 3ff.; "Monuments to Power," *Economist* 397, no. 8704 (October 16, 2010): 103.
13. Crandall A. Shifflett, *Coal Towns: Life, Work, and Culture in Company Towns of Southern Appalachia, 1880–1960* (Knoxville: University of Tennessee Press, 1991), 37–38, 54.
14. Margaret Crawford, *Building the Workingman's Paradise: The Design of American Company Towns* (New York: Verso, 1995), 37; Richard J. Clyne, *Coal People: Life in Southern Colorado's Company Towns, 1890–1930* (Denver: Colorado Historical Society, 1999), 30.
15. Rhinehart, *A Way of Work*, 11, 42, 45.
16. Shifflett, *Coal Towns*, 35, 54; Clyne, *Coal People*, 19–21, 68–69.
17. Floyd, "Thurber, Texas," 23, 25; Floyd's thesis includes what is the only known photograph of the Johnson Coal Mining Company commissary, figure 19 on page 25; Richard F. Selcer, *Legendary Watering Holes: The Saloons That Made Texas Famous* (College Station: Texas A&M University Press, 2004), 238; Gentry, "Thurber," 8, 126–27; Hardman, *Fire in a Hole!* 94–95; see also *Texas & Pacific Coal Company v. Thomas Lawson*, case no. 346 (Nov. 1895), Supreme Court of Texas Records, 1838–1945, trial transcript, State Archives, Texas State Library, Austin, Texas.
18. "Annual Report of the Texas and Pacific Coal Company to the Stockholders for the Year Ending December 31, 1889," box 1, folder 3, Texas and Pacific Coal Company Records, S1021.2.
19. Ibid.
20. Rhinehart, *A Way of Work*, 11; Shifflett, *Coal Towns*, 35.
21. "Annual Report of the Texas and Pacific Coal Company to the Stockholders for the Year Ending December 31, 1889," box 1, folder 3, unpaged, Texas and Pacific Coal Company Records, S1021.2; Rhinehart, *A Way of Work*, 47–48; *Texas & Pacific v. Lawson*; Ruby J. Schmidt, "Thurber Chronology," Ruby J. Schmidt Collection, W. K. Gordon Center for Industrial History of Texas, Tarleton State

University, Mingus, Texas, hereafter referred to as the Ruby J. Schmidt Collection; Hardman, *Fire in a Hole!* 117; Leo S. Bielinski, *The Thurber Connection* (Fort Worth: privately printed, 1999), 179.

22. "Annual Report of the Texas and Pacific Coal Company to the Stockholders for the Year Ending December 31, 1889," box 1, folder 3, unpaged, Texas and Pacific Coal Company Records, S1021.2.
23. Ibid.
24. "Coal Mine Strike," *Dallas Morning News,* September 13, 1903, p. 1; "Strike of Miners," *Dallas Morning News,* September 11, 1903, p. 9; Gentry, "Thurber," 106; Gomer Gower to Mary J. Gentry, January 18, 1945, letter, in Gentry, "Thurber," 235–36; Marilyn D. Rhinehart, "'Underground Patriots': Thurber Coal Miners and the Struggle for Individual Freedom, 1888–1903," *Southwestern Historical Quarterly* 92 (April 1989): 520–21; Rhinehart, *A Way of Work,* 45–46; Roscoe Hayden Sherrill, by Ann Clark, Biographical Data Information Sheet and Questionnaire (based on interview), box 2, folder 1, Thurber, Texas, Collection, S1076.1, Southwest Collection, Texas Tech University Libraries, Texas Tech University, Lubbock, Texas, hereafter cited as the Thurber, Texas, Collection, S1076.1.
25. *Texas & Pacific v. Lawson,* pp. 269, 271
26. Hut Brock, by Karl Andrews, Biographical Data Information Sheet and Questionnaire (based on interview), box 3, folder 12, unpaged, Thurber, Texas, Collection, S1076.1; *Texas & Pacific v. Lawson,* pp. 269, 271; "TP's Birthplace," *TP Voice* 2, no. 3 (May–June 1966): 5–6; Skaggs, "To Build a Barony," 254–55; Charlie S. Wilkins, "Thurber: A Sociological Study of a Company-Owned Town" (master's thesis, University of Texas, 1929), 6; Rhinehart, "Underground Patriots," 521–22; Rhinehart, *A Way of Work,* 46; Price V. Fishback, "Did Coal Miners 'Owe Their Souls to the Company Store'? Theory and Evidence from the Early 1900s," *Journal of Economic History* 46, no. 4 (December 1986): 1021. The first quotation is from "TP's Birthplace," 6, and the second quotation is from Wilkins, "Thurber," 6.
27. *Texas & Pacific v. Lawson,* pp. 307, 322; Gentry, "Thurber," 90–91; Hardman, *Fire in a Hole!* 94–95.
28. Gentry, "Thurber," 91; W. John L. Sullivan, *Twelve Years in the Saddle for Law and Order on the Frontiers of Texas* (Austin: Von Boeckmann-Jones, 1909), 34–35.
29. Sullivan, *Twelve Years in the Saddle,* 33, 35–36.
30. *Texas & Pacific v. Lawson,* pp. 261, 284, 286–87, 290, 328, 335, 530; *Texas & Pacific v. Lawson* in *Southwestern Reporter,* vol. 34, *March 9–April 20, 1896* (St. Paul, MN: West Publishing Company, 1906), 919–21.
31. "Annual Report of the Texas and Pacific Coal Co. for the Year 1890," box 1, folder 3, 8–9, Texas and Pacific Coal Company Records, S1021.2; Rhinehart, *A Way of Work,* 65; Hardman, *Fire in a Hole!* 95.

32. "The Thurber Camp," *Dallas Morning News,* September 20, 1897, p. 4; "The Thurber Mines," *Fort Worth Mail-Telegram,* May 14, 1896, Historical Edition, sec. 2; Gentry, "Thurber," 25ff.; Rhinehart, *A Way of Work,* 19–20, 22.
33. "The Thurber Mines," *Fort Worth Mail-Telegram,* May 14, 1896, Historical Edition, sec. 2.

Chapter 2

1. "Annual Report of the Texas and Pacific Coal Company to the Stockholders for the Year Ending December 31, 1889," box 1, folder 3, Texas and Pacific Coal Company Records, S1021.2, unpaged.
2. Texas and Pacific Coal Company, "The Texas Pacific Coal Co. Carry the Largest Stock of Goods" (advertisement), (Thurber, Texas: Texas and Pacific Coal Company, [early 1890s]), Articles, 1890–1990, box 1, folder 17, Thurber Historical Association Records, AR399, Special Collections Division, University of Texas at Arlington Libraries, University of Texas at Arlington, Arlington, Texas.
3. "Annual Report of the Texas and Pacific Coal Company to the Stockholders for the Year Ending December 31, 1889," unpaged; "Annual Report of the Texas and Pacific Coal Co. for the Year 1890," pp. 5–6, 8–9; "Annual Report of the Texas and Pacific Coal Co. for the Year 1891," pp. 5, 8–9; "Annual Report of the Texas and Pacific Coal Co. to the Stockholders for the Year Ending Dec. 31, 1892," p. 10; "Annual Report of the Texas & Pacific Coal Co. and Texas Pacific Mercantile & Manufacturing Co. to the Stockholders for the Year Ending December 31, 1894," pp. 3–4, 10; the previous five sources are found in box 1, folder 3, Texas and Pacific Coal Company Records, S1021.2; Hall, "Data Submitted by Thos. R. Hall," in Studdard, *Life of the Texas Pacific Coal & Oil Co.,* 43–44; Hardman, *Boom Town,* 45; Texas and Pacific Coal Company, "The Texas Pacific Coal Co. Carry the Largest Stock of Goods" (advertisement), (Thurber, Texas: Texas and Pacific Coal Company, [early 1890s]), Articles, 1890–1990, box 1, folder 17, Thurber Historical Association Records, AR399, Special Collections Division, University of Texas at Arlington Libraries, University of Texas at Arlington, Arlington, Texas.
4. Hardman, *Fire in a Hole!* 92–93; Hall, "Data Submitted by Thos. R. Hall," in Studdard, *Life of the Texas Pacific Coal & Oil Co.,* 44; Gentry, "Thurber," 112–13, 124; "Annual Report of the Texas and Pacific Coal Company to the Stockholders for the Year Ending December 31, 1889," box 1, folder 3, unpaged; "Annual Report of the Texas and Pacific Coal Co., to the Stockholders for the Year Ending Dec. 31, 1892," p. 11; "Annual Report of the Texas & Pacific Coal Co. and Texas Pacific Mercantile & Manufacturing Co. to the Stockholders for the Year Ending December 31, 1894," p. 10; the previous three sources are found in box 1, folder 3, Texas and Pacific Coal Company Records, S1021.2; Price V. Fishback, *Soft*

Coal, Hard Choices: The Economic Welfare of Bituminous Coal Miners, 1890–1930 (New York: Oxford University Press, 1992), 3–5, 135.

5. Gentry, "Thurber," 112–13, 124; Hardman, *Fire in a Hole!* 92–93; George B. Studdard, interview by Richard Mason, February 13, 1981, Fort Worth, Texas, Oral History Collection, Southwest Collection, Texas Tech University Libraries, Texas Tech University, Lubbock, Texas; Edgar E. Bryant, interview by T. Lindsay Baker, July 15, 2004, W. K. Gordon Center for Industrial History of Texas, Tarleton State University, Mingus, Texas, transcript, p. 23; Edgar E. Bryant, interview by T. Lindsay Baker, August 25, 2004, W. K. Gordon Center for Industrial History of Texas, Tarleton State University, Mingus, Texas, transcript, p. 9; Joseph Lopushansky and Michael Lopushansky, "Mining Town Terms," *American Speech* 4, no. 5 (June 1929): 370.

6. Gomer Gower to Mary J. Gentry, letter, August 14, 1944, in Gentry, "Thurber," 231–32; Rhinehart, *A Way of Work,* 32–33; "Annual Report of the Texas and Pacific Coal Company to the Stockholders for the Year Ending December 31, 1889," unpaged; "Annual Report of the Texas and Pacific Coal Co. for the Year 1890," p. 9; "Annual Report of the Texas and Pacific Coal Co. for the Year 1891," p. 9; "Annual Report of the Texas and Pacific Coal Co. to the Stockholders for the Year Ending Dec. 31, 1892," p. 10; "Annual Report of the Texas & Pacific Coal Co. and Texas Pacific Mercantile & Manufacturing Co. to the Stockholders for the Year Ending December 31, 1894," p. 10; the previous five sources are found in box 1, folder 3, Texas and Pacific Coal Company Records, S1021.2; William K. Gordon, "Data Submitted by W. K. Gordon, Sec. V. P. & G. M., for the Texas & Pacific Coal Company's Twenty-fifth Anniversary Souvenir, Thurber, Texas, July 4, 1913," in Studdard, *Life of the Texas Pacific Coal & Oil Co.,* 20; Dick Naylor, "Thurber," *Dallas Morning News,* January 11, 1892, p. 5.

7. Dick Naylor, "Thurber," *Dallas Morning News,* January 11, 1892, p. 5; Hardman, *Fire in a Hole!* 116; Homer Stephen, *Fragments of History, Erath County: Philosophical Essays, Cities of the Immortal Dead* (Stephenville, TX: privately printed, 1966), p. 21; all quotations are from Naylor, "Thurber."

8. Gentry, "Thurber," 65, 69; Rhinehart, *A Way of Work,* 80; "Annual Report of the Texas & Pacific Coal Co. and Texas Pacific Mercantile & Manufacturing Co. to the Stockholders for the Year Ending December 31, 1894," box 1, folder 3, pp. 3–5, Texas and Pacific Coal Company Records, S1021.2; "May Quit at Thurber," *Dallas Morning News,* June 4, 1894, p. 1.

9. Gentry, "Thurber," 65–77; Rhinehart, *A Way of Work,* 81; Hardman, *Fire in a Hole!* 34–36.

10. Gentry, "Thurber," 65–77; Dick King, "Rascals and Rangers," *True West* 22 (March–April 1975), 11–13; Rhinehart, *A Way of Work,* 81; Hardman, *Fire in a Hole!* 34–36.

11. Affidavit filed by W. K. Gordon in the injunction brought by Bruce and Stewart

against the Texas and Pacific Coal Company, in the Adjutant General Records, State Archives, Texas State Library, Austin, Texas, quoted in Gentry, "Thurber," 71.

12. Gentry, "Thurber," 65–77; King, "Rascals and Rangers," 11–13; Rhinehart, *A Way of Work,* 81–82; Hardman, *Fire in a Hole!* 34–36.
13. Gentry, "Thurber," 74.
14. "Annual Report of the Texas & Pacific Coal Co. and Texas Pacific Mercantile & Manufacturing Co. to the Stockholders for the Year Ending December 31, 1894," box 1, folder 3, pp. 3–5, Texas and Pacific Coal Company Records, S1021.2; King, "Rascals and Rangers," 11–13; William Hunter McLean, *From Ayr to Thurber: Three Hunter Brothers and the Winning of the West* (Fort Worth: News Printing Company, 1978), 34.
15. Gentry, "Thurber," 74.
16. "May Quit at Thurber," *Dallas Morning News,* June 4, 1894, p. 1; King, "Rascals and Rangers," 11–13; Hardman, *Fire in a Hole!* 34–36.
17. Report, W. J. McDonald to W. H. Mabry, July 1, 1894, General Correspondence, Adjutant General Records, State Archives, Texas State Library, Austin.
18. "Minutes: Directors and Stockholders Meetings, Date of Incorporation September 28, 1894 to April 21, 1920," Ledger 691, p. 1, Texas and Pacific Coal Company Records, S1021.1; "Texas Pacific Mercantile and Manufacturing Company: Minutes, 1894–1898," Series VI, B, 3, pp. 1–4, Miles B. Hart Collection; "Annual Report of the Texas & Pacific Coal Co. and Texas Pacific Mercantile & Manufacturing Co. to the Stockholders for the Year Ending December 31, 1894," box 1, folder 3, pp. 3–5; "Annual Report of the Texas & Pacific Coal Company for the Fiscal Year Ended December 31st, 1903," box 1, folder 7, unpaged; "Directors' Meeting Minutes, 1894–1906," box 5, folder 27, p. 1; the preceding three items are from the Texas and Pacific Coal Company Records, S1021.2; see also Shifflett, *Coal Towns,* chap. 9, and Fishback, "Did Coal Miners," which discuss the relationships between coal companies and their subsidiary mercantile concerns. The quotation is from "Annual Report of the Texas & Pacific Coal Co. and Texas Pacific Mercantile & Manufacturing Co. to the Stockholders for the Year Ending December 31, 1894." For insight into Hunter's character and disposition towards unions, see Skaggs, "To Build a Barony," McLean, *From Ayr to Thurber,* and Gower to Gentry, August 14, 1944, letter, in Gentry, "Thurber," 228–34.
19. "Directors' Meeting Minutes, 1894–1906," box 5, folder 27, pp. 1–6, Texas and Pacific Coal Company Records, S1021.2; "Minutes: Directors and Stockholders Meetings, Date of Incorporation September 28, 1894 to April 21, 1920," Ledger 691, pp. 1–4, 9, 151, Texas and Pacific Coal Company Records, S1021.1; "Texas Pacific Mercantile and Manufacturing Company: Minutes, 1894–1898," Series VI, B, 3, pp. 1–4, Miles B. Hart Collection.

20. "Minutes: Directors and Stockholders Meetings, Date of Incorporation September 28, 1894 to April 21, 1920," Ledger 691, pp. 1–2.

21. "Directors and Stockholders, 1888–1909," Ledger 440, Texas and Pacific Coal Company Records, S1021.1, pp. 48–49; W. T. League, Fort Worth, Texas, to Texas & Pacific Coal Company, Fort Worth, Texas, September 24, 1894, typewritten letter signed, box 5, folder 27; "Directors' Meeting Minutes, 1894–1906," box 5, folder 27, p. 1; the previous two sources are from the Texas and Pacific Coal Company Records, S1021.2; "Texas and Pacific Coal Company, Stockholders and Directors' Meetings Minutes, 1888–1904," Series VI, B, 4, Miles B. Hart Collection; *Texas Miner* (Thurber, Texas), September 29, 1894, vol. 1, no. 37; *Texas Miner* (Thurber, Texas), October 6, 1894, vol. 1, no. 38; the previous two sources are found in Thurber Newspaper Collection, Special Collections, Dick Smith Library, Tarleton State University, Stephenville, Texas.

22. "Annual Report of the Texas & Pacific Coal Co. and Texas Pacific Mercantile & Manufacturing Co. to the Stockholders for the Year Ending December 31, 1894," pp. 3, 13; "Annual Report of the Texas & Pacific Coal Co. to the Stockholders for the Year Ending December 31, 1895," box 1, folder 3, p. 4; the previous two sources are found in box 1, folder 3, Texas and Pacific Coal Company Records, S1021.2; "Revenue and Expense Journal, 1894–1898," Ledger 637, Texas and Pacific Coal Company Records, S1021.1; Rhinehart, *A Way of Work,* 46.

23. "Down in a Coal Mine," *Dallas Morning News,* June 19, 1894, p. 4.

24. Ibid.

25. R. D. Hunter, "Thurber Coal Mines," *Dallas Morning News,* July 19, 1895, p. 4.

26. Ibid.

27. Ibid.

28. Edgar L. Marston, New York, New York, to William K. Gordon, Thurber, Texas, February 2, 1916, typewritten letter signed, letterpress copy, Correspondence Files, vol. 1, February 1, 1916 to January 12, 1917, pp. 4–5, Series VI, A, p. 1, Miles B. Hart Collection.

29. Frank Martin, by Ruth Hosey, Biographical Data Information Sheet and Questionnaire (based on interview), box 2, folder 1, p. 3, Thurber, Texas, Collection, S1076.1.

30. "Minutes: Directors and Stockholders Meetings, Date of Incorporation September 28, 1894 to April 21, 1920," Ledger 691, pp. 9, 55, 151, Texas and Pacific Coal Company Records, S1021.1; Edgar L. Marston, New York, New York, to Ed Britton, Thurber, Texas, March 30, 1917, typewritten letter signed, letterpress copy, Correspondence Files, vol. 2, January 15, 1917 to November 23, 1917, pp. 164–66, Series VI, A, p. 2, Miles B. Hart Collection.

Chapter 3

1. U.S. Department of the Interior, National Park Service, National Register of

Historic Places, Thurber Historic District Nomination, 1979, typescript, unpaged, Office of the Keeper of the National Register of Historic Places, National Park Service, Washington, DC, hereafter referred to as the Thurber Historic District Nomination; Sanborn Map Company, *Thurber, Erath County, Texas,* January 1905, 1:50, Library of Congress, available at "Digital Sanborn Map Collection, 1867–1970–Texas," ProQuest UMI, sheet 1, hereafter referred to as the Sanborn Map Collection; "Annual Report of the Texas & Pacific Coal Co. to the Stockholders for the Year Ending December 31, 1896," box 1, folder 3, p. 3, Texas and Pacific Coal Company Records, S1021.2; Spratt, *Thurber, Texas,* 12; Hardman, *Fire in a Hole!* 109; "Mineral Well at Thurber," *Dallas Morning News,* July 28, 1896, p. 3; unidentified newspaper clipping from the *Texas Mining and Trade Journal* (Thurber, Texas), June 8, 1901, Texas and Pacific Company Clipping Scrapbook (1900–1901), unpaged, Series VII, Miles B. Hart Collection; "The Thurber Mines," *Fort Worth Mail-Telegram,* May 14, 1896, Historical Edition, sec. 2, unpaged.

2. "Mineral Well at Thurber," *Dallas Morning News,* July 28, 1896, p. 3.
3. "The Thurber Mines," *Fort Worth Mail-Telegram,* May 14, 1896, Historical Edition, sec. 2, unpaged.
4. "The Thurber Mines," *Fort Worth Mail-Telegram,* May 14, 1896, Historical Edition, sec. 2, unpaged; "Invited to Confer," *Dallas Morning News,* September 18, 1903, p. 2; "Voucher Record, 1899–1902," Ledger 673, pp. 21–23, 109–10, Texas and Pacific Coal Company Records, S1021.1; Hooks, "Thurber," 13; "The Grocery Department Is Again Running . . . ," newspaper clipping from the *Texas Mining and Trade Journal* (Thurber, Texas), November 2, 1901, Texas and Pacific Company Clipping Scrapbook (1900–1901), unpaged, Series VII, Miles B. Hart Collection; Leo S. Bielinski, "Beer, Booze, Bootlegging and Bocci Ball in Thurber-Mingus," 78; Valentine J. Belfiglio, *The Italian Experience in Texas* (Austin: Eakin Press, 1995), 112; "As Others See Us," newspaper clipping from the *Texas Mining and Trade Journal* (Thurber, Texas), June 2, 1900, Texas and Pacific Company Clipping Scrapbook (1900–1901), unpaged, Series VII, Miles B. Hart Collection; Gentry, "Thurber," 108. The quotation is from "As Others See Us."
5. "The Thurber Mines," *Fort Worth Mail-Telegram,* May 14, 1896, Historical Edition, sec. 2, unpaged; Hall, "Data Submitted by Thos. R. Hall," in Studdard, *Life of the Texas Pacific Coal & Oil Co.,* 43–44; Studdard, *Life of the Texas Pacific Coal & Oil Co.,* 74–75; Hardman, *Boom Town,* 46–47; "Ed S. Britton, Ex-Ranger, Dies in Strawn," *Dallas Morning News,* June 12, 1948, sec. 2, p. 5; John Miller Morris, *A Private in the Texas Rangers: A. T. Miller of Company B, Frontier Battalion* (College Station: Texas A&M University Press, 2001), 271; "Ed Britton," Texas Adjutant General Service Records, 1836–1935, FB 401-144, Adjutant General Records, State Archives, Texas State Library, Austin, Texas; Studdard, interview; "Annual

Report of the Texas & Pacific Coal Company for the Fiscal Year Ended December 31st, 1903," box 1, folder 7, unpaged; "1915 Annual Report," box 1, folder 10, unpaged; the last two sources are from the Texas and Pacific Coal Company Records, S1021.2.

6. George B. Studdard, *Life of the Texas Pacific Coal & Oil Co.: 1888–1963* (Fort Worth: privately printed, 1992), 74–75.

7. "The Thurber Mines," *Fort Worth Mail-Telegram,* May 14, 1896, Historical Edition, sec. 2, unpaged; Studdard, *Life of the Texas Pacific Coal & Oil Co.,* 74–75. The quotation is from "The Thurber Mines."

8. Studdard, *Life of the Texas Pacific Coal & Oil Co.,* 74–75; Hardman, *Boom Town,* 46–47; "Ed S. Britton, Ex-Ranger, Dies in Strawn," *Dallas Morning News,* June 12, 1948, sec. 2, p. 5; T. P. M. & M. Co., "Grocery Department" (advertisement), *Texas Mining and Trade Journal* (Thurber, Texas), October 25, 1902, whole no. 323, Bound Issues, Series IX, E, Miles B. Hart Collection.

9. "1901," box 1, folder 3, unpaged, Texas Pacific Coal and Oil Company Financial Material, AR386, Special Collections Division, University of Texas at Arlington Libraries, University of Texas at Arlington, Arlington, Texas, hereafter referred to as Texas Pacific Coal and Oil Company Financial Material, AR386; "Data Submitted by W. K. Gordon," in Studdard, *Life of the Texas Pacific Coal & Oil Co.,* 25; "Texas Fires, Texas and Pacific Mercantile Company Suffers a Heavy Loss at Thurber," *Dallas Morning News,* February 26, 1902, p. 1; "Thurber's Great Fire," newspaper clipping from the *Fort Worth Register,* ca. February 26 [1902], Texas and Pacific Company Clipping Scrapbook (1900–1904), p. 19, Series VII, Miles B. Hart Collection.

10. "Fire . . . ," *Texas Mining and Trade Journal* (Thurber, Texas), March 1, 1902, whole no. 293, Bound Issues, Series IX, E, Miles B. Hart Collection.

11. "Annual Report of the Texas & Pacific Coal Company for the Fiscal Year Ended December 31st, 1902," box 1, folder 6, Texas and Pacific Coal Company Records, S1021.2; "Data Submitted by W. K. Gordon," in Studdard, *Life of the Texas Pacific Coal & Oil Co.,* 25; "Thurber's Great Fire," newspaper clipping from the *Fort Worth Register,* ca. February 26 [1902], Texas and Pacific Company Clipping Scrapbook (1900–1904), p. 19, Series VII, Miles B. Hart Collection.

12. "Fire . . . ," *Texas Mining and Trade Journal* (Thurber, Texas), March 1, 1902, whole no. 293, Bound Issues, Series IX, E, Miles B. Hart Collection.

13. Ibid.

14. "Thurber's Great Fire," newspaper clipping from the *Fort Worth Register,* ca. February 26 [1902], Texas and Pacific Company Clipping Scrapbook (1900–1904), p. 19, Series VII, Miles B. Hart Collection; "Data Submitted by W. K. Gordon," in Studdard, *Life of the Texas Pacific Coal & Oil Co.,* 25; "Fire . . . ," *Texas Mining and Trade Journal* (Thurber, Texas), March 1, 1902, whole no. 293, Bound Issues, Series IX, E, Miles B. Hart Collection.

15. "Fire . . . ," *Texas Mining and Trade Journal* (Thurber, Texas), March 1, 1902, whole no. 293, Bound Issues, Series IX, E, Miles B. Hart Collection.

16. Edgar L. Marston, New York, New York to William K. Gordon, Thurber, Texas, December 21, 1899, typewritten letter signed, box 1, folder 19, E. L. Marston Correspondence, E. L. Marston and W. K. Gordon, December 1899, W. K. Gordon, Sr., Papers, AR421, Special Collections Division, University of Texas at Arlington Libraries, University of Texas at Arlington, Arlington, Texas, hereafter referred to as the W. K. Gordon, Sr., Papers, AR421; "Annual Report of the Texas & Pacific Coal Company for the Fiscal Year Ended December 31st, 1902," box 1, folder 6, unpaged; "Annual Report of the Texas & Pacific Coal Company for the Year 1907," box 1, folder 9, unpaged; the previous two sources are from the Texas and Pacific Coal Company Records, S1021.2; "Thurber's Great Fire," newspaper clipping from the *Fort Worth Register,* ca. February 26 [1902], Texas and Pacific Company Clipping Scrapbook (1900–1904), p. 19, Series VII, Miles B. Hart Collection; William K. Gordon, "Data Submitted by W. K. Gordon," in Studdard, *Life of the Texas Pacific Coal & Oil Co.,* 25–26; C. Richard King, *A Lodge in a Company-Owned Town: Solomon Lodge no. 813, Thurber, Texas,* Tarleton State University Dick Smith Library Keepsake no. 2 ([Stephenville, Texas: Tarleton State University, 2005]), unpaged; Sanborn Map Company, *Thurber, Erath County, Texas,* January 1905, 1:50, Digital Sanborn Map Collection, sheet 1; Gentry, "Thurber," 111–12; "Cash and Check Sales Record, 1897–1907," Ledger 606, pp. 228–73, Texas and Pacific Coal Company Records, S1021.1; Bielinski, "The Italian Presence," 37.

17. "The Thurber Mines," *Fort Worth Mail-Telegram,* May 14, 1896, Historical Edition, sec. 2, unpaged; "To the Stockholders of the Texas & Pacific Coal Company: The Results of Operations for the Year Ending December 21, 1913," box 1, folder 10, p. 2, Texas and Pacific Coal Company Records, S1021.2; "Property Report, June 1st, 1900," in "Additions to Property and Various Inventories, 1900–1932," Ledger 602; "Cash and Check Sales Record, 1897–1907," Ledger 606, pp. 228–73; the previous two sources are from the Texas and Pacific Coal Company Records, S1021.1; Victor Lucadello, "Lucadello Memoir," unpaged, Ruby J. Schmidt Collection; Spratt, *Thurber, Texas,* 28, 66, 70; "Local Notes," *Texas Miner* (Thurber, Texas), May 25, 1895, vol. 2, no. 19, p. 9; T. P. M. & M. Co., "Hardware Department" (advertisement), *Texas Mining and Trade Journal* (Thurber, Texas), January 13, 1900, vol. 4, no. 26, whole no. 182, p. 11; the preceding two sources are from Thurber Newspaper Collection, Special Collections, Dick Smith Library, Tarleton State University, Stephenville, Texas, hereafter referred to as the Thurber Newspaper Collection; "Voucher Record, 1899–1902," Ledger 673, pp. 21–23, Texas and Pacific Coal Company Records, S1021.1; "'Expansion' Is the Word," clipping from the *Texas Mining and Trade Journal* (Thurber, Texas), September 8, 1900, Texas and Pacific Company

Clipping Scrapbook (1900–1901), unpaged, Series VII, Miles B. Hart Collection; Sanborn Map Company, *Thurber, Erath County, Texas,* January 1905, 1:50, Digital Sanborn Map Collection, sheet 1; Sanborn Map Company, *Thurber, Erath County, Texas,* April 1911, 1:50, Digital Sanborn Map Collection, sheet 1; Gordon, "Data Submitted by W. K. Gordon," in Studdard, *Life of the Texas Pacific Coal & Oil Co.,* 26; Studdard, *Life of the Texas Pacific Coal & Oil Co.,* 86–88; Spratt, *Thurber, Texas,* 93.

18. "The Thurber Mines," *Fort Worth Mail-Telegram,* May 14, 1896, Historical Edition, sec. 2, unpaged; "To the Stockholders of the Texas & Pacific Coal Company: The Results of Operations for the Year Ending December 21, 1913," box 1, folder 10, p. 2, Texas and Pacific Coal Company Records, S1021.2; "Down in a Coal Mine," *Dallas Morning News,* June 19, 1894, p. 4; "Voucher Record, 1899–1902," Ledger 673, pp. 21–23, Texas and Pacific Coal Company Records, S1021.1; "As Others See Us," newspaper clipping from the *Texas Mining and Trade Journal* (Thurber, Texas), June 2, 1900, Texas and Pacific Company Clipping Scrapbook (1900–1901), unpaged, Series VII, Miles B. Hart Collection; R. D. Hunter, "Thurber Coal Mines," *Dallas Morning News,* July 19, 1895, p. 4; Spratt, *Thurber, Texas,* 12, 28, 66, 70; T. P. M. & M. Co., "Market Department" (advertisement), *The Thurber Journal,* vol. 9, no. 49, August 1, 1907, box 1, folder 11, Thurber, Texas, Collection, S1076.1; "'Expansion' Is the Word," clipping from the *Texas Mining and Trade Journal* (Thurber, Texas), September 8, 1900, Texas and Pacific Company Clipping Scrapbook (1900–1901), unpaged, Series VII, Miles B. Hart Collection; "Sales at Fort Worth," *Dallas Morning News,* December 9, 1902, p. 13; T. P. M. & M. Co., "Market and Cold Storage Dept." (advertisement), *Texas Mining and Trade Journal* (Thurber, Texas), January 13, 1900, vol. 4, no. 26, whole no. 182, p. 9, Thurber Newspaper Collection; John S. Spratt, Sr., *The Road to Spindletop: Economic Change in Texas, 1875–1901* (Austin: University of Texas Press, 1970), 53; "Annual Report of the Texas & Pacific Coal Company for the Fiscal Year Ended December 31st, 1902," box 1, folder 6, Texas and Pacific Coal Company Records, S1021.2; "Meeting of Department Managers Held Thursday Evening, April 27, 1905," T. P. M. & M.–Minutes, Mary Jane Gentry Collection, AR 95-13, Special Collections Division, University of Texas at Arlington Libraries, University of Texas at Arlington, Arlington, Texas, hereafter referred to as the Mary Jane Gentry Collection, AR 95-13 (this collection is now processed and known as the Thurber, Texas, Collection, AR506); Sanborn Map Company, *Thurber, Erath County, Texas,* January 1905, 1:50, Digital Sanborn Map Collection, sheet 1; Sanborn Map Company, *Thurber, Erath County, Texas,* April 1911, 1:50, Digital Sanborn Map Collection, sheet 1; "Annual Report of the Texas & Pacific Coal Company for the Year 1906," box 1, folder 9, p. 1, Texas and Pacific Coal Company Records, S1021.2; "Cash and Check Sales Record,

1897–1907," Ledger 606, pp. 228–73, Texas and Pacific Coal Company Records, S1021.1; Hardman, *Fire in a Hole!* 110–11; Studdard, *Life of the Texas Pacific Coal & Oil Co.*, 86–88; Bryant, interview by Baker, July 15, 2004, transcript, p. 20, W. K. Gordon Center for Industrial History of Texas, Tarleton State University, Mingus, Texas.

19. "The Thurber Mines," *Fort Worth Mail-Telegram*, May 14, 1896, Historical Edition, sec. 2, unpaged; Sanborn Map Company, *Thurber, Erath County, Texas*, January 1905, 1:50, Digital Sanborn Map Collection, sheet 1; Sanborn Map Company, *Thurber, Erath County, Texas*, April 1911, 1:50, Digital Sanborn Map Collection, sheet 1; "Texas Pacific Mercantile and Manufacturing Company, Additions to Property for the Year 1909," in "Additions to Property and Various Inventories, 1900–1932," Ledger 602, Texas and Pacific Coal Company Records, S1021.1; T. P. M. & M. Co., "Cold in the Head" (advertisement), *Texas Mining and Trade Journal* (Thurber, Texas), January 27, 1900, vol. 4, no. 28, whole no. 184, p. 12, Thurber Newspaper Collection; "Texas & Pacific Coal Company and Controlled Companies President's Annual Report 1909," box 1, folder 9, unpaged, Texas and Pacific Coal Company Records, S1021.2; T. P. M. & M. Co., "Dr. Binney's Iron Tonic" (advertisement), *Texas Mining and Trade Journal* (Thurber, Texas), August 2, 1902, whole no. 311, Bound Issues, Series IX, E, Miles B. Hart Collection; Gordon, "Data Submitted by W. K. Gordon," in Studdard, *Life of the Texas Pacific Coal & Oil Co.*, 26; Spratt, *Thurber, Texas*, 58–59; Studdard, *Life of the Texas Pacific Coal & Oil Co.*, 94–95; Studdard, interview; "Sales by Departments Summary, Accounting Dept., 1923–1925," Ledger 650; "Property Report, June 1st, 1900," in "Additions to Property and Various Inventories, 1900–1932," Ledger 602; "Voucher Record, 1899–1902," Ledger 673, pp. 21–24; the previous three sources are from the Texas and Pacific Coal Company Records, S1021.1; Bryant, interview by Baker, July 15, 2004, transcript, p. 22; "Cash and Check Sales Record, 1897–1907," Ledger 606, pp. 228–73, Texas and Pacific Coal Company Records, S1021.1; Bielinski, *The Thurber Connection*, 213.

20. "Cash and Check Sales Record, 1897–1907," Ledger 606, pp. 208, 228–73, Texas and Pacific Coal Company Records, S1021.1; Gordon Baines, "Notes on Thurber, Texas," box 3, folder 1, unpaged, Thurber, Texas, Collection, S1076.1; "The Grocery Department Is Again Running . . . ," newspaper clipping from the *Texas Mining and Trade Journal* (Thurber, Texas), November 2, 1901, Texas and Pacific Company Clipping Scrapbook (1900–1901), unpaged, Series VII, Miles B. Hart Collection; Gordon, "Data Submitted by W. K. Gordon," in Studdard, *Life of the Texas Pacific Coal & Oil Co.*, 26; Gentry, "Thurber," 112–113; Hardman, *Fire in a Hole!* 91–92; Texas and Pacific Coal Company, [New York, NY], *Sketch Map of Thurber, Tex.*, September 1916, 1:200, Bennett Family Collection, W. K. Gordon

Center for Industrial History of Texas, Tarleton State University, Mingus, Texas, hereafter referred to as the Bennett Family Collection; "Meeting of Department Managers Held Wednesday Evening May 3, 1905," T. P. M. & M.–Minutes, Mary Jane Gentry Collection, AR 95-13; Hooks, "Thurber," 6; Bielinski, *The Thurber Connection,* 135, 189, 210. TPM&M opened this general store in the recently closed Lizard Saloon building.

21. "Texas Pacific Mercantile and Manufacturing Company: Minutes, 1894–1898," Series VI, B, 3, pp. 1–4, Miles B. Hart Collection; "Annual Report of the Texas & Pacific Coal Co. and Texas Pacific Mercantile & Manufacturing Co. to the Stockholders for the Year Ending December 31, 1894," box 1, folder 3, pp. 3–5; "Annual Report of the Texas & Pacific Coal Company for the Fiscal Year Ended December 31st, 1903," box 1, folder 7, unpaged; "Directors' Meeting Minutes, 1894–1906," box 5, folder 27, p. 1; the preceding three items are from the Texas and Pacific Coal Company Records, S1021.2; "Cash and Check Sales Record, 1894–1895," Ledger 605, Texas and Pacific Coal Company Records, S1021.1.
22. "Property Report, June 1st, 1900," "Texas Pacific Mercantile & Manufacturing Co. Inventory Saloon Equipment, Month of January, 1915," "Additions to Property Accounts. Year 1904," and "Inventory Fixtures and Equipment, Dec 31, 1904, Saloon #3," in "Additions to Property and Various Inventories, 1900–1932," Ledger 602, Texas and Pacific Coal Company Records, S1021.1; Rhinehart, *A Way of Work,* 65–66; Hardman, *Fire in a Hole!* 95–96; photocopies of Saloon Ledger Covers, box 1, folder 2, Don Woodard Papers, S1617.1, Southwest Collection, Texas Tech University Libraries, Texas Tech University, Lubbock, Texas.
23. "Property Report, June 1st, 1900," "Texas Pacific Mercantile & Manufacturing Co. Inventory Saloon Equipment, Month of January, 1915," "Additions to Property Accounts. Year 1904," and "Inventory Fixtures and Equipment, Dec 31, 1904, Saloon #3," in "Additions to Property and Various Inventories, 1900–1932," Ledger 602, Texas and Pacific Coal Company Records, S1021.1; Rhinehart, *A Way of Work,* 65–66; Hardman, *Fire in a Hole!* 95–96; "Annual Report of the Texas and Pacific Coal Company for the Year Ended December 31, 1899," box 1, folder 4, p. 27; "Annual Report of the Texas and Pacific Coal Co. for the Year 1890," box 1, folder 3, 8–9; the previous two sources are from the Texas and Pacific Coal Company Records, S1021.2; Lawrence Santi, interview by George Green, February 15, 1974, Mingus, Texas, transcript, p. 4, HD8083.T4 T47 no. 41, p. 10, Texas Labor Archives Oral Histories, Special Collections Division, University of Texas at Arlington Libraries, University of Texas at Arlington, Arlington, Texas; "Cash and Check Sales Record, 1894–1895," Ledger 605; "Cash and Check Sales Record, 1897–1907," Ledger 606, pp. 83, 128–71, 352; the previous two sources are from the Texas and Pacific Coal Company Records, S1021.1.

24. "Inventory Fixtures and Equipment, Dec 31, 1904, Saloon #3," in "Additions to Property and Various Inventories, 1900–1932," Ledger 602, Texas and Pacific Coal Company Records, S1021.1; "Annual Report of the Texas and Pacific Coal Company for the Year Ended December 31, 1899," box 1, folder 4, p. 27, Texas and Pacific Coal Company Records, S1021.2; "Cash and Check Sales Record, 1897–1907," Ledger 606, pp. 83, 128–71, 352, Texas and Pacific Coal Company Records, S1021.1; "1901," box 1, folder 3, unpaged, Texas Pacific Coal and Oil Company Financial Material, AR386.

25. "Saloon no. 1," unpaged, Mary Jane Gentry Collection, AR 95-13, Texas Pacific Coal Company, "To the Boy's in the Camp" (advertisement), *Texas Miner* (Thurber, Texas), March 3, 1894, vol. 1, no. 7, p. 6; Dallas Brewing Company, "Dallas Brewing Company" (advertisement), *Texas Miner* (Thurber, Texas), October 13, 1894, vol. 1, no. 39, p. 20; the previous two items are to be found in the Thurber Newspaper Collection; Carl Crow, "Thurber Might Furnish Liquor Problem Solution. Largest Saloon in Texas Requires Only One Officer to Preserve Peace," *Fort Worth Star-Telegram,* February 2, 1910; Literary Production, Willie M. Floyd Papers, Southwest Collection, Texas Tech University Libraries, Texas Tech University, Lubbock, Texas (hereafter referred to as the "Willie M. Floyd Papers"); Gentry, "Thurber," 91–92; Floyd, "Thurber, Texas," 31; Rhinehart, *A Way of Work,* 25, 65–66; Hardman, *Fire in a Hole!* 95–96; Spratt, *Thurber, Texas,* 14–15; Leo S. Bielinski, "Beer, Booze, Bootlegging and Bocci Ball in Thurber-Mingus," *West Texas Historical Association Year Book* 59 (1983): 76; Bielinski, *The Thurber Connection,* 170–71; Belfiglio, *The Italian Experience in Texas,* 86; Studdard, *Life of the Texas Pacific Coal & Oil Co.,* 71.

26. "Property Report, June 1st, 1900," in "Additions to Property and Various Inventories, 1900–1932," Ledger 602; "Voucher Record, 1899–1902," Ledger 673, pp. 21–23, 110; "Voucher Record, 1903–1905," Ledger 674, p. 5; the previous three sources are from the Texas and Pacific Coal Company Records, S1021.1; Carl Crow, "Thurber Might Furnish Liquor Problem Solution. Largest Saloon in Texas Requires Only One Officer to Preserve Peace," *Fort Worth Star-Telegram,* February 2, 1910; Gentry, "Thurber," 91–92; Floyd, "Thurber, Texas," 31; Rhinehart, *A Way of Work,* 25, 65–66; Hardman, *Fire in a Hole!* 95–96; Spratt, *Thurber, Texas,* 14–15; Bielinski, "Beer, Booze, Bootlegging and Bocci Ball in Thurber-Mingus," 76; Bielinski, *The Thurber Connection,* 170–71; Belfiglio, *The Italian Experience in Texas,* 86; Studdard, *Life of the Texas Pacific Coal & Oil Co.,* 71. Studdard (p. 71) has a photograph of a hexagonal token with the words "THURBER SALOON" on the obverse, and "GOOD FOR ONE 12½¢ DRINK" on the reverse. Aside from this photograph, no other source mentions these tokens, including all the extant company records investigated.

27. "Cash and Check Sales Record, 1897–1907," Ledger 606, pp. 56–79; "Cash and

Check Sales Record, 1894–1895," Ledger 605, p. 23; the previous two sources are from the Texas and Pacific Coal Company Records, S1021.1.

28. Floyd, "Thurber, Texas," 70, 72; Hardman, *Fire in a Hole!* 96–97; Nathan Washington Marston, *The Marston Genealogy* (South Lubec, ME: privately printed, 1888), 59.
29. Floyd, "Thurber, Texas," 73.
30. Edgar L. Marston, New York, New York, to Thomas R. Tennant, Thurber, Texas, March 7, 1905, typewritten letter signed, in Floyd, "Thurber, Texas," 72.
31. Floyd, "Thurber, Texas," 70, 72; Hardman, *Fire in a Hole!* 96–97.
32. "A Sunday at Thurber," newspaper clipping from the *Fort Worth Register,* ca. July 5, 1900, Texas and Pacific Company Clipping Scrapbook (1900–1904), pp. 16–18, Series VII, Miles B. Hart Collection.
33. "Criminal Docket 1897–1901, Erath County," pp. 176ff., Mary Jane Gentry Collection; Andrew T. Albright household, 1910 U.S. Census, Palo Pinto County, Texas, population schedule, Justice Precinct 3, enumeration district 185, supervisor's district 16, page 62, sheet 11a, dwelling 206, family 206, National Archives micropublication T624, roll 1583; Carl Crow, "Thurber Might Furnish Liquor Problem Solution. Largest Saloon in Texas Requires Only One Officer to Preserve Peace," *Fort Worth Star-Telegram,* February 2, 1910.
34. "Annual Report of the Texas & Pacific Coal Company for the Fiscal Year Ended December 31st, 1903," box 1, folder 7, Texas and Pacific Coal Company Records, S1021.2; "Erath County Went Dry," *Dallas Morning News,* March 17, 1902, p. 9; "Thurber Was Excluded, Prohibition Election Ordered for Every Other Erath County Precinct," *Dallas Morning News,* February 17, 1902, p. 8; Hardman, *Fire in a Hole!* 95.
35. Hardman, *Fire in a Hole!* 95.
36. "The Observation of an Old Line Pro," handbill, n.p., [June 1903], Texas and Pacific Company Clipping Scrapbook (1900–1904), p. 24, Series VII, Miles B. Hart Collection.
37. Crow, "Thurber Might Furnish Liquor Problem Solution."
38. "The Observation of an Old Line Pro."
39. "That 'Funeral' Procession," clipping from *The Empire* (Stephenville, Texas), June 4, 1903, Texas and Pacific Company Clipping Scrapbook (1900–1904), p. 22, Series VII, Miles B. Hart Collection.
40. William K. Gordon, Thurber, Texas, to Edgar L. Marston, New York, New York, August 8, 1911, typewritten letter, carbon copy, box 1, folder 25, p. 2, E. L. Marston Correspondence, E. L. Marston and W. K. Gordon, August–October 1911, W. K. Gordon, Sr., Papers, AR421; *United Mine Workers' Journal,* September 24, 1903, in Allen, *Chapters in the History of Organized Labor in Texas,* 95; "Local Notes," *Texas Miner* (Thurber, Texas), July 20, 1895, vol. 2, no. 27, p. 10; "For or

Against Prohibition," *Texas Miner* (Thurber, Texas), July 27, 1895, vol. 2, no. 28, p. 9; "County Site News," *Texas Miner* (Thurber, Texas), August 3, 1895, vol. 2, no. 29, p. 7; the three previous items are found in the Thurber Newspaper Collection.

41. "For or Against Prohibition," *Texas Miner* (Thurber, Texas), July 27, 1895, vol. 2, no. 28, p. 9, Thurber Newspaper Collection.
42. "Local Notes," *Texas Miner* (Thurber, Texas), July 20, 1895, vol. 2, no. 27, p. 10; "For or Against Prohibition," *Texas Miner* (Thurber, Texas), July 27, 1895, vol. 2, no. 28, p. 9; "County Site News," *Texas Miner* (Thurber, Texas), August 3, 1895, vol. 2, no. 29, p. 7; the three previous items are found in the Thurber Newspaper Collection; Crow, "Thurber Might Furnish Liquor Problem Solution."
43. Untitled tally of 1904 Erath County prohibition election results, literary production, Mary Jane Gentry Collection, AR 95-13; "Erath County Dry," *Dallas Morning News,* June 12, 1904, p. 7; "Pros Carry Erath County," *Dallas Morning News,* June 12, 1904, p. 6. Fewer Thurberites voted in this election than before, possibly because miners did not feel obligated to toe the company line after unionization in 1903; see Rhinehart, *A Way of Work,* 53ff.
44. "Inventory Fixtures and Equipment, Dec. 31, 1904, Saloon #4," in "Additions to Property and Various Inventories, 1900–1932," Ledger 602; "Texas Pacific Mercantile & Manufacturing Co. Inventory Saloon Equipment, Month of January, 1915," in "Additions to Property and Various Inventories, 1900–1932," Ledger 602; "Cash and Check Sales Record, 1897–1907," Ledger 606, pp. 176–221; the previous three sources are from Texas and Pacific Coal Company Records, S1021.1; "Annual Report of the Texas & Pacific Coal Company for the Fiscal Year Ended December 31st, 1904," box 1, folder 7, p. 20, Texas and Pacific Coal Company Records, S1021.2; Texas and Pacific Coal Company, *Sketch Map of Thurber, Tex.,* September 1916, 1:200, Bennett Family Collection, W. K. Gordon Center for Industrial History of Texas, Tarleton State University, Mingus, Texas; Hardman, *Fire in a Hole!* 96–97; Floyd, "Thurber, Texas," 70–71.
45. "Burglar and Hatchet; Safe Open; $980 Gone Saloon at Thurber Robbed with Simple Equipment Which," *Fort Worth Star-Telegram,* December 28, 1910.
46. Gordon to Marston, August 8, 1911, W. K. Gordon, Sr., Papers, AR421; Grace Groves, untitled memoir, typescript with irregular pagination, [ca. 1974–1975], box 1, folder 14, Thurber Historical Association Records, AR399, Special Collections Division, University of Texas at Arlington Libraries, University of Texas at Arlington, Arlington, Texas. Quotation is from the Grace Groves memoir.
47. Necah Stewart Furman, *Walter Prescott Webb: His Life and Impact* (Albuquerque: University of New Mexico Press, 1976), 52–54; Walter Prescott Webb, "Texas

Collection," *Southwestern Historical Quarterly* 43, no. 1 (July 1939): 93–94.

48. Furman, *Walter Prescott Webb,* 54.

49. *Sketch Map of Thurber, Tex.;* Gentry, "Thurber," 130; Hardman, *Fire in a Hole!* 96–97; Floyd, "Thurber, Texas," 70–71; Rhinehart, *A Way of Work,* 65; Walter Kostiha to Dan K. Utley and Leo S. Bielinski, interview, March 6, 1999, Strawn, Texas, interview 9 in *Thurber Oral History Project: Edited and Excerpted Transcripts* ([Thurber, Texas]: Thurber Historical Association, Inc., [2008]), irregular pagination; Webb, "Texas Collection," 94. Quotation is from Webb, 94.

50. "Inventory Fixtures and Equipment, Dec 31, 1904, Saloon #3," in "Additions to Property and Various Inventories, 1900–1932," Ledger 602; "Cash and Check Sales Record, 1897–1907," Ledger 606, pp. 83, 128–71, 176–221, 228–73, 352; the previous two sources are from the Texas and Pacific Coal Company Records, S1021.1; "Annual Report of the Texas and Pacific Coal Company for the Year Ended December 31, 1899," box 1, folder 4, p. 27; "Annual Report of the Texas & Pacific Coal Company for the Fiscal Year Ended December 31st, 1904," box 1, folder 7, p. 20; the previous two sources are from the Texas and Pacific Coal Company Records, S1021.2; "1901," box 1, folder 3, unpaged, Texas Pacific Coal and Oil Company Financial Material, AR386, Special Collections Division, University of Texas at Arlington Libraries, University of Texas at Arlington, Arlington, Texas; Spratt, *Thurber, Texas,* 15; Literary Production, Willie M. Floyd Papers; Floyd, "Thurber, Texas," 31; Gentry, "Thurber," 130.

51. "Palo Pinto Campaign," *Dallas Morning News,* November 23, 1905, p. 12; "County Boundary Line," *Dallas Morning News,* September 2, 1906, p. 8; "Contest Line of County," *Dallas Morning News,* January 9, 1907, p. 7; "Surveyors Split Thurber," *Dallas Morning News,* January 15, 1907, p. 9; Gordon to Marston, August 8, 1911; William K. Gordon, Thurber, Texas, to Edgar L. Marston, New York, New York, August 27, 1911, typewritten letter, carbon copy, box 1, folder 25, pp. 2–3; the previous two sources are from the E. L. Marston Correspondence, E. L. Marston and W. K. Gordon, August–October 1911, W. K. Gordon, Sr., Papers, AR421.

52. Independent Good Templar Society, *Proceedings of the Grand Lodge of Texas I. O. G. T.: Fourteenth Annual Session Held in Thurber, Texas, July 23 and 24th, 1907* (Dallas: privately printed, 1907), unpaged, located in the Willie M. Floyd Papers; Rhinehart, *A Way of Work,* 64.

53. Gordon to Marston, August 8, 1911; Gordon to Marston, August 27, 1911; the previous two sources are from the E. L. Marston Correspondence, E. L. Marston and W. K. Gordon, August–October 1911, W. K. Gordon, Sr., Papers, AR421; K. Austin Kerr, "Prohibition," in *The New Handbook of Texas* (Austin: Texas State Historical Association, 1996), 5:355.

54. Gordon to Marston, August 8, 1911, E. L. Marston Correspondence, E. L. Marston and W. K. Gordon, August–October 1911, W. K. Gordon, Sr., Papers, AR421.

55. "Palo Pinto County Votes Prohibition," *Dallas Morning News,* November 15, 1914, p. 6; John Leffler, "Palo Pinto County," in *The New Handbook of Texas,* 5:29–31; Gordon to Marston, August 27, 1911, E. L. Marston Correspondence, E. L. Marston and W. K. Gordon, August–October 1911, W. K. Gordon, Sr., Papers, AR421; Floyd, "Thurber, Texas," 70; Hardman, *Fire in a Hole!* 97.

56. "Cash and Check Sales Record, 1914–1927," Ledger 608, pp. 10–11; "Revenue and Expense Journal, 1915–1917," Ledger 643, p. 2; the previous two sources are from the Texas and Pacific Coal Company Records, S1021.1; "1915 Annual Report," box 1, folder 10, Texas and Pacific Coal Company Records, S1021.2; Floyd, "Thurber, Texas," 70; Hardman, *Fire in a Hole!* 97–98.

57. Gentry, "Thurber," 93; Ken Jones, *From Boom Town to Ghost Town,* [Tarleton State University Dick Smith Library Keepsake No. 1] ([Stephenville, TX]: Tarleton State University, [2002]), unpaged; Bielinski, *The Thurber Connection,* 171; Spratt, *Thurber, Texas,* 15; Rhinehart, *A Way of Work,* 100.

58. Texas Historical Commission, *Texas Historic Sites Atlas,* s.v. "Site of Snake Saloon," Marker no. 4888, erected 1995, Palo Pinto County, 0.25 mile north of IH 20 on FM 108 at south county line, http://atlas.thc.state.tx.us/common/viewform.asp?atlas_num=5363004888&site_name=Snake+Saloon,+Site+of&class=5000 (accessed February 21, 2006).

59. "Revenue and Expense Journal, 1915–1917," Ledger 643, p. 2, Texas and Pacific Coal Company Records, S1021.1.

60. "Texas Pacific Mercantile and Manufacturing Company, Additions to Property for the Year 1915," in "Additions to Property and Various Inventories, 1900–1932," Ledger 602, Texas and Pacific Coal Company Records, S1021.1.

61. Sadie Markland Plummer, by Ruth Hosey, Biographical Data Information Sheet and Questionnaire (based on interview), box 2, folder 1, Thurber, Texas, Collection, S1076.1, Southwest Collection, Texas Tech University Libraries, Texas Tech University, Lubbock, Texas; George B. Studdard, interview by Richard Mason, February 13, 1981, Fort Worth, Texas, Oral History Collection, Southwest Collection, Texas Tech University Libraries, Texas Tech University, Lubbock, Texas; Hardman, *Fire in a Hole!* 97–98.

62. "Did Not Violate Revenue Laws. Acquitted of Charge by Jury in Federal Court," *Fort Worth Register,* November 28, 1900, morning edition; Spratt, *Thurber, Texas,* 15–16; King, "Rascals and Rangers," 6–13, 40, 44; Lucadello, "Lucadello Memoir," unpaged, Ruby J. Schmidt Collection; Hardman, *Fire in a Hole!* 97–98; Belfiglio, *The Italian Experience,* 85–86; *The Italian Texans* (San Antonio: University of Texas Institute of Texan Cultures at San Antonio, 1987), 11–12; Bielinski, "Beer, Booze, Bootlegging and Bocci Ball in Thurber-Mingus"; Spratt, *Thurber, Texas,* 15–16.

63. Lucadello, "Lucadello Memoir," unpaged, Ruby J. Schmidt Collection.

64. Lucadello, "Lucadello Memoir," unpaged, Ruby J. Schmidt Collection; Belfiglio,

The Italian Experience, 85–86; *The Italian Texans*, 11–12; Bielinski, "Beer, Booze, Bootlegging and Bocci Ball in Thurber-Mingus"; Spratt, *Thurber, Texas*, 15–16; Studdard, interview; "Much Liquor Is Found at Thurber," *Dallas Morning News*, November 11, 1921, p. 16. LeAnna Schooley and Dr. T. Lindsay Baker, curator and director, respectively, of Tarleton State University's W. K. Gordon Center for Industrial History of Texas have discovered and photographed ruins of rock-lined depressions that may represent the remains of cellars in the western section of Thurber, where most of the Italians lived (LeAnna Schooley, e-mail message to author, July 11, 2008; T. Lindsay Baker, e-mail message to author, July 29, 2008).

65. Walter Kostiha to Dan K. Utley and Leo S. Bielinski, interview, March 6, 1999, Strawn, Texas, interview 9 in *Thurber Oral History Project: Edited and Excerpted Transcripts* ([Thurber, TX]: Thurber Historical Association, Inc., [2008]), irregular pagination.
66. Dean Hiatt to Dan K. Utley and Leo S. Bielinski, interview, March 28, 1999, Peaster, Texas, interview 8 in *Thurber Oral History Project: Edited and Excerpted Transcripts* ([Thurber, TX]: Thurber Historical Association, Inc., [2008]), irregular pagination.
67. Bielinski, "Beer, Booze, Bootlegging and Bocci Ball in Thurber-Mingus," 81.
68. Edgar L. Marston, New York, New York, to Ed Britton, Thurber, Texas, June 15, 1916, typewritten letter signed, letterpress copy, Correspondence Files, vol. 1, February 1, 1916 to January 12, 1917, p. 298, Series VI, A, Miles B. Hart Collection.
69. Studdard, interview; Bielinski, "Beer, Booze, Bootlegging and Bocci Ball in Thurber-Mingus."
70. Hiatt, interview.

Chapter 4

1. "Minutes: Directors and Stockholders Meetings, Date of Incorporation September 28, 1894 to April 21, 1920," Ledger 691, pp. 1–2, 9; "Rent Book, 1924," Ledger 339; "Payroll Book, Mine, 1915," Ledger 133; the previous three sources are from the Texas and Pacific Coal Company Records, S1021.1; "Annual Report of the Texas and Pacific Coal Co. for the Year 1891," box 1, folder 3, p. 5; "Annual Report of the Texas & Pacific Coal Co. to the Stockholders for the Year Ending December 31, 1896," box 1, folder 3, p. 3; the previous two sources are from the Texas and Pacific Coal Company Records, S1021.2; S. Mims, Fort Worth, Texas, to William K. Gordon, Thurber, Texas, August 25, 1894, typewritten letter signed, box 2, folder 8, Other Business Correspondence, Texas & Pacific Coal Company, June 1890–December 1899, W. K. Gordon, Sr., Papers, AR421; James Hayes Quarles, "Wonderful Exodus of Thurber Miners," unidentified Fort

Worth newspaper clipping, September 15, 1903, Texas and Pacific Company Clipping Scrapbook (Strike, Sep. 1903), unpaged, Series VII, Miles B. Hart Collection; Hardman, *Fire in a Hole!* 105–8; Gentry, "Thurber," 175; Lucadello, "Lucadello Memoir," unpaged, Ruby J. Schmidt Collection.

2. "Annual Report of the Texas & Pacific Coal Co. to the Stockholders for the Year Ending December 31, 1896," box 1, folder 3, p. 3; "Annual Report of the Texas and Pacific Coal Company for the Year Ended December 31, 1899," box 1, folder 4, pp. 8, 29; "Annual Report of the Texas & Pacific Coal Company for the Year 1908," box 1, folder 9, unpaged; "Texas & Pacific Coal Company and Controlled Companies President's Annual Report 1910," box 1, folder 9, unpaged; "1915 Annual Report," box 1, folder 10, unpaged; "1916 Annual Report," box 1, folder 10, unpaged; the previous six sources are from the Texas and Pacific Coal Company Records, S1021.2; "Texas Pacific Mercantile and Manufacturing Company, Additions to Property for the Year 1919," in "Additions to Property and Various Inventories, 1900–1932," Ledger 602; "Texas Pacific Mercantile and Manufacturing Company, Additions to Property for the Year 1912," in "Additions to Property and Various Inventories, 1900–1932," Ledger 602; "Texas Pacific Mercantile and Manufacturing Company, Additions to Property for the Year 1915," in "Additions to Property and Various Inventories, 1900–1932," Ledger 602; the previous three sources are from the Texas and Pacific Coal Company Records, S1021.1; "The Ice Plant . . . ," newspaper clipping from the *Texas Mining and Trade Journal* (Thurber, Texas), January 19, 1901, Texas and Pacific Company Clipping Scrapbook (1900–1901), unpaged, Series VII; Quarles, "Wonderful Exodus of Thurber Miners," unidentified Fort Worth newspaper clipping, September 15, 1903, Texas and Pacific Company Clipping Scrapbook (Strike, Sep. 1903), unpaged, Series VII; the previous two sources are from the Miles B. Hart Collection; "New Ice Factories," *Ice and Refrigeration* 10, no. 1 (January 1896): 36; "The Thurber Mines," *Fort Worth Mail-Telegram,* May 14, 1896, Historical Edition, sec. 2, unpaged; Gentry, "Thurber," 155–57; Studdard, *Life of the Texas Pacific Coal & Oil Co.,* 82–83; Hardman, *Fire in a Hole!* 108–10; Kate Oliver, "Museum Stirs Memories of Thurber," *Abilene Reporter-News,* September 4, 1966, sec. C, p. 1.

3. "Annual Report of the Texas and Pacific Coal Company for the Year Ended December 31, 1899," box 1, folder 4, p. 26, Texas and Pacific Coal Company Records, S1021.2; S. Mims, Fort Worth, Texas, to William K. Gordon, Thurber, Texas, June 1, 1899, typewritten letter signed, box 2, folder 8, Other Business Correspondence, Texas and Pacific Coal Company, June 1890–December 1899, W. K. Gordon, Sr., Papers, AR421; R. D. Hunter, "Thurber Coal Mines," *Dallas Morning News,* July 19, 1895, p. 4; Texas and Pacific Coal Company, [New York, NY], *Sketch Map of Thurber, Tex.,* September 1916, 1:200, Bennett Family

Collection; Joe David Grimshaw, "Hard, Heavy Lifting: The Manufacture of Bricks at Thurber, Texas" (master's thesis, Tarleton State University, 2004), 52ff.; Arden Jean Schuetz and Wilma Jean Schuetz, *People-Events and Erath County, Texas* (Stephenville, TX: privately published, 1972), 155; Pauline Naylor, "Photo Recalls Stage Coach Days in Coal Mining Town," clipping from unidentified San Angelo, Texas, newspaper, about December 1, 1976, W. K. Gordon, Jr., Scrapbook, p. 39, Oversize box 386, Special Collections Division, University of Texas at Arlington Libraries, University of Texas at Arlington, Arlington, Texas; Hall, "Data Submitted by Thos. R. Hall," in Studdard, *Life of the Texas Pacific Coal & Oil Co.*, 44; Studdard, *Life of the Texas Pacific Coal & Oil Co.*, 100; E. G. Senter, "A Pioneer Texas Industry," *Texas Farm and Ranch*, January 22, 1898, reprinted in *Texas Mining and Trade Journal* (Thurber, Texas), October 1, 1898, vol. 3, no. 11, whole no. 115, pp. 12–13, Thurber Newspaper Collection; Schmidt, "Thurber Chronology," unpaged; *Gordon v. Texas & Pacific Mercantile & Mfg. Co.* in *Southwestern Reporter*, vol. 190, *January 17— February 7, 1917* (St. Paul, MN: West Publishing Company, 1917), 748–51; Hardman, *Fire in a Hole!* 104–5; Bielinski, *The Thurber Connection*, 178; Spratt, *Thurber, Texas*, 29, 55.

4. Lucadello, "Lucadello Memoir," unpaged, Ruby J. Schmidt Collection.
5. Ibid.
6. "Property Report, June 1st, 1900," in "Additions to Property and Various Inventories, 1900–1932," Ledger 602, Texas and Pacific Coal Company Records, S1021.1.
7. "The Thurber Mines," *Fort Worth Mail-Telegram*, May 14, 1896, Historical Edition, sec. 2, unpaged.
8. "Rent Book, 1910," Ledger 325; "Time Book, 1911–1914," Ledger 651, p. 158; the previous two sources are from the Texas and Pacific Coal Company Records, S1021.1; Baines, "Notes on Thurber, Texas," box 3, folder 1, unpaged, Thurber, Texas, Collection, S1076.1; Bryant, interview by Baker, July 15, 2004, transcript, pp. 17–18; Bryant, interview by Baker, August 25, 2004, transcript, p. 10; the previous two sources are at the W. K. Gordon Center for Industrial History of Texas, Tarleton State University, Mingus, Texas; "To Our Citizens," *Texas Miner* (Thurber, Texas), March 3, 1894, vol. 1, no. 7, p. 9, Thurber Newspaper Collection; Rhinehart, *A Way of Work*, 42–43; Studdard, *Life of the Texas Pacific Coal & Oil Co.*, 103–4; Hardman, *Fire in a Hole!* 100–103; Bielinski, *The Thurber Connection*, 208.
9. "Time Book, 1911–1914," Ledger 651, pp. 159, 163; "Time Book, 1920–1923," Ledger 653, pp. 1–5; the previous two sources are from the Texas and Pacific Coal Company Records, S1021.1; "Annual Report of the Texas and Pacific Coal Company for the Year Ended December 31, 1899," box 1, folder 4, p. 29, Texas and Pacific Coal Company Records, S1021.2; Sanborn Map Company, *Thurber, Erath County, Texas*, January 1905, 1:50, Digital Sanborn Map Collection, sheet 2;

Sanborn Map Company, *Thurber, Erath County, Texas,* April 1911, 1:50, Digital Sanborn Map Collection, sheet 3; Sanborn Map Company, *Thurber, Erath County, Texas,* January 1905, 1:50, Digital Sanborn Map Collection, sheet 3; Sanborn Map Company, *Thurber, Erath County, Texas,* April 1911, 1:50, Digital Sanborn Map Collection, sheet 4; Texas and Pacific Coal Company, [New York, NY], *Sketch Map of Thurber, Tex.,* September 1916, 1:200, Bennett Family Collection; Edgar L. Marston, New York, New York, to W. K. Gordon, Thurber, Texas, February 9, 1917, typewritten letter signed, letterpress copy, Correspondence Files, vol. 2, January 15, 1917 to November 23, 1917, pp. 48–49, Series VI, A, Miles B. Hart Collection; "The Thurber Mines," *Fort Worth Mail-Telegram,* May 14, 1896, Historical Edition, sec. 2, unpaged; Floyd, "Thurber, Texas," 61; Rhinehart, *A Way of Work,* 22–23, 32; Spratt, *Thurber, Texas,* 70–71; Studdard, *Life of the Texas Pacific Coal & Oil Co.,* 100–101, 106. The quotation is from Studdard, *Life of the Texas Pacific Coal & Oil Co.,* 106.

10. "Notice to Cotton Raisers," *Texas Miner* (Thurber, Texas), September 8, 1894, vol. 1, no. 34, p. 6, Thurber Newspaper Collection.
11. "Property Report, June 1st, 1900," in "Additions to Property and Various Inventories, 1900–1932," Ledger 602; "Texas Pacific Mercantile and Manufacturing Company, Additions to Property for the Year 1915," in "Additions to Property and Various Inventories, 1900–1932," Ledger 602; the previous two sources are from the Texas and Pacific Coal Company Records, S1021.1; "Receipt of Cotton Sold," box 1, folder 2, Thurber, Texas, Collection, S1076.1; "Annual Report of the Texas & Pacific Coal Co. and Texas Pacific Mercantile & Manufacturing Co. to the Stockholders for the Year Ending December 31, 1894," box 1, folder 3, p. 11; "1915 Annual Report," box 1, folder 10; "1916 Annual Report," box 1, folder 10; the previous three sources are from the Texas and Pacific Coal Company Records, S1021.2; Sanborn Map Company, *Thurber, Erath County, Texas,* January 1905, 1:50, Digital Sanborn Map Collection, sheet 2; Sanborn Map Company, *Thurber, Erath County, Texas,* April 1911, 1:50, Digital Sanborn Map Collection, sheet 3; Texas and Pacific Coal Company, [New York, NY], *Sketch Map of Thurber, Tex.,* September 1916, 1:200, Bennett Family Collection; "Notice to Cotton Raisers," *Texas Miner* (Thurber, Texas), September 8, 1894, vol. 1, no. 34, p. 6; "Cotton Ginning in Thurber," *Texas Miner* (Thurber, Texas), October 27, 1894, vol. 1, no. 41, p. 5; "Cotton Planters," *Texas Miner* (Thurber, Texas), January 12, 1895, vol. 1, no. 52, p. 6; the previous three articles are from the Thurber Newspaper Collection; R. D. Hunter, "Thurber Coal Mines," *Dallas Morning News,* July 19, 1895, p. 4; Spratt, *Thurber, Texas,* 74–75, 119; Spratt, *The Road to Spindletop,* 53. For more on cotton ginning in Texas, see Karen Gerhardt Britton, *Bale o' Cotton: The Mechanical Art of Cotton Ginning* (College Station: Texas A&M University Press, 1992).
12. "Time Book, 1911–1914," Ledger 651, p. 163, Texas and Pacific Coal Company

Records, S1021.1; "Annual Report of the Texas & Pacific Coal Company for the Fiscal Year Ended December 31st, 1903," box 1, folder 7, unpaged; "Annual Report of the Texas and Pacific Coal Company for the Year Ended December 31, 1899," box 1, folder 4, p. 28; "1916 Annual Report," box 1, folder 10, unpaged; the previous three sources are from the Texas and Pacific Coal Company Records, S1021.2; S. Mims, Fort Worth, Texas, to William K. Gordon, Thurber, Texas, August 25, 1894, typewritten letter signed, box 2, folder 8, Other Business Correspondence, Texas and Pacific Coal Company, June 1890–December 1899, W. K. Gordon, Sr., Papers, AR421; Schmidt, "Thurber Chronology," unpaged, Ruby J. Schmidt Collection; Edgar L. Marston, New York, New York, to Ed Britton, Thurber, Texas, May 18, 1916, typewritten letter signed, letterpress copy, Correspondence Files, vol. 1, February 1, 1916 to January 12, 1917, pp. 215–16, Series VI, A; Edgar L. Marston, New York, New York, to Ed Britton, Thurber, Texas, May 12, 1917, typewritten letter signed, letterpress copy, Correspondence Files, vol. 2, January 15, 1917 to November 23, 1917, p. 249, Series VI, A; Edgar L. Marston, New York, New York, to Ed Britton, Thurber, Texas, November 9, 1917, typewritten letter signed, letterpress copy, Correspondence Files, vol. 2, January 15, 1917 to November 23, 1917, p. 651, Series VI, A; Quarles, "Wonderful Exodus of Thurber Miners," unidentified Fort Worth newspaper clipping, September 15, 1903, Texas and Pacific Company Clipping Scrapbook (Strike, Sep. 1903), unpaged, Series VII; the previous four sources are from the Miles B. Hart Collection; Floyd, "Thurber, Texas," 61; Senter, "A Pioneer Texas Industry," *Texas Farm and Ranch,* January 22, 1898, reprinted in *Texas Mining and Trade Journal* (Thurber, Texas), October 1, 1898, vol. 3, no. 11, whole no. 115, pp. 12–13, Thurber Newspaper Collection; Texas and Pacific Coal Company, [New York, NY], *Sketch Map of Thurber, Tex.,* September 1916, 1:200, Bennett Family Collection; "The Thurber Mines," *Fort Worth Mail-Telegram,* May 14, 1896, Historical Edition, sec. 2, unpaged; "The Thurber Camp," *Dallas Morning News,* September 20, 1897, p. 4; Hardman, *Fire in a Hole!* 110–11; Spratt, *Thurber, Texas,* 31–32. The quotation is from Edgar L. Marston, New York, New York, to Ed Britton, Thurber, Texas, May 12, 1917, typewritten letter signed.

13. "Annual Report of the Texas and Pacific Coal Company for the Year Ended December 31, 1899," box 1, folder 4, p. 27, Texas and Pacific Coal Company Records, S1021.2; "Rent Book, 1910," Ledger 325, pp. 289–90ff., Texas and Pacific Coal Company Records, S1021.1; "1900," box 1, folder 3, unpaged, Texas Pacific Coal and Oil Company Financial Material, AR386; S. Mims, Fort Worth, Texas, to William K. Gordon, Thurber, Texas, August 25, 1894, typewritten letter signed, box 2, folder 8, Other Business Correspondence, Texas & Pacific Coal Company, June 1890–December 1899, W. K. Gordon, Sr., Papers, AR421.
14. "Farms!" *Texas Miner* (Thurber, Texas), February 3, 1894, vol. 1, no. 3, p. 7, Thurber Newspaper Collection.

15. "Annual Report of the Texas and Pacific Coal Company for the Year Ended December 31, 1899," box 1, folder 4, p. 27; "1916 Annual Report," box 1, folder 10, unpaged; the previous two sources are from the Texas and Pacific Coal Company Records, S1021.2; "Accounts Receivable Ledger, Farm and Pasture Rent, 1918–1920," Ledger 2, pp. 31, 58, 175, 184, 204, *passim;* "Rent Book, 1910," Ledger 325, pp. 289–90ff.; the previous two entries are from the Texas and Pacific Coal Company Records, S1021.1; "1900," box 1, folder 3, unpaged, Texas Pacific Coal and Oil Company Financial Material, AR386; S. Mims, Fort Worth, Texas, to William K. Gordon, Thurber, Texas, August 25, 1894, typewritten letter signed, box 2, folder 8, Other Business Correspondence, Texas and Pacific Coal Company, June 1890–December 1899, W. K. Gordon, Sr., Papers, AR421; "Farms!" *Texas Miner* (Thurber, Texas), February 3, 1894, vol. 1, no. 3, p. 7; "Local Notes," *Texas Miner* (Thurber, Texas), April 21, 1894, vol. 1, no. 12, p. 8; the previous two sources are from the Thurber Newspaper Collection; "Meeting of Department Managers Held Thursday Evening, April 27, 1905," T. P. M. & M.–Minutes, Mary Jane Gentry Collection, AR 95-13; Lucadello, "Lucadello Memoir," unpaged, Ruby J. Schmidt Collection; "The Thurber Mines," *Fort Worth Mail-Telegram,* May 14, 1896, Historical Edition, sec. 2, unpaged; R. D. Hunter, "Thurber Coal Mines," *Dallas Morning News,* July 19, 1895, p. 4; "The Thurber Camp," *Dallas Morning News,* September 20, 1897, p. 4; Floyd, "Thurber, Texas," 61; Bielinski, *The Thurber Connection,* 125; Leo S. Bielinski, "The Polish People of Thurber," *Polish Footprints* 21, no. 2 (Summer 2004): 3; Hardman, *Fire in a Hole!* 110–12; Studdard, *Life of the Texas Pacific Coal & Oil Co.,* 105.
16. "The Thurber Mines," *Fort Worth Mail-Telegram,* May 14, 1896, Historical Edition, sec. 2, unpaged; Julius Cahn, *Julius Cahn's Official Theatrical Guide,* vol. 6, *1901–1902* (New York: Publication Office, Empire Theatre Building, 1901), 669; "Brown's in Town" newspaper clipping from the *Texas Mining and Trade Journal* (Thurber, Texas), October 12, 1901, Texas and Pacific Company Clipping Scrapbook (1900–1901), unpaged, Series VII, Miles B. Hart Collection; "Meeting of the Mercantile Co., Held at the Opera House, Wednesday Night, May 10, 1905," T. P. M. & M.–Minutes; Thurber High School Graduation Invitation, 1930; the previous two sources are from the Mary Jane Gentry Collection, AR 95-13; "1916 Annual Report," box 1, folder 10, unpaged, Texas and Pacific Coal Company Records, S1021.2; Schmidt, "Thurber Chronology," unpaged; Lucadello, "Lucadello Memoir," unpaged; the previous two sources are from the Ruby J. Schmidt Collection; C. Richard King, "Opera Houses in West Texas," *West Texas Historical Association Year Book* 38 (1962): 100–101; Belfiglio, *The Italian Experience in Texas,* 115; Gentry, "Thurber," 163–167; Hardman, *Fire in a Hole!* 119–20; Bielinksi, *The Thurber Connection,* 175–77; John N. Cravens, "Two Miners

and Their Families in the Thurber-Strawn Coal Mines, 1905–1918," *West Texas Historical Association Year Book* 45 (1969), 118; Hooks, "Thurber," 10; Studdard, *Life of the Texas Pacific Coal & Oil Co.*, 81; Schuetz and Schuetz, *People-Events and Erath County,* 155; Edgar L. Marston, New York, New York, to Ed Britton, Thurber, Texas, May 18, 1916, typewritten letter signed, letterpress copy, Correspondence Files, Vol. 1, February 1, 1916 to January 12, 1917, pp. 215–16, Series VI, A, Miles B. Hart Collection; William Knox Gordon, Jr., Biographical Data Information Sheet and Questionnaire (based on interview), box 2, folder 1, Thurber, Texas, Collection, S1076.1; Cyrus Mowers household, 1910 U.S. Census, Erath County, Texas, Thurber Town, population schedule, Justice Precinct 7, enumeration district 30, supervisor's district 12, page 27, sheet 27a, dwelling 490, family 529, National Archives micropublication T624, roll 1551.

17. Edgar L. Marston, New York, New York, to Ed Britton, Thurber, Texas, May 18, 1916, typewritten letter signed, letterpress copy, Correspondence Files, Vol. 1, February 1, 1916 to January 12, 1917, pp. 215–216, Series VI, A, Miles B. Hart Collection.
18. William K. Gordon, Thurber, Texas, to Edgar L. Marston, New York, New York, January 10, 1900, typewritten letter, carbon copy, box 1, folder 20, E. L. Marston Correspondence, E. L. Marston and W. K. Gordon, January–July 1900, W. K. Gordon, Sr., Papers, AR421; *Texas Miner* (Thurber, Texas), January 27, 1894, vol. 1, no. 2; "Thurber E La Colonia Italiana," *Texas Miner* (Thurber, Texas), March 3, 1894, vol. 1, no. 7, p. 5; "Local Notes," *Texas Miner* (Thurber, Texas), March 3, 1894, vol. 1, no. 7, p. 5; "Send the Miner Back Home," *Texas Miner* (Thurber, Texas), March 24, 1894, vol. 1, no. 10, p. 5; Senter, "A Pioneer Texas Industry," *Texas Farm and Ranch,* January 22, 1898, reprinted in *Texas Mining and Trade Journal* (Thurber, Texas), October 1, 1898, vol. 3, no. 11, whole no. 115, pp. 12–13; the previous five sources are from the Thurber Newspaper Collection; Rhinehart, *A Way of Work,* 53–54; Hardman, *Boom Town,* 26–27; Hardman, *Fire in a Hole!* 112–13; Spratt, *Thurber, Texas,* 71; Studdard, *Life of the Texas Pacific Coal & Oil Co.,* 99.
19. "Thurber E La Colonia Italiana," *Texas Miner* (Thurber, Texas), March 3, 1894, vol. 1, no. 7, p. 5.
20. "Local Notes," *Texas Miner* (Thurber, Texas), March 3, 1894, vol. 1, no. 7, p. 5, Thurber Newspaper Collection.
21. William K. Gordon, Thurber, Texas, to Edgar L. Marston, New York, New York, January 10, 1900, typewritten letter, carbon copy, box 1, folder 20, E. L. Marston Correspondence, E. L. Marston and W. K. Gordon, January–July 1900, W. K. Gordon, Sr., Papers, AR421.
22. Edgar L. Marston, New York, New York, to Ed Britton, Thurber, Texas, March 19, 1918, typewritten letter signed, letterpress copy, Correspondence Files, Vol. 3, November 24, 1917 to September 17, 1918, pp. 301–302, Series VI, A;

Edgar L. Marston, New York, New York, to John D. Rockefeller, Jr., New York, New York, September 6, 1916, typewritten letter signed, letterpress copy, Correspondence Files, Vol. 1, February 1, 1916 to January 12, 1917, p. 447, Series VI, A; the previous two sources are from the Miles B. Hart Collection; "1916 Annual Report," box 1, folder 10, unpaged, Texas and Pacific Coal Company Records, S1021.2; "Texas Pacific Mercantile and Manufacturing Company, Additions to Property for the Year 1908," in "Additions to Property and Various Inventories, 1900–1932," Ledger 602, Texas and Pacific Coal Company Records, S1021.1; Sanborn Map Company, *Thurber, Erath County, Texas,* January 1905, 1:50, Digital Sanborn Map Collection, sheet 1; Sanborn Map Company, *Thurber, Erath County, Texas,* April 1911, 1:50, Digital Sanborn Map Collection, sheet 1; Rhinehart, *A Way of Work,* 53–54; Hardman, *Boom Town,* 26–27; Hardman, *Fire in a Hole!* 112–113; Spratt, *Thurber, Texas,* 71; Studdard, *Life of the Texas Pacific Coal & Oil Co.,* 99.

23. "Annual Report of the Texas & Pacific Coal Co. and Texas Pacific Mercantile & Manufacturing Co. to the Stockholders for the Year Ending December 31, 1894," box 1, folder 3, pp. 2–3; "Texas and Pacific Coal Company Annual Report to the Stockholders for the Year Ended December 31st, 1898," box 1, folder 3, unpaged; the previous two sources are from the Texas and Pacific Coal Company Records, S1021.2; "The Thurber Mines," *Fort Worth Mail-Telegram,* May 14, 1896, Historical Edition, sec. 2, unpaged; "Hotel Knox Inventory, October 1st 1904," in "Additions to Property and Various Inventories, 1900–1932," Ledger 602; "Property Report, June 1st, 1900," in "Additions to Property and Various Inventories, 1900–1932," Ledger 602; the previous two sources are from the Texas and Pacific Coal Company Records, S1021.1; "The New Hotel Knox," *Texas Miner* (Thurber, Texas), October 13, 1894, vol. 1, no. 21, p. supplement; "Local Notes," *Texas Miner* (Thurber, Texas), October 13, 1894, vol. 1, no. 39, p. 6; "Local Notes," *Texas Miner* (Thurber, Texas), February 16, 1895, vol. 2, no. 5, p. 10; Senter, "A Pioneer Texas Industry," *Texas Farm and Ranch,* January 22, 1898, reprinted in *Texas Mining and Trade Journal* (Thurber, Texas), October 1, 1898, vol. 3, no. 11, whole no. 115, pp. 12–13; T. P. M. & M. Co., "Now Open" (advertisement), *Texas Mining and Trade Journal* (Thurber, Texas), January 13, 1900, vol. 4, no. 26, whole no. 182, p. 20; the previous five sources are from the Thurber Newspaper Collection; *Texas Mining and Trade Journal,* February 27, 1898 in Gentry, "Thurber," 150; "Our 'Gusher' Gushes Mo [*sic*] More," newspaper clipping from the *Texas Mining and Trade Journal* (Thurber, Texas), May 18, 1901, Texas and Pacific Company Clipping Scrapbook (1900–1901), unpaged, Series VII, Miles B. Hart Collection; R. F. Binney, interview by Richard Mason, January 15, 1982, Arlington, Texas, Oral History Collection, Southwest Collection, Texas Tech University Libraries, Texas Tech University, Lubbock, Texas; Sanborn Map Company, *Thurber, Erath County, Texas,* January 1905, 1:50,

Digital Sanborn Map Collection, sheet 1; Sanborn Map Company, *Thurber, Erath County, Texas,* April 1911, 1:50, Digital Sanborn Map Collection, sheet 1; Gordon, "Data Submitted by W. K. Gordon," in Studdard, *Life of the Texas Pacific Coal & Oil Co.,* 26; Gentry, "Thurber," 150–52; Schuetz and Schuetz, *People-Events and Erath County,* 155; Hardman, *Fire in a Hole!* 104–05; Bielinski, *The Thurber Connection,* 177–78.

24. Sanborn Map Company, *Thurber, Erath County, Texas,* January 1905, 1:50, Digital Sanborn Map Collection, sheet 1; Sanborn Map Company, *Thurber, Erath County, Texas,* April 1911, 1:50, Digital Sanborn Map Collection, sheet 1; "To the Stockholders of the Texas & Pacific Coal Company: The Results of Operations for the Year Ending December 21, 1913," box 1, folder 10; "1915 Annual Report," box 1, folder 10, unpaged; "1916 Annual Report," box 1, folder 10, unpaged; the previous three sources are from Texas and Pacific Coal Company Records, S1021.2; "Invited to Confer," *Dallas Morning News,* September 18, 1903, p. 2; Cantey H. Ferchill, "A Survey and Comparison of the Cultural Landscapes of Two Early-Twentieth Century Coal-Mining Communities: Thurber, Texas and Buxton, Iowa" (master's thesis, University of Texas at Arlington, 1995), 134; Floyd, "Thurber, Texas," 93; Studdard, *Life of the Texas Pacific Coal & Oil Co.,* 80, 94–95; Bielinski, *The Thurber Connection,* 208, 211.

25. D. H. Killar, "The Germ Theory: What Profits It?" *The Medical Brief,* quoted in W. A. Burr, "General Medicine," *The Critique* 7, no. 3 (March 15, 1900): 85–86.

26. *Texas & Pacific Coal Co. v. Connaughton* in *Southwestern Reporter,* vol. 50, *April 5–May 29, 1899* (St. Paul, MN: West Publishing Company, 1899), 173–75.

27. "To the Stockholders of the Texas & Pacific Coal Company: The Results of Operations for the Year Ending December 21, 1913," box 1, folder 10; "1915 Annual Report," box 1, folder 10, unpaged; "1916 Annual Report," box 1, folder 10, unpaged; the previous three sources are from the Texas and Pacific Coal Company Records, S1021.2; "Invited to Confer," *Dallas Morning News,* September 18, 1903, p. 2; Ferchill, "A Survey and Comparison," 134; Studdard, *Life of the Texas Pacific Coal & Oil Co.,* 80, 94–95; Bielinski, *The Thurber Connection,* 208, 211.

28. "Rent Book, 1924," Ledger 339, pp. 414–20, Texas and Pacific Coal Company Records, S1021.1; Sanborn Map Company, *Thurber, Erath County, Texas,* January 1905, 1:50, Digital Sanborn Map Collection, sheet 1; Sanborn Map Company, *Thurber, Erath County, Texas,* April 1911, 1:50, Digital Sanborn Map Collection, sheet 1; William Knox Gordon, Jr., Biographical Data Information Sheet and Questionnaire (based on interview), box 2, folder 1, Thurber, Texas, Collection, S1076.1; Robert E. Ayers, 1910 U.S. Census, Erath County, Texas, Thurber Town, population schedule, Justice Precinct 7, enumeration district 30, supervisor's district 12, page 16, sheet 16b, dwelling 281, family 311, National Archives micropublication T624, roll 1551; "General Ledger Subsidiary, A-60 Physical Property–Town and Farm Department, All Properties–Texas, January 1, 1924 to

December 31, 1937," unpaged, Bennett Family Collection; Ferchill, "A Survey and Comparison," 134; Floyd, "Thurber, Texas," 93; Studdard, *Life of the Texas Pacific Coal & Oil Co.*, 80, 94–95; Bielinski, *The Thurber Connection*, 211.

29. "Time Book, 1911–1914," Ledger 651, pp. 159, 163; "Time Book, 1920–1923," Ledger 653, pp. 1–5; the previous two sources are from the Texas and Pacific Coal Company Records, S1021.1; "Directors' Meeting Minutes, 1894–1906," box 5, folder 27, pp. 1–6, Texas and Pacific Coal Company Records, S1021.2.

Chapter 5

1. "TP's Birthplace," 5; 1900 U.S. Census, Erath County, Texas, Thurber, population schedule, Justice Precinct 7, National Archives micropublication T623, computer analysis of database for Thurber by the author; Rhinehart, *A Way of Work*, 12–15; Hardman, *Fire in a Hole!* 127; Grimshaw, "Hard, Heavy Lifting," chap. 5; Lucadello, "Lucadello Memoir," unpaged, Ruby J. Schmidt Collection.
2. 1900 U.S. Census, Erath County, Texas, Thurber, population schedule, Justice Precinct 7, National Archives micropublication T623, computer analysis of database for Thurber by the author; 1910 U.S. Census, Erath County, Texas, Thurber Town, population schedule, Justice Precinct 7, National Archives micropublication T624, computer analysis of database for Thurber by the author; "Time Book, 1911–1914," Ledger 651; "Time Book, 1920–1923," Ledger 653; "Payroll Book, Mine, 1900–1902," Ledger 121; "Cash and Check Sales Record, 1897–1907," Ledger 606, pp. 208, 228–73; the previous four sources are from the Texas and Pacific Coal Company Records, S1021.1; Texas and Pacific Coal Company, [New York, NY], *Sketch Map of Thurber, Tex.*, September 1916, 1:200, Bennett Family Collection; "Meeting of Department Managers held Wednesday Evening May 3, 1905," T. P. M. & M.–Minutes, Mary Jane Gentry Collection, AR 95-13; Hooks, "Thurber," 6–7; Rhinehart, *A Way of Work*, 12–15; Gentry, "Thurber," 112–113; Hardman, *Fire in a Hole!* 91–92.
3. William Knox Gordon, Jr., Biographical Data Information Sheet and Questionnaire (based on interview), box 2, folder 1, Thurber, Texas, Collection, S1076.1; Lillie Ivey Gibson, interview by T. Lindsay Baker and LeAnna S. Schooley, February 28, 2006, Stephenville, Texas, notes, W. K. Gordon Center for Industrial History of Texas, Tarleton State University, Mingus, Texas; Santi, interview by George Green, transcript, p. 6; Rhinehart, "Underground Patriots," 516; Hooks, "Thurber," 6–7; "Cash and Check Sales Record, 1897–1907," Ledger 606, pp. 208, 228–73, Texas and Pacific Coal Company Records, S1021.1; Gentry, "Thurber," 112–13; Hardman, *Fire in a Hole!* 91–92; Texas and Pacific Coal Company, [New York, NY], *Sketch Map of Thurber, Tex.*, September 1916, 1:200, Bennett Family Collection; "Meeting of Department Managers held Wednesday Evening May 3, 1905," T. P. M. & M.–Minutes, Mary Jane Gentry Collection, AR 95-13; Bielinski, *The Thurber Connection*, 135, 189, 210.

4. "The Thurber Mines," *Fort Worth Mail-Telegram,* May 14, 1896, Historical Edition, sec. 2, unpaged; Rhinehart, "Underground Patriots," 516, 518; Rhinehart, *A Way of Work,* 30–31, 44–45, 60–61; Hardman, *Fire in a Hole!* 119–20, 124–25; "Thurber E La Colonia Italiana," *Texas Miner* (Thurber, Texas), March 3, 1894, vol. 1, no. 7, p. 5; Senter, "A Pioneer Texas Industry," *Texas Farm and Ranch,* January 22, 1898, reprinted in *Texas Mining and Trade Journal* (Thurber, Texas), October 1, 1898, vol. 3, no. 11, whole no. 115, pp. 12–13; the previous two sources, and other examples of society columns as well as Italian and Polish articles, can be found in the Thurber Newspaper Collection; Grimshaw, "Hard, Heavy Lifting," chap. 5; "Time Book, 1911–1914," Ledger 651, pp. 157–64; "Voucher Record, 1903–1905," Ledger 674, p. 5; the previous two sources are from the Texas and Pacific Coal Company Records, S1021.1; William Preston Powers, "The Subversion of 'Gordon's Kingdom': The Unionization of the Texas and Pacific Coal Mines at Thurber, Texas, 1888–1903" (master's thesis, University of Texas at Arlington, 1989), 48, 90–91; *By-Laws of the R. D. Hunter Fishing & Boating Club, Thurber, Texas* (Thurber, TX: Texas Pacific Mercantile and Manufacturing Company, 1904), 3–4, 16, W. K. Gordon Center for Industrial History of Texas, Tarleton State University, Mingus, Texas.
5. Bielinski, "The Italian Presence," 35; 1900 U.S. Census, Erath County, Texas, Thurber, population schedule, Justice Precinct 7, National Archives micropublication T623, computer analysis of database for Thurber by the author; 1910 U.S. Census, Erath County, Texas, Thurber Town, population schedule, Justice Precinct 7, National Archives micropublication T624, computer analysis of database for Thurber by the author; Mary Britton household, 1880 U.S. Census, Parker County, Texas, population schedule, Weatherford, enumeration district H-Ward, supervisor's district 3, page 329, sheet 19, family 174; National Archives micropublication T9, roll 1322; Morris, *A Private in the Texas Rangers,* 271; "Meeting of the Mercantile Co., Held at the Opera House, Wednesday Night, May 10, 1905," T. P. M. & M.–Minutes, Mary Jane Gentry Collection, AR 95-13; "Time Book, 1911–1914," Ledger 651, pp. 157–64; "Time Book, 1920–1923," Ledger 653, pp. 1–5; the previous two sources are from the Texas and Pacific Coal Company Records, S1021.1; "Made a Change in Business All Around," clipping from the *Texas Mining and Trade Journal* (Thurber, Texas), September 8, 1900, Texas and Pacific Company Clipping Scrapbook (1900–1901), unpaged, Series VII, Miles B. Hart Collection; "Newsclippings in Regard to Mr. A. B. Marston's Death, December 8, 1902," Marston Family Scrapbooks, NC449, unpaged, Special Collections Department, University of Nevada–Reno Library, University of Nevada–Reno, Reno, Nevada; "Coal Man's Sudden Death," *New York Times,* December 9, 1902, p. 1; "Marston's Sudden Death," *Dallas Morning News,* December 10, 1902, p. 2; "Death of Mr. Marston," *Dallas Morning News,* December 9, 1902, p. 4; Marston, *The Marston Genealogy,* 59, 67; Lena R. Lewis, *Erath County: A Compilation* (Stephenville, TX: privately printed, 1940), 154.

6. Maroney, "The Unionization of Thurber," 28; "Thurber on Strike," *United Mine Workers' Journal,* September 24, 1903; Gentry, "Thurber," 106; Gomer Gower to Mary J. Gentry, January 18, 1945, letter, in Gentry, "Thurber," 235–36; Rhinehart, "Underground Patriots," 520–522; Rhinehart, *A Way of Work,* 45–46; *Texas & Pacific v. Lawson,* pp. 269, 271; "Country Buyers in Thurber," clipping from the *Texas Mining and Trade Journal* (Thurber, Texas), October 6, 1900, Texas and Pacific Company Clipping Scrapbook (1900–1901), unpaged, Series VII, Miles B. Hart Collection; Hut Brock, by Karl Andrews, Biographical Data Information Sheet and Questionnaire (based on interview), box 3, folder 12, unpaged, Thurber, Texas, Collection, S1076.1; Skaggs, "To Build a Barony," 254–55; Fishback, "Did Coal Miners 'Owe Their Souls to the Company Store'?" 1021.

7. "Meeting of Department Managers Held Thursday Evening, June 1, 1905," unpaged, T. P. M. & M.–Minutes, Mary Jane Gentry Collection, AR 95-13.

8. Ibid.

9. Ibid.

10. Ibid.

11. Bernice Bearden, "Mingus Founded in 1890," in *History of Palo Pinto County, Texas* (Dallas: Curtis Media Corporation, 1986), 533; Leo S. Bielinski, "Mingus: Little Known Facts about a Well Known Town," in *History of Palo Pinto County, Texas* (Dallas: Curtis Media Corporation, 1986), 534–36; Cravens, "Two Miners," 119; "News from Mingus," *Dallas Morning News,* January 10, 1899, p. 4; "Mingus Matters," *Dallas Morning News,* November 20, 1897, p. 2; "Annual Report of the Texas & Pacific Coal Co. to the Stockholders for the Year Ending December 31, 1897," box 1, folder 3, unpaged, Texas and Pacific Coal Company Records, S1021.2; Spratt, *Thurber, Texas,* 7.

12. "Annual Report of the Texas & Pacific Coal Co. to the Stockholders for the Year Ending December 31, 1897," box 1, folder 3, unpaged, Texas and Pacific Coal Company Records, S1021.2.

13. "Annual Report of the Texas and Pacific Coal Company for the Year Ended December 31, 1899," box 1, folder 4, p. 8, Texas and Pacific Coal Company Records, S1021.2.

14. Bearden, "Mingus Founded in 1890," 533; Bielinski, "Mingus," 534–36; Cravens, "Two Miners," 119; Joe Ronchetti household, 1900 U.S. Census, Palo Pinto County, Texas, population schedule, Justice Precinct 3, enumeration district 121, supervisor's district 4, page 124, sheet 5, dwelling 96, family 96; James Corona household, 1900 U.S. Census, Palo Pinto County, Texas, population schedule, Justice Precinct 3, enumeration district 121, supervisor's district 4, page 124, sheet 5, dwelling 96, family 97; Bartester Mazzano household, 1900 U.S. Census, Palo Pinto County, Texas, population schedule, Justice Precinct 3, enumeration district 121, supervisor's district 4, page 124, sheet 5, dwelling 97, family 98; George Sealfi household, 1900 U.S. Census, Palo Pinto County, Texas, popula-

tion schedule, Justice Precinct 3, enumeration district 121, supervisor's district 4, page 124, sheet 5, dwelling 98, family 99; the previous four records can all found in National Archives micropublication T623, roll 1663; Bielinski, "The Italian Presence," 35; Jarrard Foster, Thurber, Texas, to J. W. Everman, Dallas, Texas, September 19, 1899, autograph letter signed, pp. 14–15, Teddy Rowland Collection, W. K. Gordon Center for Industrial History of Texas, Tarleton State University, Mingus, Texas; Spratt, *Thurber, Texas,* 7.

15. "Strike of Miners," *Dallas Morning News,* September 11, 1903, p. 9.
16. Ibid.
17. "Coal Mine Strike," *Dallas Morning News,* September 13, 1903, p. 1.
18. "Thurber on Strike," *United Mine Workers' Journal,* September 24, 1903.
19. Ibid.
20. "Strike of Miners," *Dallas Morning News,* September 11, 1903, p. 9.
21. David Corbin, *Life, Work, and Rebellion in the Coal Fields: The Southern West Virginia Miners, 1880–1922* (Urbana: University of Illinois Press, 1981), 10.
22. Powers, "The Subversion of 'Gordon's Kingdom,'" 49–50.
23. Leo S. Bielinski, *The Back Road to Thurber* (Baird, TX: Joy Presswork Collection, 1993), 152—53.
24. William P. Dillingham, et al., *Reports of the Immigration Commission: Immigrants in Industry,* part 1, vol. 1, *Bituminous Coal Mining* (Washington, DC: Government Printing Office, 1911), 95.
25. Ibid., 327.
26. Fishback, "Did Coal Miners," 1012; see also Fishback, *Soft Coal, Hard Choices,* chap. 8.
27. "Strike of Miners," *Dallas Morning News,* September 11, 1903, p. 9.
28. "She Tells of First Trouble," unidentified newspaper clipping, ca. September 1903, Texas and Pacific Company Clipping Scrapbook (Strike, Sep. 1903), unpaged, Series VII, Miles B. Hart Collection.
29. Ibid.; W. K. Gordon, "No Smallpox at Thurber," *Dallas Morning News,* March 30, 1901, p. 7.
30. "She Tells of First Trouble," unidentified newspaper clipping, ca. September 1903, Texas and Pacific Company Clipping Scrapbook (Strike, Sep. 1903), unpaged, Series VII, Miles B. Hart Collection; "The Check System," newspaper clipping from the *Fort Worth Telegram,* ca. September 1903, Texas and Pacific Company Clipping Scrapbook (1900–1904), p. 10, Series VII; James Hayes Quarles, "Town of Thurber May Be Abandoned," unidentified Fort Worth newspaper clipping, September 16, 1903, Texas and Pacific Company Clipping Scrapbook (Strike, Sep. 1903), unpaged, Series VII; James Hayes Quarles, "Wonderful Exodus of Thurber Miners," unidentified Fort Worth newspaper clipping, September 15, 1903, Texas and Pacific Company Clipping Scrapbook (Strike, Sep. 1903), unpaged, Series VII; "She Tells of First Trouble," unidentified

newspaper clipping, ca. September 1903, Texas and Pacific Company Clipping Scrapbook (Strike, Sep. 1903), unpaged, Series VII; the previous four sources are from the Miles B. Hart Collection; "Invited to Confer," *Dallas Morning News,* September 18, 1903, p. 2; S. E. Stelle Brooks, by Karl Andrews, Biographical Data Information Sheet and Questionnaire (based on interview), box 3, folder 12; Lorene Smith Dobson, by Ann Clark, Biographical Data Information Sheet and Questionnaire (based on interview), box 3, folder 12; Irene Ryan Laird, by Ann Clark, Biographical Data Information Sheet and Questionnaire (based on interview), box 3, folder 13; Mary Williams Merritt, by Ann Clark, Biographical Data Information Sheet and Questionnaire (based on interview), box 3, folder 13; Aurora Catherine Marchioni Maldino, by Karl Andrews, Biographical Data Information Sheet and Questionnaire (based on interview), box 2, folder 1; the previous five sources are from the Thurber, Texas, Collection, S1076.1.

31. William K. Gordon, Thurber, Texas, to Edgar L. Marston, New York, New York, March 1, 1908, typewritten letter, carbon copy, box 1, folder 22, E. L. Marston Correspondence, E. L. Marston and W. K. Gordon, December 1906–March 1908, W. K. Gordon, Sr., Papers, AR421.
32. Ibid.
33. J'Nell L. Pate, "Rock Creek Community and Mines in Parker County," *West Texas Historical Association Year Book* 80 (2004): 41–52; the quotation is from p. 47.
34. S. E. Stelle Brooks, by Karl Andrews, Biographical Data Information Sheet and Questionnaire (based on interview), box 3, folder 12; Lorene Smith Dobson, by Ann Clark, Biographical Data Information Sheet and Questionnaire (based on interview), box 3, folder 12; Irene Ryan Laird, by Ann Clark, Biographical Data Information Sheet and Questionnaire (based on interview), box 3, folder 13; Mary Williams Merritt, by Ann Clark, Biographical Data Information Sheet and Questionnaire (based on interview), box 3, folder 13; Aurora Catherine Marchioni Maldino, by Karl Andrews, Biographical Data Information Sheet and Questionnaire (based on interview), box 2, folder 1; the previous five sources are from the Thurber, Texas, Collection, S1076.1.
35. William Knox Gordon, Jr., Biographical Data Information Sheet and Questionnaire (based on interview), box 2, folder 1; Conia Duke McKinnon, by Cathy Sue Wincovitch, Biographical Data Information Sheet and Questionnaire (based on interview), box 2, folder 1; Roscoe Hayden Sherrill, by Ann Clark, Biographical Data Information Sheet and Questionnaire (based on interview), box 2, folder 1; Earl L. Brown, by Ruth Hosey, Biographical Data Information Sheet and Questionnaire (based on interview), box 3, folder 12; John Douglas Conn, by Penny Green, Biographical Data Information Sheet and Questionnaire (based on interview), box 3, folder 12; Ruth Elaine Calloway Costa, by Ann Clark, Biographical Data Information Sheet and Questionnaire (based on interview), box 3, folder 12; the previous six sources are from the Thurber, Texas, Collec-

tion, S1076.1; there are other examples in the same collection; Higginbotham's Company, "Some Sound Facts" (advertisement), *Stephenville Empire,* October 9, 1896, unpaged; Higginbotham's Company, "Well, Here They Go!" (advertisement), *Stephenville Empire,* December 4, 1896, unpaged; T. P. M. & M. Co., "Grocery Department" (advertisement), *Texas Miner* (Thurber, Texas), October 20, 1894, vol. 1, no. 40, p. 18; "Down in a Coal Mine," *Dallas Morning News,* June 19, 1894, p. 4; James Hayes Quarles, "Town of Thurber May Be Abandoned," unidentified Fort Worth newspaper clipping, September 16, 1903, Texas and Pacific Company Clipping Scrapbook (Strike, Sep. 1903), unpaged, Series VII; James Hayes Quarles, "Wonderful Exodus of Thurber Miners," unidentified Fort Worth newspaper clipping, September 15, 1903, Texas and Pacific Company Clipping Scrapbook (Strike, Sep. 1903), unpaged, Series VII; the previous two sources are from the Miles B. Hart Collection.

36. "Down in a Coal Mine," *Dallas Morning News,* June 19, 1894, p. 4.

37. William Knox Gordon, Jr., Biographical Data Information Sheet and Questionnaire (based on interview), box 2, folder 1; T. P. M. & M. Co., "Grocery Department" (advertisement), *Texas Miner* (Thurber, Texas), October 20, 1894, vol. 1, no. 40, p. 18; Spratt, *Thurber, Texas,* 14, 64.

38. *George Scalfi et al. v. John R. Graves,* in *Texas Civil Appeals Report,* vol. 31, *Cases Argued and Adjudged in the Courts of Civil Appeals of the State of Texas during the Early Part of the Year 1903* (Austin: Gammel-Statesman Publishing Company, 1903), 667–70; *George Scalfi & Co. et al. v. State of Texas,* in *Texas Civil Appeals Report,* vol. 31, 671–75.

39. "The Observation of an Old Line Pro," handbill, n.p., [June 1903], Texas and Pacific Company Clipping Scrapbook (1900–1904), p. 24, Series VII, Miles B. Hart Collection.

40. Schuetz and Schuetz, *People-Events and Erath County, Texas,* 150.

41. Ibid.

42. "Thurber on Strike," *United Mine Workers' Journal,* September 24, 1903, in Allen, *Chapters in the History of Organized Labor in Texas,* 94–95; "Payroll Book, Mine, 1900–1902," Ledger 121; "Payroll Book, Mine, 1903," Ledger 122; "Payroll Book, Mine, 1904–1905," Ledger 123; "Payroll Book, Mine, 1910," Ledger 128; the previous four sources are from the Texas and Pacific Coal Company Records, S1021.1; William K. Gordon, Thurber, Texas, to Edgar L. Marston, New York, New York, December 5, 1899, typewritten letter, carbon copy, box 1, folder 19, p. 2, E. L. Marston Correspondence, E. L. Marston and W. K. Gordon, December 1899, W. K. Gordon, Sr., Papers, AR421; Powers, "The Subversion of 'Gordon's Kingdom,'" 45–49; Rhinehart, *A Way of Work,* 32–33; "The Strike at Thurber," newspaper clipping from the *Empire* (Stephenville, Texas), September 17, 1903, Texas and Pacific Company Clipping Scrapbook (1900–1904), p. 40, Series VII,

Miles B. Hart Collection; T. P. M. & M. Co., "Employes [*sic*] can find . . ." (advertisement), *Texas Mining and Trade Journal* (Thurber, Texas), October 6, 1900, Texas and Pacific Company Clipping Scrapbook (1900–1901), unpaged, Series VII, Miles B. Hart Collection; "New Incorporations," *Dallas Morning News,* March 17, 1907, p. 2; "The Thurber Camp," *Dallas Morning News,* September 20, 1897, p. 4; Fishback, "Did Coal Miners," 1028; Bielinski, *The Thurber Connection,* 72–74; Spratt, *Thurber, Texas,* 13–14; "Annual Report of the Texas & Pacific Coal Company for the Fiscal Year Ended December 31st, 1902," box 1, folder 6, Texas and Pacific Coal Company Records, S1021.2.

43. "The Thurber Camp," *Dallas Morning News,* September 20, 1897, p. 4.
44. "Annual Report of the Texas & Pacific Coal Company for the Fiscal Year Ended December 31st, 1902," box 1, folder 6, Texas and Pacific Coal Company Records, S1021.2.
45. "The Strike at Thurber," newspaper clipping from the *Empire* (Stephenville, Texas), September 17, 1903, Texas and Pacific Company Clipping Scrapbook (1900–1904), p. 40, Series VII, Miles B. Hart Collection.
46. "Thurber on Strike," *United Mine Workers' Journal,* September 24, 1903.
47. See various instances in "Payroll Book, Mine, 1900–1902," Ledger 121; "Payroll Book, Mine, 1903," Ledger 122; "Payroll Book, Mine, 1904–1905," Ledger 123; "Payroll Book, Mine, 1910," Ledger 128; the previous four sources are from the Texas and Pacific Coal Company Records, S1021.1; Eliot Lord, John J. D. Trenor, and Samuel J. Barrows, *The Italian in America* (New York: B. F. Buck & Company, 1905), 110–13. See also Fishback, *Soft Coal, Hard Choices,* chap. 8.
48. "Thurber on Strike," *United Mine Workers' Journal,* September 24, 1903, in Allen, *Chapters in the History of Organized Labor in Texas,* 94–95; "Invited to Confer," *Dallas Morning News,* September 18, 1903, p. 2; "Strike of Miners," *Dallas Morning News,* September 11, 1903, p. 9; "Settling Thurber Trouble," *Fort Worth Star-Telegram,* September 20, 1903, p. 1.
49. "Settling Thurber Trouble," *Fort Worth Star-Telegram,* September 20, 1903, p. 1.
50. Stefan Nesterowicz, *Notatki z podróży po północnej i środkowej Ameryce* [Travel notes through northern and middle America] (Toledo, OH: A. A. Paryski, 1909), 157; Stefan Nesterowicz, *Travel Notes,* trans. and ed. Marion Moore Coleman (Cheshire, CT: Cherry Hill Books, 1970), 79.
51. "Union Makes Good," *Dallas Morning News,* September 17, 1903, p. 2; "Settling Thurber Trouble," *Fort Worth Star-Telegram,* September 20, 1903, p. 1; "From Thurber, Texas," *Official Journal: Amalgamated Meat Cutters and Butcher Workmen of North America* 7, no. 6 (April 1906): 34; "Contract Firm Agreements," *Machinists' Monthly Journal* 19, no. 10 (October 1907): 970; Allen, *Chapters in the History of Organized Labor in Texas,* 146–47; "Meeting of Department Managers Held Thursday Evening, June 1, 1905," unpaged, T. P. M. & M.–Minutes, Mary

Jane Gentry Collection, AR 95-13; "Annual Report of the Texas & Pacific Coal Company for the Fiscal Year Ended December 31st, 1903," box 1, folder 7, unpaged, Texas and Pacific Coal Company Records, S1021.2; "May Ask for Conference," clipping from the *Dallas Times-Herald,* ca. September 13, 1903, Texas and Pacific Company Clipping Scrapbook (1900–1904), p. 10, Series VII; "Thurber Is Now a Deserted Village," clipping from the *Fort Worth Register,* ca. September 15, 1903, Texas and Pacific Company Clipping Scrapbook (1900–1904), p. 11, Series VII; "Miners Hold a Mass Meeting," unidentified newspaper clipping, ca. September 12, 1903, Texas and Pacific Company Clipping Scrapbook (1900–1904), p. 12, Series VII; the previous three sources are from the Miles B. Hart Collection; Gentry, "Thurber," 93–94.

52. "Annual Report of the Texas & Pacific Coal Company for the Fiscal Year Ended December 31st, 1903," box 1, folder 7, unpaged, Texas and Pacific Coal Company Records, S1021.2.
53. "Cash and Check Sales Record, 1894–1895," Ledger 605, pp. 22–45; "Cash and Check Sales Record, 1897–1907," Ledger 606, pp. 56–79, 228–73; "Cash and Check Sales Record, 1908–1914," Ledger 607, pp. 74–108; "Cash and Check Sales Record, 1914–1927," Ledger 608, pp. 10–43; the previous four sources are from the Texas and Pacific Coal Company Records, S1021.1; "Meeting of Department Managers Held Thursday Evening, June 1, 1905," unpaged, T. P. M. & M.–Minutes, Mary Jane Gentry Collection, AR 95-13.
54. Bearden, "Mingus Founded in 1890," in *History of Palo Pinto County, Texas,* 533; Leo S. Bielinski, "The Immigrants of Southwest Palo Pinto County: The Italians," in *History of Palo Pinto County, Texas,* 638–639; Leo S. Bielinski, "The Immigrants of Southwest Palo Pinto County: The Lebanese," in *History of Palo Pinto County, Texas,* 536–37; "Mingus or Thurber Junction, Texas Business and Professional Directory 1908," USGenWeb Archives, http://files.usgwarchives.net/tx/erath/history/mingus.txt (accessed January 29, 2012); Bielinski, "Mingus," 534–36; Spratt, *Thurber, Texas,* 14, 62–64.
55. William K. Gordon, Thurber, Texas, to Edgar L. Marston, New York, New York, August 8, 1911, typewritten letter, carbon copy, box 1, folder 25, pp. 6–7, E. L. Marston Correspondence, E. L. Marston and W. K. Gordon, August–October 1911, W. K. Gordon, Sr., Papers, AR421.
56. William K. Gordon, Thurber, Texas, to Edgar L. Marston, New York, New York, August 8, 1911, typewritten letter, carbon copy, box 1, folder 25, pp. 6–7; William K. Gordon, Thurber, Texas, to Edgar L. Marston, New York, New York, August 27, 1911, typewritten letter, carbon copy, box 1, folder 25, p. 3; the previous two sources are from E. L. Marston Correspondence, E. L. Marston and W. K. Gordon, August–October 1911, W. K. Gordon, Sr., Papers, AR421; Bielinski, "Mingus," 534–36; Spratt, *Thurber, Texas,* 55–67.

57. "Meeting of Department Managers Held Thursday Evening, June 1, 1905," unpaged, T. P. M. & M.–Minutes, Mary Jane Gentry Collection, AR 95-13.

58. Ibid.

59. "Meeting of Department Managers Held Thursday Evening, April 27, 1905," unpaged; "Meeting of Department Managers held Wednesday Evening May 3, 1905," unpaged; "Meeting of Department Managers Held Thursday Evening, June 1, 1905," unpaged; the previous three sources are from T. P. M. & M.–Minutes, Mary Jane Gentry Collection, AR 95-13; "Revenue and Expense Journal, 1904–1906," Ledger 639; "Revenue and Expense Journal, 1906–1909," Ledger 640; "Revenue and Expense Journal, 1909–1912," Ledger 641; the previous three sources are from the Texas and Pacific Coal Company Records, S1021.1.

60. *Thomas v. State* in *Southwestern Reporter,* vol. 101, *May 8–June 5, 1907* (St. Paul, MN: West Publishing Company, 1907), 797.

61. William Knox Gordon, Jr., Biographical Data Information Sheet and Questionnaire (based on interview), box 2, folder 1, unpaged, Thurber, Texas, Collection, S1076.1.

62. Lawrence Santi, interview by Richard Mason, April 22, 1980, Houston, Texas, Oral History Collection, Southwest Collection, Texas Tech University Libraries, Texas Tech University, Lubbock, Texas.

63. William Knox Gordon, Jr., Biographical Data Information Sheet and Questionnaire (based on interview), box 2, folder 1, unpaged, Thurber, Texas, Collection, S1076.1; Lawrence Santi, interview by Richard Mason, April 22, 1980, Houston, Texas, Oral History Collection, Southwest Collection, Texas Tech University Libraries, Texas Tech University, Lubbock, Texas; Clyne, *Coal People,* 21; Shifflett, *Coal Towns,* chap. 6; "May End Coal Strike Today," *Dallas Morning News,* May 6, 1910, p. 9; "Miners Reject Proposal of T. & P. Coal Company," *Dallas Morning News,* May 8, 1910, p. 9; "Texas Coal Miners' Strike Settled," *Dallas Morning News,* June 2, 1910, p. 1; "Cash and Check Sales Record, 1908–1914," Ledger 607, pp. 74–108; "Rent Book, 1910," Ledger 325; the previous two sources are from the Texas and Pacific Coal Company Records, S1021.1; Allen, *Chapters in the History of Organized Labor in Texas,* 119; Dwight F. Henderson, "The Texas Coal Mining Industry," *Southwestern Historical Quarterly* 68, no. 2 (October 1964): 213; Price V. Fishback, "The Economics of Company Housing: Historical Perspectives from the Coal Fields," *Journal of Law, Economics, and Organization* 8, no. 2 (April 1992): 357–58.

The 1910 coal miners' strike in Texas is mentioned only in passing by Rhinehart in *A Way of Work* and in Henderson, "The Texas Coal Mining Industry." No books or scholarly treatments of Thurber discuss the two-month-long labor stoppage there in 1910. The first extensive account of labor difficulties at Thurber, Mary Jane Gentry's 1946 thesis "Thurber: The Life and Death of a Texas Town," refers to the labor actions before 1903 and after 1916 but does not remark on any in 1910. Other authors have followed her lead and left the 1910 strike unmentioned. The 1916 work stoppage is described in other works (for instance, Gentry, "Thurber," 97– 99, and Hardman, *Fire in a Hole!* 57), but it lasted only three weeks; the 1910 action lasted more than two months.

64. Green, *The Company Town,* 69–71; Clyne, *Coal People,* 22.
65. Clyne, *Coal People,* 23.
66. Ibid.
67. See the various Biographical Data Information Sheets and Questionnaires in the Thurber, Texas, Collection, S1076.1.
68. Claude Joe Marchioni, by Karl Andrews, Biographical Data Information Sheet and Questionnaire (based on interview), box 3, folder 13, unpaged, Thurber, Texas, Collection, S1076.1.
69. Frank Martin, by Ruth Hosey, Biographical Data Information Sheet and Questionnaire (based on interview), box 2, folder 1, unpaged, Thurber, Texas, Collection, S1076.1; Edgar L. Marston, New York, New York, to Ed Britton, Thurber, Texas, June 29, 1917, typewritten letter signed, letterpress copy, Correspondence Files, Vol. 2, January 15, 1917 to November 23, 1917, p. 368, Series VI, A, Miles B. Hart Collection.

Chapter 6

1. J. C. Koen, "A Social and Economic History of Palo Pinto County" (master's thesis, Hardin-Simmons University, 1949), 70; "1916 Annual Report," box 1, folder 10, Texas and Pacific Coal Company Records, S1021.2; Hooks, "Thurber," 15–16; Spratt, *Thurber, Texas,* 113–15; Boyce House, *Were You in Ranger?* (1935; repr., Ranger, TX: Ranger Historical Preservation Society, 1999), 3–9; Woodard, *Black Diamonds! Black Gold!* 100–103.
2. Edgar L. Marston, New York, New York, to John D. Rockefeller, Jr., New York, New York, September 6, 1916, typewritten letter signed, letterpress copy, Correspondence Files, Vol. 1, February 1, 1916 to January 12, 1917, p. 447, Series VI, A, Miles B. Hart Collection.
3. Edgar L. Marston, New York, New York, to William K. Gordon, Thurber, Texas, February 2, 1916, typewritten letter signed, letterpress copy, Correspondence Files, Vol. 1, February 1, 1916 to January 12, 1917, pp. 4–5, Series VI, A, Miles B. Hart Collection.
4. "Annual Report Texas Pacific Coal & Oil Company 1919," box 1, folder 10, Texas and Pacific Coal Company Records, S1021.2; Richard V. Francaviglia, "Black Diamonds to Black Gold: The Legacy of the Texas Pacific Coal and Oil Company," *West Texas Historical Association Year Book* 71 (1995): 14–16; House, *Were You in Ranger?* 3–9; Woodard, *Black Diamonds! Black Gold!* 100–110.
5. Francaviglia, "Black Diamonds and Vanishing Ruins," 58; Francaviglia, "Black

Diamonds to Black Gold," 14; "Texas Pacific Mercantile and Manufacturing Company, Additions to Property for the Year 1919," in "Additions to Property and Various Inventories, 1900–1932," Ledger 602, Texas and Pacific Coal Company Records, S1021.1; Bielinski, *The Thurber Connection,* 140–47; Edgar L. Marston, New York, New York, to Van Noy Interstate Company, Kansas City, Missouri, May 8, 1918, letter, in Bielinski, *The Thurber Connection,* 146–47; Studdard, *Life of the Texas Pacific Coal & Oil Co.,* 101; Floyd, "Thurber, Texas," 88–89; Woodard, *Black Diamonds! Black Gold!* 109–10.

6. Francaviglia, "Black Diamonds and Vanishing Ruins," 58; Francaviglia, "Black Diamonds to Black Gold," 14; Edgar L. Marston, New York, New York, to Ed Britton, Thurber, Texas, February 27, 1918, typewritten letter signed, letterpress copy, Correspondence Files, Vol. 3, November 24, 1917 to September 17, 1918, p. 283, Series VI, A, Miles B. Hart Collection; "Inventory: Car Shop, Month of January 1920," in "Additions to Property and Various Inventories, 1900–1932," Ledger 602, unpaged; "Texas Pacific Mercantile and Manufacturing Company, Additions to Property for the Year 1915," in "Additions to Property and Various Inventories, 1900–1932," Ledger 602, unpaged; the previous two sources are from the Texas and Pacific Coal Company Records, S1021.1; Bryant, interview by Baker, July 15, 2004, transcript, p. 21; George M. Carter, clipping from the *Palo Pinto County Star,* 1966, box 1, folder 11, Thurber, Texas, Collection, S1076.1; Hardman, *Fire in a Hole!* 107; Schmidt, "Thurber Chronology," unpaged, Ruby J. Schmidt Collection; Jones, *From Boom Town to Ghost Town,* unpaged.

7. "Revenue and Expense Journal, 1917–1918," Ledger 644; "Revenue and Expense Journal, 1918–1920," Ledger 645; "Revenue and Expense Journal, 1920," Ledger 646; the previous three sources are from the Texas and Pacific Coal Company Records, S1021.1; "Open Shop Fight at Thurber Mine," *Dallas Morning News,* September 14, 1921, p. 1; Floyd, "Thurber, Texas," 96; Koen, "A Social and Economic History of Palo Pinto County," 136; Francaviglia, "Black Diamonds to Black Gold," 12; Spratt, *Thurber, Texas,* 114–15. The quotation is from Frank Martin, by Ruth Hosey.

8. Frank Martin, by Ruth Hosey, Biographical Data Information Sheet and Questionnaire (based on interview), box 2, folder 1, p. 3, Thurber, Texas, Collection, S1076.1.

9. "Cash and Check Sales Record, 1914–1927," Ledger 608, pp. 200–04, Texas and Pacific Coal Company Records, S1021.1; Edgar L. Marston, New York, New York, to Ed Britton, Thurber, Texas, July 13, 1917, typewritten letter signed, letterpress copy, Correspondence Files, Vol. 2, January 15, 1917 to November 23, 1917, p. 426, Series VI, A; Edgar L. Marston, New York, New York, to Ed Britton, Thurber, Texas, March 19, 1918, typewritten letter signed, letterpress copy, Correspondence Files, Vol. 3, November 24, 1917 to September 17, 1918, pp. 301–2, Series VI, A; the previous two sources are from the Miles B. Hart

Collection; Hardman, *Fire in a Hole!* 107, 110–11; Schmidt, "Thurber Chronology," unpaged, Ruby J. Schmidt Collection; Spratt, *Thurber, Texas,* 114–15; Rhinehart, *A Way of Work,* 107–9.

10. "Open Shop Fight at Thurber Mine," *Dallas Morning News,* September 14, 1921, p. 1; "Statement of Miners' Union," *Dallas Morning News,* October 28, 1921, p. 11; Rhinehart, *A Way of Work,* 109–111; Berry, "Cooperation and Segregation," 77; Gentry, "Thurber," 122; Bielinski, *The Thurber Connection,* 160–68; Santi, interview by George Green; George N. Green, e-mail message to author, February 27, 2006; Adria Bernardi, *Houses with Names: The Italian Immigrants of Highwood, Illinois* (Chicago: University of Illinois Press, 1990), 107; Spratt, *Thurber, Texas,* 115–17. Most of those who have written about Thurber call the 1921 action a strike, although labor leaders like Santi called it a lockout at the time. Bielinski and others have followed his lead. Dr. George Green, a historian specializing in twentieth-century labor history at the University of Texas at Arlington, termed it a "defensive strike," and Lisa Berry took the middle road in her thesis, calling it a "strike/lockout."
11. "Revenue and Expense Journal, 1918–1920," Ledger 645; "Revenue and Expense Journal, 1920," Ledger 646; "Revenue and Expense Journal, 1921–1923," Ledger 647; "Revenue and Expense Journal, 1923–1925," Ledger 648; the previous four sources are from the Texas and Pacific Coal Company Records, S1021.1; Spratt, *Thurber, Texas,* 118–19; Woodard, *Black Diamonds! Black Gold!,* 115–18, 131–33; Gentry, "Thurber," 121–22, 201–2; Schmidt, "Thurber Chronology," unpaged, Ruby J. Schmidt Collection; Bryant, interview by Baker, July 15, 2004, transcript, pp. 16–17.
12. Grimshaw, "Hard, Heavy Lifting," chap. 6; Spratt, *Thurber, Texas,* 118; Hardman, *Fire in a Hole!* 110–11; "Sales by Departments Summary, Accounting Dept., 1923–1925," Ledger 650, unpaged; "Texas Pacific Mercantile and Manufacturing Company, Additions to Property for the Year 1924," in "Additions to Property and Various Inventories, 1900–1932," Ledger 602, unpaged; the previous two sources are from the Texas and Pacific Coal Company Records, S1021.1; Dean B. Hiatt, *Ever the Wildebeest: An Autobiography of a Natural Engineer* (Kerrville, TX: Kerrville Printing Company, 1979), 79; Studdard, *Life of the Texas Pacific Coal & Oil Co.,* 99; Bryant, interview by Baker, July 15, 2004, transcript, pp. 14–15; Bryant, interview by Baker, August 25, 2004, transcript, pp. 16–17.
13. "Payroll Book, Mine, 1923–1926," Ledger 139; "Payroll Book, Mine, 1927–1933," Ledger 140; the previous two sources are from the Texas and Pacific Coal Company Records, S1021.1; Hardman, *Fire in a Hole!* 93; Grimshaw, "Hard, Heavy Lifting," chap. 6; Gibson, interview by Baker and Schooley, February 28, 2006, notes.
14. "Texas Pacific Mercantile and Manufacturing Company, Additions to Property

for the Year 1926," in "Additions to Property and Various Inventories, 1900–1932," Ledger 602, Texas and Pacific Coal Company Records, S1021.1; "Thurber Gins First Bale," *Thurber Tiny Journal,* vol. 1, no. 7 (September 1930), in Gentry, "Thurber," 211; Spratt, *Thurber, Texas,* 119; Wilkins, "Thurber," 9–10.

15. Wilkins, "Thurber," 9–10.
16. T. P. M. & M. Co., "The Thurber Garage . . ." (advertisement), *Thurber Tiny Journal,* vol. 1, no. 4 (June 1930), box 1, folder 13; "The Tiny Journal Wants . . . ," *Thurber Tiny Journal,* vol. 1, no. 3 (May 1930), box 1, folder 13; the previous two sources are from the Thurber, Texas, Collection, S1076.1; *Thurber Tiny Journal,* vol. 1, no. 3 (May 1930), W. K. Gordon Center for Industrial History of Texas, Tarleton State University, Mingus, Texas; Hardman, *Fire in a Hole!* 120–21. The first quotation is from "The Tiny Journal Wants."
17. "Annual Report Texas Pacific Coal and Oil Company 1929," box 1, folder 11; "Annual Report Texas Pacific Coal and Oil Company 1930," box 1, folder 11; the previous two sources are from the Texas and Pacific Coal Company Records, S1021.2; Grimshaw, "Hard, Heavy Lifting," chap. 6; Jones, *From Boom Town to Ghost Town,* unpaged; Hiatt, *Ever the Wildebeest,* 79; Woodard, *Black Diamonds! Black Gold!* 137–47.
18. Gentry, "Thurber," 118, 213; Studdard, *Life of the Texas Pacific Coal & Oil Co.,* 89–90; Studdard, interview by Mason, Oral History Collection, Southwest Collection, Texas Tech University Libraries, Texas Tech University, Lubbock, Texas; "Block Burns at Thurber," newspaper clipping from the *Fort Worth Telegram,* September 14, 1930, box 1, folder 11, Thurber, Texas, Collection, S1076.1.
19. Studdard, *Life of the Texas Pacific Coal & Oil Co.,* 89.
20. Gentry, "Thurber," 118, 213; Studdard, *Life of the Texas Pacific Coal & Oil Co.,* 89–90; Studdard, interview by Mason, Oral History Collection, Southwest Collection, Texas Tech University Libraries, Texas Tech University, Lubbock, Texas; "Annual Report Texas Pacific Coal and Oil Company 1930," box 1, folder 11, unpaged, Texas and Pacific Coal Company Records, S1021.2; "Cash and Coupon Sales, 1930–1933," Ledger 609, pp. 1–5, Texas and Pacific Coal Company Records, S1021.1.
21. "Texas Pacific Fidelity and Surety Company, Minutes: Directors and Stockholders Meetings, 1929–1930," Ledger 597; "Insurance Policy Data, 1929–1930," Ledger 594; "Fire Suspense Account 613, 1930–1931," Wallet 39; the previous three sources are from the Texas and Pacific Coal Company Records, S1021.1; Studdard, *Life of the Texas Pacific Coal & Oil Co.,* 89–90.
22. "Texas Pacific Fidelity and Surety Company, Minutes: Directors and Stockholders Meetings, 1929–1930," Ledger 597; "Insurance Policy Data, 1929–1930," Ledger 594; "Fire Suspense Account 613, 1930–1931," Wallet 39; the previous

three sources are from the Texas and Pacific Coal Company Records, S1021.1; Studdard, *Life of the Texas Pacific Coal & Oil Co.,* 89–90. The quotations are from "Texas Pacific Fidelity and Surety Company, Minutes: Directors and Stockholders Meetings, 1929–1930," pp. 41, 63.

23. Grimshaw, "Hard, Heavy Lifting," chap. 6; Gentry, "Thurber," 202; Floyd, "Thurber, Texas," 97–98; Wilkins, "Thurber," 9; "Annual Report Texas Pacific Coal and Oil Company 1930," box 1, folder 11, unpaged; "Annual Report Texas Pacific Coal and Oil Company 1932," box 1, folder 12, unpaged; "Texas Pacific Coal and Oil Company Annual Report 1933," box 1, folder 12, unpaged; the previous three sources are from the Texas and Pacific Coal Company Records, S1021.2; "Texas and Pacific Coal and Oil Company Rent Book for Buildings, 1930–1934," box 1, folder 3, Thurber, Texas, Collection, S1076.1; "Payroll Book, Mine, 1927–1933," Ledger 140; "Texas Pacific Mercantile and Manufacturing Company: Additions to Property–Year 1930," in "Additions to Property and Various Inventories, 1900–1932," Ledger 602, unpaged; the previous two sources are from the Texas and Pacific Coal Company Records, S1021.1; Studdard, *Life of the Texas Pacific Coal & Oil Co.,* 54; "Christmas–1930," T. P. M. & M.–Minutes, Mary Jane Gentry Collection, AR 95-13; Hiatt, *Ever the Wildebeest,* 94.
24. Woodard, *Black Diamonds! Black Gold!* 151.
25. Woodard, *Black Diamonds! Black Gold!* 154–57; Spratt, *Thurber, Texas,* 126; Studdard, *Life of the Texas Pacific Coal & Oil Co.,* 54; "Directors, 1930–1939," Ledger 437, pp. 111–13, 132, Texas and Pacific Coal Company Records, S1021.1; "Texas Pacific Coal and Oil Company Annual Report 1933," box 1, folder 12, unpaged, Texas and Pacific Coal Company Records, S1021.2.
26. Gentry, "Thurber, 118–20, 202; Studdard, *Life of the Texas Pacific Coal & Oil Co.,* 54; Woodard, *Black Diamonds! Black Gold!* 157.
27. Gentry, "Thurber," 119.
28. Gentry, "Thurber," 118–20, 202; "Cash and Coupon Sales, 1930–1933," Ledger 609; "Payroll Book, Mine, 1927–1933," Ledger 140; the previous two sources are from the Texas and Pacific Coal Company Records, S1021.1; "Texas Pacific Coal and Oil Company Annual Report 1933," box 1, folder 12, unpaged, Texas and Pacific Coal Company Records, S1021.2; Studdard, *Life of the Texas Pacific Coal & Oil Co.,* 54; Woodard, *Black Diamonds! Black Gold!* 157.
29. Gentry, "Thurber," 202–205; Floyd, "Thurber, Texas," 100–04; "General Ledger Subsidiary. B-8 Transportation Equipment. B-8-B Trucks, Trailers and Tractors to B-8-D Aeroplanes-Texas. Beginning to December 31, 1938. Physical Property—Non-Operating Subsidiaries. All Properties—Texas. Beginning to December 31, 1938," account B13-B, unpaged, Texas Pacific Coal and Oil Company Collection, W. K. Gordon Center for Industrial History of Texas, Tarleton State University, Mingus, Texas; "General Ledger Subsidiary, A-60 Physical Property-Town and Farm Department, All Properties—Texas, January

1, 1924 to December 31, 1937," unpaged, Bennett Family Collection; Bryant, interview by Baker, August 25, 2004, transcript, p. 9; "Thurber & the Southwest Collection," 4–7; Schmidt, "Thurber Chronology," unpaged, Ruby J. Schmidt Collection; Jones, *From Boom Town to Ghost Town,* unpaged; Studdard, *Life of the Texas Pacific Coal & Oil Co.,* 97–98; Hiatt, *Ever the Wildebeest,* 93–103; King, *A Lodge in a Company-Owned Town,* unpaged; Thurber Historic District Nomination, typescript, unpaged; Woodard, *Black Diamonds! Black Gold!* 157; Spratt, *Thurber, Texas,* 126.

30. "Charter, 1934," box 5, folder 26, Texas and Pacific Coal Company Records, S1021.2; "Texas Charters," *Dallas Morning News,* December 19, 1934, sec. 2, p. 7; "The Thurber Mines," *Fort Worth Mail-Telegram,* May 14, 1896, Historical Edition, sec. 2, unpaged. The quotation is from "The Thurber Mines."

Epilogue

1. "General Ledger Subsidiary. B-8 Transportation Equipment. B-8-B Trucks, Trailers and Tractors to B-8-D Aeroplanes-Texas. Beginning to December 31, 1938. Physical Property—Non-Operating Subsidiaries. All Properties—Texas. Beginning to December 31, 1938," account B13-B, unpaged, Texas Pacific Coal and Oil Company Collection, W. K. Gordon Center for Industrial History of Texas, Tarleton State University, Mingus, Texas; "General Ledger Subsidiary, A-60 Physical Property-Town and Farm Department, All Properties—Texas, January 1, 1924 to December 31, 1937," unpaged, Bennett Family Collection, W. K. Gordon Center for Industrial History of Texas, Tarleton State University, Mingus, Texas; Bryant, interview, transcript, p. 9; Grady E. Daniels, interview by Kenneth W. Jones, February 14, 2001, Granbury, Texas, transcript, pp. 3, 5, 23, W. K. Gordon Center for Industrial History of Texas, Tarleton State University, Mingus, Texas; Schmidt, "Thurber Chronology," unpaged, Ruby J. Schmidt Collection; Jones, *From Boom Town to Ghost Town,* unpaged; Gentry, "Thurber," 202–205; Floyd, "Thurber, Texas," 100–104; Jon McConal, "Old Bandstand Made New Home," *Fort Worth Star-Telegram,* May 18, 1991, Metro, p. 1; "Busy Thurber's Career Ends as Ghost City," *Dallas Morning News,* May 28, 1939, sec. I, p. 4.
2. "Busy Thurber's Career Ends as Ghost City," *Dallas Morning News,* May 28, 1939, sec. I, p. 4.
3. *Stephenville Empire-Tribune,* Anniversary Edition, January 31, 1936; "Deserted Mine Yields Body," *Dallas Morning News,* November 16, 1939, sec. I, p. 5; Schmidt, "Thurber Chronology," unpaged, Ruby J. Schmidt Collection; Jones, *From Boom Town to Ghost Town,* unpaged; Boyce House, Austin, Texas, to W. K. Gordon, Fort Worth, Texas, May 20, 1940, typescript letter with enclosed newspaper clipping, W. K. Gordon, Jr., Scrapbook, Oversize box 386, Special Collections Division, University of Texas at Arlington Libraries, University of

Texas at Arlington, Arlington, Texas; "General Ledger Subsidiary, A-60 Physical Property-Town and Farm Department, All Properties-Texas, January 1, 1924 to December 31, 1937," unpaged, Bennett Family Collection; Daniels, interview by Jones, February 14, 2001, transcript, p. 23; Gentry, "Thurber," 203–4; Floyd, "Thurber, Texas," 104–7, 109–11.

4. "To Dynamite Thurber Smokestack Sunday," *Dallas Morning News,* March 25, 1937, p. 1; Dave Hall, "Dynamite Topples Once-Proud Tower in Thurber Ghost Town," *Fort Worth Press,* March 30, 1937; Hardman, *Boom Town,* 37; Hardman, *Fire in a Hole!* 84–85; Schmidt, "Thurber Chronology," unpaged, Ruby J. Schmidt Collection; Grimshaw, "Hard, Heavy Lifting," chap. 6.
5. Hall, "Dynamite Topples Once-Proud Tower in Thurber Ghost Town," *Fort Worth Press,* March 30, 1937.
6. Hardman, *Fire in a Hole!* 85.
7. "Still Prospecting: Gordon Wants to Make It 50," *Fort Worth Star-Telegram,* April 25, 1937; "Thurber to Honor Oil Man Who Wouldn't Quit Until Ranger Field Was Proved," *Dallas Times Herald,* April 28, 1937; the two preceding citations are from W. K. Gordon, Jr., Scrapbook, pp. 29–30, Oversize box 386; Floyd, "Thurber, Texas," 112–14; Hardman, *Boom Town,* 47; Hardman, *Fire in a Hole!* 136; "Busy Thurber's Career Ends as Ghost City," *Dallas Morning News,* May 28, 1939, sec. I, p. 4; T. A. Price, "Ghost City's People Return for Reunion," *Dallas Morning News,* September 5, 1939, sec. I, p. 12; "Ghost City," *Dallas Morning News,* September 8, 1939, sec. II, p. 2.
8. Price, "Ghost City's People Return for Reunion," *Dallas Morning News,* September 5, 1939, sec. I, p. 12.
9. "Busy Thurber's Career Ends as Ghost City," *Dallas Morning News,* May 28, 1939, sec. I, p. 4; "West Texas Lake Produces Fine Fishing," *Dallas Morning News,* May 7, 1939, sec. IV, p. 5; "Ghost Town," *Dallas Morning News,* May 28, 1939, Picture Section, p. 3; Frank X. Tolbert, "Does Singing Girl Haunt Town?" *Dallas Morning News,* March 25, 1955, sec. 3, p. 1; "Thurber & the Southwest Collection," *TP Voice* 14, no. 1 (January–February 1978): 4–7; "Seagram Builds an Oil Company," *Texas Parade,* July 1968, Bennett Family Collection; "'Ghost Town' of Thurber Has Colorful History," *Fort Worth Press,* June 22, 1949; "Thurber Oldtimers Set Reunion and Picnic," *Fort Worth Star-Telegram,* June 30, 1952; "Former Residents of Thurber Hold Annual Reunion," *Fort Worth Star-Telegram,* July 5, 1952; the three preceding citations are from W. K. Gordon, Jr., Scrapbook, pp. 45, 48; "Mining Town Fades into Past," *Fort Worth Star-Telegram,* August 20, 1964; Richard V. Francaviglia, "Black Diamonds and Vanishing Ruins: Reconstructing the Historic Landscape of Thurber, Texas," *Mining History Association's 1994 Annual* (1994): 51–62; Lillie Ivey Gibson, interview by T. Lindsay Baker and LeAnna S. Schooley, February 28, 2006, Stephenville, Texas, notes, W. K.

Gordon Center for Industrial History of Texas, Tarleton State University, Mingus, Texas; Walter Kostiha and Lillie Ivey Gibson, interview by Nancy Allen, July 3, 2002, Lovera's Grocery, Strawn, Texas, transcript, W. K. Gordon Center for Industrial History of Texas, Tarleton State University, Mingus, Texas; LeAnna Schooley and Gene Rhea Tucker, "Alcorn/Whitehead Timeline," December 31, 2005, in the possession of Gene Rhea Tucker. Quotation is from "Mining Town Fades into Past."

10. Floyd, "Thurber, Texas," 112–114; Hardman, *Boom Town,* 47; Hardman, *Fire in a Hole!* 136; Rex Z. Howard, *Texas Guidebook: Authentic Information about the Wonders of Texas* (Grand Prairie, TX: The Lo-Ray Co., 1954), 154; "Thurber Oldtimers Set Reunion and Picnic," *Fort Worth Star-Telegram,* June 30, 1952; "Former Residents of Thurber Hold Annual Reunion," *Fort Worth Star-Telegram,* July 5, 1952; the two preceding citations are from W. K. Gordon, Jr., Scrapbook, p. 48; Frank X. Tolbert, "Ghost Town Label Can Be Dangerous," *Dallas Morning News,* May 12, 1957, sec. 3, p. 1; "Thurber Reunion Set on Thursday," *Dallas Morning News,* July 5, 1957, sec. 3, p. 12; Autis McMahan, "Marker Dedicated to Honor Thurber," *Fort Worth Star-Telegram,* June 8, 1969, sec. C, p. 23; Webb, "Texas Collection," 93–94; "Affairs of the Association," *Southwestern Historical Quarterly* 44, no. 1 (July 1940): 136; H. Bailey Carroll and Milton R. Gutsch, "A Check List of Theses and Dissertations in Texas History Produced in the Department of History of the University of Texas," *Southwestern Historical Quarterly* 56, no. 2 (October 1952): 272.

11. Eddie S. Hughes, "Ghost Town Comes Alive Again," *Dallas Morning News,* June 13, 1965, sec. A, p. 17; "Where TPers Relax," *TP Voice* 2, no. 3 (May–June 1966): 14–15; "Thurber Lake: A TP Bonus," *TP Voice* 4, no. 3 (May–June 1968): 9–10; "A Vacation at Thurber Lake," *TP Voice* 5, no. 4 (July–August 1969): 8–9; Emily Young, "Randy Bennett Calls Thurber His Home," *Abilene Reporter-News,* November 9, 1980, sec. A, p. 19; Barry Shlachter, "Thurber's Ghosts Snoozing Quietly," undated 1986 clipping from the *Fort Worth Star-Telegram,* box 2, folder 6, Thurber Historical Association Records, AR399; "Seagram Builds an Oil Company," *Texas Parade,* July 1968, Bennett Family Collection; "Texas Pacific Trade Signed," *Dallas Morning News,* May 22, 1963, sec. 1, p. 20; "T&P Oil Company to Build Museum at Thurber," unidentified clipping, box 2, folder 6, Thurber Historical Association Records, AR399.

12. "Museum Is Planned for Ghost Town of Thurber," *Mineral Wells Index,* May 17, 1967, p. 1; "T&P Oil Company to Build Museum at Thurber," unidentified clipping, box 2, folder 6, Thurber Historical Association Records, AR399; "Thurber Group Planning Museum," *Fort Worth Star-Telegram,* June 12, 1967; Rufus Higgs, "Former Thurberites Plan Big Things for Old Mining Town," *Stephenville Daily Empire,* June 13, 1967, p. 1; "Plans Progressing for Thurber

Museum," *The Reporter* (Strawn), June 15, 1967, p. 1; "Excerpts from Business Meeting of Thurber reunion—June 11, 1967," Wallet 14, Texas and Pacific Coal Company Records, S1021.1; Dr. and Mrs. William Curry Holden, "Thurber Museum Potential," n.d., box 1, folder 13, Thurber Historical Association Records, AR399; Thurber Papers, 1967 and undated, box 73, folder 16, W. C. Holden and Frances Mayhugh Holden Papers, 1836–1989 and undated, S 455.1, Southwest Collection, Texas Tech University Libraries, Texas Tech University, Lubbock, Texas.

13. "Plans Progressing for Thurber Museum," *The Reporter* (Strawn), June 15, 1967, p. 1.
14. Office of the Secretary of State of Texas, Austin, Texas, "Certificate of Incorporation of the Thurber Historical Association, Inc.," Charter No. 257645, February 27, 1969, box 1, folder 1, Thurber Historical Association Records, AR399.
15. "Generous Gesture to Provide Thurber Group with Thurber Cemetery Deed, Road and Gate," *Stephenville Empire,* March 4, 1969, Wallet 14, Texas and Pacific Coal Company Records, S1021.1; "Marker Will Note History of Thurber," *Fort Worth Star-Telegram,* May 29, 1969; "Historical Marker to Be Placed in Thurber to Highlight Reunion," *Breckenridge American,* June 5, 1969; Bob Bain, "Smokestack at Thurber to Get Historical Marker," *Fort Worth Star-Telegram,* June 6, 1989, sec. D, p. 5; McMahan, "Marker Dedicated to Honor Thurber," *Fort Worth Star-Telegram,* June 8, 1969, sec. C, p. 23; "Historical Marker at Thurber," *TP Voice* 5, no. 4 (July–August 1969): 15; Fritz Toepperwein and Emilie Toepperwein, "Thurber Museum Study," [1969], typescript proposals for a museum at Thurber with drawings and diagrams, box 1, folder 13, Thurber Historical Association Records, AR399; Emilie Toepperwein, *Thurber Memorial Park Points of Interest,* [1969], negative photostatic copies of pencil sketch, Bennett Family Collection; Shlachter, "Thurber's Ghosts Snoozing Quietly," undated 1986 clipping from the *Fort Worth Star-Telegram,* box 2, folder 6, Thurber Historical Association Records, AR399; "Plans Progressing for Thurber Museum," *The Reporter* (Strawn), June 15, 1967, p. 1.
16. "Thurber Facilities Will Be Expanded This Summer," *TP Voice* 6, no. 4 (July–August 1970): 4–8; "Open House Marks Completion of Carrol M. Bennett Training Center," *TP Voice* 7, no. 2 (March–April 1971): 5–9; Dale E. Selzer, *A Training Center, Texas Pacific Oil Co.,* [ca. 1970], blueline copy of manuscript plan, Bennett Family Collection; Frank X. Tolbert, "Thurber's Singing Girl Ghost Not Seen Lately," *Dallas Morning News,* July 27, 1971, sec. A, p. 17; Helen Parmley, "TV Minister Evicts 'Children' from Their Thurber Commune," *Dallas Morning News,* October 2, 1971, sec. D, p. 1; Shlachter, "Thurber's Ghosts Snoozing Quietly," undated 1986 clipping from the *Fort Worth Star-Telegram,* box 2, folder 6, Thurber Historical Association Records, AR399; Michael Pellecchia and Dave Ferman, "On the Road to Salvation," *Fort Worth Star-Telegram,* October 8,

1989, sec. G, p. 1; Texas Highway Department, *Interstate Highway 20, Thurber Area C,* [ca. 1970], 1:100, photostatic copy of an aerial photograph, Bennett Family Collection; Humble Oil and Refining Company, Houston, Texas, *Station Type: Special Design Thurber, Texas,* May 8, 1972, photostatic copy of a manuscript plan, Bennett Family Collection; Martha Hand, "'Children of God' Evicted from Ranch," *Odessa American* (Odessa, TX), October 1, 1971; David E. Van Zandt, "The Children of God," in *America's Alternative Religions,* ed. Timothy Miller, 127–32 (New York: SUNY Press, 1995), 127–28; "Thurber & the Southwest Collection," 4–7; U.S. Department of the Interior, National Park Service, National Register of Historic Places, Thurber Historic District Nomination, 1979, typescript, Office of the Keeper of the National Register of Historic Places, National Park Service, Washington, DC.

17. Jane Baskett, "Permit for Coal Mining Near Thurber Issued," *Abilene Reporter-News,* May 9, 1979; Emily Young, "Coal Flows Again through Thurber's Veins," *Abilene Reporter-News,* November 9, 1980, sec. A, p. 19; "Coal Mine to Expand," unidentified clipping, December 15, 1980; "The Cost of Oil . . . ," unidentified clipping, December 19, 1980; the previous two citations are from Thurber, Texas Vertical File, Southwest Collection, Texas Tech University Libraries, Texas Tech University, Lubbock, Texas; Shlachter, "Thurber's Ghosts Snoozing Quietly," undated 1986 clipping from the *Fort Worth Star-Telegram,* box 2, folder 6, Thurber Historical Association Records, AR399; Young, "Randy Bennett Calls Thurber His Home," *Abilene Reporter-News,* November 9, 1980, sec. A, p. 19; Studdard, *Life of the Texas Pacific Coal & Oil Co.,* 157; Woodard, *Black Diamonds! Black Gold!* 267; Bill Whitaker, "Stenholm Placing Hope in Next Session," *Abilene Reporter-News,* undated clipping; Kent Biffle, "Ghost City Becomes Alive at Reunion," *Dallas Morning News,* June 19, 1988, sec. A, p. 41; Terry Goodrich, "Ballad of Thurber," *Fort Worth Star-Telegram,* January 2, 1989, sec. 2, p. 1; Thurber Lake Family Resort, "Thurber Lake Family Resort" (advertisement brochure), Thurber Lake Resort file, Mrs. W. K. Gordon, Jr., Papers, W. K. Gordon Center for Industrial History of Texas, Tarleton State University, Mingus, Texas; Bill Fairley, "Historic Thurber Down, Not Out," *Fort Worth Star-Telegram,* March 28, 2001, sec. B, p. 7; Jean Simmons, "Competing Restaurants Give Entrée into Thurber's Coal Town Past," *Dallas Morning News,* August 2, 1998, sec. G, p. 1.

The forty-six-minute video *Thurber, Texas: Boom Town to Ghost Town, 1886–1936,* was updated in 1991 and is now available on DVD as well as VHS. For more information on the creation of the video, as well as the (sometimes questionable) attempts of the Thurber Historical Association to make Thurber into a state park, consult the Ruby Schmidt Collection and Mrs. W. K. Gordon, Jr., Papers at the W. K. Gordon Center and the Thurber Historical Association Records, AR399, at the University of Texas at Arlington.

18. Simmons, "Competing Restaurants Give Entrée into Thurber's Coal Town Past," *Dallas Morning News*, August 2, 1998, sec. G, p. 1; Erick Krapf, "Fire Destroys Landmark," *Stephenville Empire-Tribune*, January 16, 1992, p.1; Steve Nash, "Blaze Destroys Historic Smokestack Restaurant between Abilene and Dallas Fed Travelers for Years," *Abilene Reporter-News*, January 16, 1992, sec. A, p.1; Greg Orwig, "Smoke Stack Fire Took More Than Restaurant from Thurber," *Abilene Reporter-News*, January 17, 1992, sec. A, p. 9; Amy Keen, "Blaze Destroys Eatery," *Fort Worth Star-Telegram*, January 17, 1992, sec. Metro, p. 19; Thurber Historical Association, "Souvenir Program for Dedication of Thurber Cemetery Monument," Cemetery file, Mrs. W. K. Gordon, Jr., Papers; "Thurber's Curious Graveyard Symbolic of a Curious Town," *Victoria Advocate* (Victoria, TX), June 1, 2005, p. 4; *Thurber, Texas: Demise of Thurber Cemetery and Interments* (Gordon, TX: Thurber Historical Association, 1990); Gerron S. Hite, Cemetery Preservation Coordinator, Texas Historical Commission, History Programs Division, Austin, Texas, to Louis Scopel, Medowlakes, Texas, February 25, 2000, typewritten letter signed, Cemetery file, Mrs. W. K. Gordon, Jr., Papers; Ruby Schmidt, Fort Worth, Texas, to Bishop Joseph P. Delaney, Fort Worth, Texas, October 10, 1990, typewritten letter signed, box 1, folder 5, Thurber Historical Association Records, AR399; Jon McConal, "Well-traveled Church Returns to Former Coal-mining Town," *Fort Worth Star-Telegram*, August 7, 1993, sec. Metro, p. 28; Donnis Baggett, "See? Thurber's a Very Visible Ghost Town," *Dallas Morning News*, March 13, 1994, sec. Texas & Southwest, p. 46A; Deana Totzke, "Traditional Latin Mass to Highlight Annual Reunion of Ghost Mining Town," *Stephenville Empire-Tribune*, June 9, 1995; Francaviglia, "Black Diamonds to Black Gold," 7–20; Francaviglia, "Black Diamonds and Vanishing Ruins," 51–62; Fairley, "Historic Thurber Down, Not Out," *Fort Worth Star-Telegram*, March 28, 2001, sec. B, p. 7; Hollace Weiner, "Ceremony to Mark Bustling History of Ghost Town Thurber," *Fort Worth Star-Telegram*, October 12, 1995, sec. Texas, p. 18; Deana Totzke, "Thurber's Glory Recalled," *Stephenville Empire-Tribune*, October 13, 1995, p. 1; Joyce Whitis, "Thurber Remembered with Historical Markers," *Stephenville Empire-Tribune*, November 30, 1995, sec. Cross Timbers Senior Living, p. 11; Tommy Wells, "State Unveils Eight Historical Markers in Thurber Area," *Quad City Messenger* (Gordon), October 19, 1995, p. 1.

19. Elk Castle Hunters Club, "The Ultimate Outdoor Experience . . ." (advertisement brochure), Greystone Castle file, Mrs. W. K. Gordon, Jr., Papers; Jerry Circelli, "Land Castle: The Medieval Turrets Rising Near the Ghost Town of Thurber Are No Highway Mirage," *Fort Worth Star-Telegram*, September 24, 1997, sec. Life & Arts, p. 1; Simmons, "Competing Restaurants Give Entrée into Thurber's Coal Town Past," *Dallas Morning News*, August 2, 1998, sec. G, p. 1; Richard C. Rome, Landscape Architects, Inc., "Thurber Visioning/Goals-Settings

Workshop," March 7, 1997, Gordon Center creation history file, Mrs. W. K. Gordon, Jr., Papers; Murphy & Orr Exhibits, "W. K. Gordan [*sic*] Center for Industrial History of Texas: A Museum & Visitor Center" (Forest Park, GA: Murphy & Orr Exhibits, 2001), W. K. Gordon Center for Industrial History of Texas, Tarleton State University, Mingus, Texas; Bill Hanna, "Tarleton to Establish Center in Thurber," *Fort Worth Star-Telegram,* February 7, 2001, sec. Metro, p. 1; "Gordon Research Center, Museum Plans Finalized," *Stephenville Empire-Tribune,* February 8, 2001, sec. A, p. 1; Fairley, "Historic Thurber Down, Not Out," *Fort Worth Star-Telegram,* March 28, 2001, sec. B, p. 7; Diane Jennings, "Ghost Town Alive with Controversy," *Fort Worth Star-Telegram,* June 2, 2002, sec. Texas & Southwest, p. 45A; Diane Jennings, "Museum to Bring Texas Ghost Town Alive but Some Residents Miffed That Outsiders Are in Charge," *Houston Chronicle,* June 9, 2002, sec. A, p. 47; "Mining History: Industrial History Recreated in Thurber at New Tarleton Museum," *The J-TAC* (Tarleton State University, Stephenville), September 19, 2002, p. 1; Art Chapman, "New Museum Preserves Memories of Thurber," *Fort Worth Star-Telegram,* October 27, 2002, sec. Metro, p. 5; Deborah Voorhees, "Thurber, Texas, Museum," *Dallas Morning News,* January 3, 2003, sec. Guide, p. 29; Ann P. White, "Thurber Recalls Glory Days," *Houston Chronicle,* March 9, 2003, sec. Texas Magazine, p. 14.

BIBLIOGRAPHY

Archival Sources

Indiana University Archives, Indiana University, Bloomington, Indiana, Charles W. Cushman Collection

Library of Congress, Sanborn Map Collection

Nita Stewart Haley Memorial Library, Midland, Texas, Miles B. Hart Collection

Southwest Collection, Texas Tech University Libraries, Texas Tech University, Lubbock, Texas

- Don Woodard Papers, S1617.1
- Texas and Pacific Coal Company Records, S1021.1
- Texas and Pacific Coal Company Records, S1021.2
- Thurber, Texas, Collection, S1076.1
- Thurber, Texas, Photograph Collection, SWCPC 209
- Thurber, Texas, Vertical File
- W. C. Holden and Frances Mayhugh Holden Papers, S455.1
- William Whipple Johnson Papers, S496.1
- Willie M. Floyd Collection

Special Collections, Dick Smith Library, Tarleton State University, Stephenville, Texas

- Cross Timbers Historical Images Project
- Thurber Newspaper Collection

Special Collections Department, University of Nevada–Reno Library, University of Nevada–Reno, Reno, Nevada

- Marston Family Scrapbooks, NC449

Special Collections Division, University of Texas at Arlington Libraries, University of Texas at Arlington, Arlington, Texas

Texas Pacific Coal and Oil Company Financial Material
Thurber Historical Association Records, AR399
Thurber, Texas, Collection AR506 (formerly Mary Jane Gentry Collection, AR 95-13)
Thurber, Texas, Photograph Collection, AR88
W. K. Gordon, Jr., Scrapbook, Oversize Box 386
W. K. Gordon, Sr., Papers, AR421

W. K. Gordon Center for Industrial History of Texas, Tarleton State University, Mingus, Texas
Bennett Family Collection
Eugene Proctor Collection
James Lorenz Collection
Mrs. W. K. Gordon, Jr., Papers
Raymond Thomas Collection
Ruby J. Schmidt Collection
Teddy Rowland Collection
Texas Pacific Coal and Oil Company Collection

Interviews

Southwest Collection, Texas Tech University Libraries, Texas Tech University, Lubbock, Texas: Oral History Collection
Binney, R. F.
Santi, Lawrence
Studdard, George B.

W. K. Gordon Center for Industrial History of Texas, Tarleton State University, Mingus, Texas
Bryant, Edgar E.
Daniels, Grady E.
Gibson, Lillie Ivey
Kostiha, Walter, and Lillie Ivey Gibson

Special Collections Division, University of Texas at Arlington Libraries, University of Texas at Arlington, Arlington, Texas: Texas Labor Archives Oral Histories
Santi, Lawrence

Government Publications and Records

Dillingham, William P., et al. *Reports of the Immigration Commission: Immigrants in Industry.* Part 1, vol. 1, *Bituminous Coal Mining.* Washington, DC: Government Printing Office, 1911.

"Ed Britton." Texas Adjutant General Service Records, 1836–1935. FB 401-144. Adjutant General Records, State Archives, Texas State Library, Austin, Texas.

George Scalfi et al. v. John R. Graves. In *Texas Civil Appeals Report.* Vol. 31, *Cases Argued and Adjudged in the Courts of Civil Appeals of the State of Texas during the Early Part of the Year 1903.* Austin: Gammel-Statesman Publishing Company, 1903.

George Scalfi & Co. et al. v. State of Texas. In *Texas Civil Appeals Report.* Vol. 31, *Cases Argued and Adjudged in the Courts of Civil Appeals of the State of Texas during the Early Part of the Year 1903.* Austin: Gammel-Statesman Publishing Company, 1903.

Gordon v. Texas & Pacific Mercantile & Mfg. Co. In *Southwestern Reporter.* Vol. 190, *January 17– February 7, 1917.* St. Paul, MN: West Publishing Company, 1917.

Report, W. J. McDonald to W. H. Mabry, July 1, 1894, General Correspondence. Adjutant General Records, State Archives, Texas State Library, Austin, Texas.

Shumard, George G. *A Partial Report on the Geology of Western Texas Consisting of a General Geological Report and a Journal of Geological Observations Along the Routes Traveled by the Expedition between Indianola, Texas, and the Valley of the Mimbres, New Mexico, During the Years 1855 and 1856.* Austin: State Printing Office, 1886.

Southwestern Reporter. Vol. 34, *March 9–April 20, 1896.* St. Paul, MN: West Publishing Company, 1906.

Southwestern Reporter. Vol. 50, *April 5–May 29, 1899.* St. Paul, MN: West Publishing Company, 1899.

Southwestern Reporter. Vol. 101, *May 8–June 5, 1907.* St. Paul, MN: West Publishing Company, 1907.

Southwestern Reporter. Vol. 190, *January 17–February 7, 1917.* St. Paul, MN: West Publishing Company, 1917.

Texas. Erath County, Texas. 1900 U.S. Census, Thurber, population schedule. Micropublication T624. National Archives, Washington, DC.

Texas. Erath County, Texas. 1910 U.S. Census, Thurber Town, population schedule. Micropublication T624, roll 1551. National Archives, Washington, DC.

Texas. Palo Pinto County, Texas. 1900 U.S. Census, Thurber, population schedule. Micropublication T624, roll 1551. National Archives, Washington, DC.

Texas. Palo Pinto County. 1910 U.S. Census, population schedule. Micropublication T624, roll 1583. National Archives, Washington, DC.

Texas. Parker County. 1880 U.S. Census, population schedule. Micropublication T9, roll 1322. National Archives, Washington, DC.

Texas Civil Appeals Report. Vol. 31, *Cases Argued and Adjudged in the Courts of Civil Appeals of the State of Texas during the Early Part of the Year 1903.* Austin: Gammel-Statesman Publishing Company, 1903.

Texas & Pacific Coal Co. v. Connaughton. In *Southwestern Reporter.* Vol. 50, *April 5–May 29, 1899.* St. Paul, MN: West Publishing Company, 1899.

Texas & Pacific Coal Company v. Thomas Lawson. Case no. 346, Supreme Court of Texas Records, 1838–1945. Trial transcript. Texas State Library and Archives, Austin, Texas.

Texas & Pacific Coal Company v. Thomas Lawson. In *Southwestern Reporter.* Vol. 34, *March 9–April 20, 1896.* St. Paul, MN: West Publishing Company, 1906.

Thomas v. State. In *Southwestern Reporter.* Vol. 101, *May 8–June 5, 1907.* St. Paul, MN: West Publishing Company, 1907.

U. S. Department of the Interior. National Park Service. National Register of Historic Places. Thurber Historic District Nomination, 1979. Typescript. Office of the Keeper of the National Register of Historic Places. National Park Service. Washington, DC.

Newspapers

Abilene Reporter-News (Abilene, TX)

Breckenridge American (Breckenridge, TX)

Dallas Morning News

Dallas Times Herald

Fort Worth Mail-Telegram

Fort Worth Press

Fort Worth Star-Telegram

Fort Worth Weekly Gazette

Houston Chronicle

The J-TAC (Tarleton State University, Stephenville, TX)

Mineral Wells Index (Mineral Wells, TX)

New York Times

Odessa American (Odessa, TX)

Quad City Messenger (Gordon, TX)

The Reporter (Strawn, TX)

Stephenville Daily Empire (Stephenville, TX)

Stephenville Empire (Stephenville, TX)

Stephenville Empire-Tribune (Stephenville, TX)

Victoria Advocate (Victoria, TX)

Theses and Dissertations

Berry, Tonja Lisa. "Cooperation and Segregation: A History of North Central Texas Coal-Mining Towns, Organized Labor, and the Mexican Workforce." Master's thesis, University of Texas at Arlington, 2004.

Ferchill, Cantey H. "A Survey and Comparison of the Cultural Landscapes of Two Early-Twentieth Century Coal-Mining Communities: Thurber, Texas and Buxton, Iowa." Master's thesis, University of Texas at Arlington, 1995.

Floyd, Willie M. "Thurber, Texas: An Abandoned Coal Field Town." Master's thesis, Southern Methodist University, 1939.

Gentry, Mary Jane. "Thurber: The Life and Death of a Texas Town." Master's thesis, University of Texas, 1946.

Grimshaw, Joe David. "Hard, Heavy Lifting: The Manufacture of Bricks at Thurber, Texas." Master's thesis, Tarleton State University, 2004.

Koen, J. C. "A Social and Economic History of Palo Pinto County." Master's thesis, Hardin-Simmons University, 1949.

Maroney, James C. "Organized Labor in Texas, 1900–1929." PhD diss., University of Houston, 1975.

Powers, William Preston. "The Subversion of 'Gordon's Kingdom': The Unionization of the Texas and Pacific Coal Mines at Thurber, Texas, 1888–1903." Master's thesis, University of Texas at Arlington, 1989.

Rhinehart, Marilyn D. "A Way of Work and a Way of Life: Coal Mining and Coal Miners in Thurber, Texas, 1888–1926." PhD diss., University of Houston, 1988.

Spoede, Robert William. "William Whipple Johnson: An Enterprising Man." Master's thesis, Hardin-Simmons University, 1968.

Tucker, Gene Rhea. "Oysters, Macaroni, and Beer: The Texas Pacific Mercantile and Manufacturing Company of Thurber, Texas." Master's thesis, Tarleton State University, 2006.

Wilkins, Charlie S. "Thurber: A Sociological Study of a Company-Owned Town." Master's thesis, University of Texas, 1929.

Books

Allen, Ruth A. *Chapters in the History of Organized Labor in Texas.* Austin: University of Texas, 1941.

Bernardi, Adria. *Houses with Names: The Italian Immigrants of Highwood, Illinois.* Chicago: University of Illinois Press, 1990.

Bielinski, Leo S. *The Back Road to Thurber.* Baird, TX: Joy Presswork Collection, 1993.

———. *The Thurber Connection.* Fort Worth: privately printed, 1999.

Britton, Karen Gerhardt. *Bale o' Cotton: The Mechanical Art of Cotton Ginning.* College Station: Texas A&M University Press, 1992.

Cahn, Julius. *Julius Cahn's Official Theatrical Guide.* Vol. 6, *1901–1902.* New York: Publication Office, Empire Theatre Building, 1901.

Clyne, Richard J. *Coal People: Life in Southern Colorado's Company Towns, 1890–1930.* Denver: Colorado Historical Society, 1999.

Corbin, David. *Life, Work, and Rebellion in the Coal Fields: The Southern West Virginia Miners, 1880–1922.* Urbana: University of Illinois Press, 1981.

Crawford, Margaret. *Building the Workingman's Paradise: The Design of American Company Towns.* New York: Verso, 1995.

Fishback, Price Van Meter. *Soft Coal, Hard Choices: The Economic Welfare of Bituminous Coal Miners, 1890-1930.* New York: Oxford University Press, 1992.

Francaviglia, Richard V. *Hard Places: Reading the Landscape of America's Historic Mining Districts.* Iowa City: University of Iowa Press, 1997.

Furman, Necah Stewart. *Walter Prescott Webb: His Life and Impact.* Albuquerque: University of New Mexico Press, 1976.

Gentry, Mary Jane. *The Birth of a Texas Ghost Town: Thurber, 1886–1933.* College Station: Texas A&M University Press, 2008.

Green, Hardy. *The Company Town: The Industrial Edens and Satanic Mills That Shaped the American Economy.* New York: Basic Books, 2010.

Hardman, Weldon B. *Boom Town: The Story of Thurber.* Wichita Falls, TX: Johnnie Barley Printing Company, 1937.

———. *Fire in a Hole!* Gordon, TX: Thurber Historical Association, 1975.

Hiatt, Dean B. *Ever the Wildebeest: An Autobiography of a Natural Engineer.* Kerrville, TX: Kerrville Printing Company, 1979.

House, Boyce. *Were You in Ranger?* 1935. Reprint, Ranger, TX: Ranger Historical Preservation Society, 1999.

Howard, Rex Z. *Texas Guidebook: Authentic Information about the Wonders of Texas.* Grand Prairie, TX: The Lo-Ray Co., 1954.

Jones, Ken. *From Boom Town to Ghost Town.* [Tarleton State University Dick Smith Library Keepsake No. 1]. [Stephenville, TX]: Tarleton State University, [2002].

Lewis, Lena R. *Erath County: A Compilation.* Stephenville, TX: privately printed, 1940.

Lord, Eliot, John J. D. Trenor, and Samuel J. Barrows. *The Italian in America.* New York: B. F. Buck & Company, 1905.

Marston, Nathan Washington. *The Marston Genealogy.* South Lubec, ME: privately printed, 1888.

McLean, William Hunter. *From Ayr to Thurber: Three Hunter Brothers and the Winning of the West.* Fort Worth: News Printing Company, 1978.

Miller, Timothy, ed. *America's Alternative Religions.* New York: SUNY Press, 1995.

Morris, John Miller. *A Private in the Texas Rangers: A. T. Miller of Company B, Frontier Battalion.* College Station: Texas A&M University Press, 2001.

Nesteŕowicz, Stefan. *Notatki z podró ży po północnej i środkowej Ameryce* [Travel notes through northern and middle America]. Toledo, OH: A. A. Paryski, 1909.

———. *Travel Notes.* Translated and edited by Marion Moore Coleman. Cheshire, CT: Cherry Hill Books, 1970.

Rhinehart, Marilyn D. *A Way of Work and a Way of Life: Coal Mining in Thurber, Texas, 1888–1926.* College Station: Texas A&M University Press, 1992.

Schuetz, Arden Jean, and Wilma Jean Schuetz. *People-Events and Erath County, Texas.* Stephenville, TX: privately published, 1972.

Selcer, Richard F. *Legendary Watering Holes: The Saloons That Made Texas Famous.* College Station: Texas A&M University Press, 2004.

Shifflett, Crandall A. *Coal Towns: Life, Work, and Culture in Company Towns of Southern Appalachia, 1880–1960.* Knoxville: University of Tennessee Press, 1991.

Smith, Larry Lane. *Historic Coal Mines in Texas: An Annotated Bibliography.* Austin: Railroad Commission of Texas, 1980.

Spratt, John S., Sr. *The Road to Spindletop: Economic Change in Texas, 1875–1901.* Austin: University of Texas Press, 1970.

———. *Thurber, Texas: The Life and Death of a Company Coal Town.* Edited by Harwood P. Hinton. 1986. Reprint, Abilene, TX: State House Press, 2005.

Stephen, Homer. *Fragments of History, Erath County: Philosophical Essays, Cities of the Immortal Dead.* Stephenville, TX: privately printed, 1966.

Studdard, George B. *Life of the Texas Pacific Coal & Oil Co.: 1888–1963.* Fort Worth: privately printed, 1992.

Sullivan, W. John L. *Twelve Years in the Saddle for Law and Order on the Frontiers of Texas.* 1909. Reprint, *Twelve Years in the Saddle with the Texas Rangers,* Lincoln: University of Nebraska Press, 2001.

Thurber, Texas: Demise of Thurber Cemetery and Interments. Gordon, TX: Thurber Historical Association, 1990.

Woodard, Don. *Black Diamonds! Black Gold! The Saga of Texas Pacific Coal and Oil Company.* Lubbock: Texas Tech University Press, 1998.

Articles

"Affairs of the Association." *Southwestern Historical Quarterly* 44, no. 1 (July 1940): 134–38.

Bearden, Bernice. "Mingus Founded in 1890." In *History of Palo Pinto County, Texas,* 533. Dallas: Curtis Media Corporation, 1986.

Bielinski, Leo S. "Beer, Booze, Bootlegging and Bocci Ball in Thurber-Mingus." *West Texas Historical Association Year Book* 59 (1983): 75–89.

———. "The Immigrants of Southwest Palo Pinto County: The Italians." In *History of Palo Pinto County, Texas,* 638–39. Dallas: Curtis Media Corporation, 1986.

———. "The Immigrants of Southwest Palo Pinto County: The Lebanese." In *History of Palo Pinto County, Texas,* 536-37. Dallas: Curtis Media Corporation, 1986.

———. "The Italian Presence in the Coal Camp of Thurber, Texas." *West Texas Historical Association Year Book* 80 (2004): 33–40.

———. "Mingus: Little Known Facts about a Well Known Town." In *History of Palo Pinto County, Texas,* 534–36. Dallas: Curtis Media Corporation, 1986.

———. "The 1903 Thurber Coal Miners' Meeting at Rocky Creek Bridge and Its Significance in the Southwest Labor Movement." *West Texas Historical Association Year Book* 71 (1995): 36–43.

———. "The Polish People of Thurber." *Polish Footprints* 21, no. 2 (Summer 2004): 2–20.

Burr, W. A. "General Medicine." *The Critique* 7, no. 3 (March 15, 1900): 85–89.

Carroll, H. Bailey, and Milton R. Gutsch. "A Check List of Theses and Dissertations in Texas History Produced in the Department of History of the University of Texas." *Southwestern Historical Quarterly* 56, no. 2 (October 1952): 254–308.

"Contract Firm Agreements." *Machinists' Monthly Journal* 19, no. 10 (October 1907): 970.

Cravens, John N. "Two Miners and Their Families in the Thurber-Strawn Coal Mines, 1905–1918." *West Texas Historical Association Year Book* 45 (1969): 115-26.

Crawford, Brad. "Black Diamonds: A Researcher Shines Light on African-American Coal Miners' Invisible Lives." *Family Tree Magazine* (February 2006): 8–9.

Fishback, Price V. "Did Coal Miners 'Owe Their Souls to the Company Store'? Theory and Evidence from the Early 1900s." *Journal of Economic History* 46, no. 4 (December 1986): 1011–29.

———. "The Economics of Company Housing: Historical Perspectives from the Coal Fields." *Journal of Law, Economics, and Organization* 8, no. 2 (April 1992): 346–65.

Floyd, Willie M. "Thurber, Texas, an Abandoned Coal Field Town." *Texas Geographic Magazine* 3, no. 2 (Autumn 1939): 1–21.

Francaviglia, Richard V. "Black Diamonds and Vanishing Ruins: Reconstructing the Historic Landscape of Thurber, Texas." *Mining History Association's 1994 Annual* (1994): 51–62.

———. "Black Diamonds to Black Gold: The Legacy of the Texas Pacific Coal and Oil Company." *West Texas Historical Association Year Book* 71 (1995): 7–20.

"From Thurber, Texas." *Official Journal: Amalgamated Meat Cutters and Butcher Workmen of North America* 7, no. 6 (April 1906): 34.

Gordon, William K. "Data Submitted by W. K. Gordon, Sec. V. P. & G. M., for the Texas & Pacific Coal Company's Twenty-fifth Anniversary Souvenir, Thurber, Texas, July 4, 1913." In *Life of the Texas Pacific Coal & Oil Co.: 1888–1963,* by George B. Studdard, 17–36. Fort Worth: privately printed, 1992.

Hall, Thomas R. "Data Submitted by Thos. R. Hall, Cashier and Paymaster, for the Texas & Pacific Coal Company's Twenty-fifth Anniversary Souvenir, Thurber, Texas, July 30, 1913." In *Life of the Texas Pacific Coal & Oil Co.: 1888–1963,* by George B. Studdard, 40–46. Fort Worth: privately printed, 1992.

Henderson, Dwight F. "The Texas Coal Mining Industry." *Southwestern Historical Quarterly* 68, no. 2 (October 1964): 207–19.

"Historical Marker at Thurber." *TP Voice* 5, no. 4 (July–August 1969): 15.

Hooks, Michael Q. "Thurber: A Unique Texas Community." *Panhandle-Plains Historical Review* 56 (1983): 1–17.

Kerr, K. Austin. "Prohibition." In *The New Handbook of Texas,* 5:355. Austin: Texas State Historical Association, 1996.

King, C. Richard. "Opera Houses in West Texas." *West Texas Historical Association Year Book* 38 (1962): 97–110.

King, Dick [C. Richard]. "Rascals and Rangers." *True West* 22 (March–April 1975): 6–13, 40, 44.

Leffler, John. "Palo Pinto County." In *The New Handbook of Texas,* 5:29–31. Austin: Texas State Historical Association, 1996.

Lopushansky, Joseph, and Michael Lopushansky. "Mining Town Terms." *American Speech* 4, no. 5 (June 1929): 368–74.

Maroney, James C. "The Unionization of Thurber, 1903." *Red River Valley Historical Review* 4 (Spring 1979): 27–32.

"Monuments to Power." *Economist* 397, no. 8704 (October 16, 2010): 103.
"New Ice Factories." *Ice and Refrigeration* 10, no. 1 (January 1896): 35–36.
"Open House Marks Completion of Carrol M. Bennett Training Center." *TP Voice* 7, no. 2 (March–April 1971): 5–9.
Rhinehart, Marilyn D. "'Underground Patriots': Thurber Coal Miners and the Struggle for Individual Freedom, 1888–1903." *Southwestern Historical Quarterly* 92 (April 1989): 509–42.
"Seagram Builds an Oil Company." *Texas Parade,* July 1968. Bennett Family Collection.
Skaggs, Jimmy M. "To Build a Barony: Colonel Robert D. Hunter." *Arizona and the West* 15 (Autumn 1973): 245–56.
"Thurber Facilities Will Be Expanded This Summer." *TP Voice* 6, no. 4 (July–August 1970): 4–8.
"Thurber and the Southwest Collection." *TP Voice* 14, no. 1 (January–February 1978): 4–7.
"Thurber Lake: A TP Bonus." *TP Voice* 4, no. 3 (May–June 1968): 9–10.
"Thurber on Strike." *United Mine Workers' Journal,* September 24, 1903.
"TP's Birthplace." *TP Voice* 2, no. 3 (May–June 1966): 4–13.
Utley, Dan K. "The Children of Thurber." *Sound Historian* 7 (2001): 29–51.
"A Vacation at Thurber Lake." *TP Voice* 5, no. 4 (July–August 1969): 8–9.
Webb, Walter Prescott. "Texas Collection." *Southwestern Historical Quarterly* 43, no. 1 (July 1939): 85–107.
"Where TPers Relax." *TP Voice* 2, no. 3 (May–June 1966): 14–15.

INDEX

Page numbers in **boldface** refer to photographs

ABOUT THE AUTHOR

Gene Rhea Tucker, originally from Killeen, Texas, earned the BA and MA degrees in history from Tarleton State University and the PhD in transatlantic history from the University of Texas at Arlington. While at Tarleton he was a graduate assistant at the W. K. Gordon Center for Industrial History of Texas, a museum documenting the boomtown-turned-ghost town of Thurber. He is a professor at various institutions in Texas.